DISCONTINUOUS CHANGE

David A. Nadler
Robert B. Shaw
A. Elise Walton
and Associates

DISCONTINUOUS CHANGE

*Leading Organizational
Transformation*

Jossey-Bass Publishers • San Francisco

Excerpt from Howard, 1992, in Chapter 9 is reprinted by permission of *Harvard Business Review.* "The CEO as Organizational Architect" by R. Howard, *70* (5). Copyright © 1992 by the President and Fellows of Harvard College; all rights reserved.

Excerpts in Chapter 14 from "A Week of Woe for the CEO" by Bill Saporito are from *Fortune,* Feb. 22, 1993. © 1993 Time Inc. All rights reserved.

Excerpts in Chapter 14 from "Shareholder Sues Utility" are from *The New York Times,* June 11, 1993. Copyright © 1993 by The New York Times Company. Reprinted by permission.

Substantial discounts on bulk quantities of Jossey-Bass books are available to corporations, professional associations, and other organizations. For details and discount information, contact the special sales department at Jossey-Bass Inc., Publishers. (415) 433–1740; Fax (415) 433-0499.

For sales outside the United States, please contact your local Simon & Schuster International Office.

T͡CF Manufactured in the United States of America on Lyons Falls Pathfinder Tradebook. This paper is acid-free and 100 percent totally chlorine-free.

Library of Congress Cataloging-in-Publication Data

Nadler, David.
    Discontinuous change : leading organizational transformation / David A. Nadler, Robert B. Shaw, A. Elise Walton, and associates. — 1st ed.
      p. cm.—(The Jossey-Bass management series)
    Includes bibliographical references and index.
    ISBN 0-7879-0042-7
    1. Organizational change—Management. 2. Strategic planning.
  I. Shaw, Robert B., date. II. Walton, A. Elise, date.
  III. Title. IV. Series.
  HD58.8.N298   1994   94-30752
  658.4'063—dc20 CIP

FIRST EDITION
HB Printing 10 9 8 7 6 5 4 3 2   *Code 94126*

The Jossey-Bass
Management Series

Contents

Preface

Delta Consulting Group is a firm whose practice focuses on the management of strategic organizational change. The basic thrust of Delta's work is to provide counsel to managers in understanding, managing, and effectively leading their organizations through periods of significant transition. Our work with clients typically leads to the development of a long-term intensive consulting relationship where we collaborate closely with senior management while working throughout the organization.

Delta's practice combines two very different and usually separate perspectives. We have a strategic view of business, seeing organizations as economic and social entities that are constantly dealing with the demands, threats, and opportunities posed by the larger environment, and making longer-term choices about how to respond to that environment. Thus we begin with a senior management "point of view," thinking about the organization at a strategy and policy level. At the same time, we focus on the behavioral dynamics of organizations. We think of organizations as complex yet active systems of human behavior. This behavioral perspective is central to how we view change and the process of leadership in organizations.

Discontinuous Change consolidates ten years of our experience with organizational change. We decided to write this book upon coming to the realization that the type of organizational change we have been seeing as consultants has shifted. In particular, we have been seeing more senior leaders faced with the need to create a radical and integrated change agenda that would alter the basic identity of their firms. The commonly accepted change-management techniques were insufficient to meet that challenge. Thus, this book offers a new view on large-scale change—one that builds on approaches used in the past but that is intended to assist those faced with the need for more extreme and far-reaching change. Our intent is to give those with responsibility for large organizations a map for thinking about change and a tested tool kit for managing change in their companies.

Over the past five years, we have noticed an increasing amount of dramatic change in our major clients, changes that alter the fundamental essence of their organizations. Such profound change is full of risk. Companies that succeed are those that—as individuals and organizations—become change-capable. Change-capable organizations recognize change as a constant element of the landscape, and stability as the exception. They define changes as opportunities, rather than threats. They work to turn change to their advantage. In many cases, they actively and deliberately create change so that they can then capitalize on it. Their strength lies not in order and structure but in responsiveness and flexibility.

Practice into Theory

We wrote this book with the goal of turning practice into theory. Although much has been written about change, we believe we have a unique perspective and some fresh ideas about change, based on our experience with large-scale change efforts. The change literature does not always translate well into the everyday world of day-to-day, moment-to-moment leadership. The language of the latest theories is often too obtuse or complex for most executives, who do not, for example, find a 2 percent difference in measured attitudes from one intervention over another particularly compelling.

As consultants to senior managers engaged in change, we find ourselves continually faced with the need to design just-in-time interventions that will create new behaviors immediately. We are pressed to action before we can evaluate elaborate theories and their implications. This yields a pragmatic, practitioners' approach to change—complete with trade-offs faced by those whose feet are in the fire. Often, the tried-and-true techniques, some generated decades ago, are the most powerful. Other times, we find new ideas and approaches are needed and work with clients to create pragmatic approaches to change leadership.

This book should be regarded as a set of propositions based on our participation in change initiatives. It is theory in use, built on trial-and-error learning. It is our attempt as practitioners to articulate our insights and build generalizations based on what we have learned through our "in-close" experience with organizational change.

Audience and Purpose

We wrote this book with several readers in mind. Perhaps the one who will benefit most is the senior executive who is involved in or undertaking a major change. This executive could be a first-time leader or a more experienced change manager. We hope this reader will gain from the experiences of other senior executives and pick up practical insights as well.

Another reader is the person who assists senior executives in managing change, perhaps a staff assistant who gets involved in the core activities of senior leadership. This individual may act as a catalyst, identifying and selling the need for change, or may be involved in the planning or implementation of change.

A third reader is someone interested in the theory and practice of change. This reader will gain the most from the reported experiences, ideas, and techniques. However, readers looking for broad cross-comparisons of change models or meta-analytic assessment of change intervention effectiveness are likely to be disappointed. The authors of these chapters use a shared model of organizations, change, and corollary techniques. Thus, we do not address the current theoretical debates about the the power of different approaches.

All these readers can use the book for several purposes. First, the book provides a diagnostic framework that can help organizations and individuals understand what type of change they face. It should help individuals assess the challenges that lie ahead for their organization, build understanding about the nature of the change, and evaluate choices. The book should help the reader recognize the need for dramatic change before it becomes a crisis—avoiding reactive change in favor of proactive strategic change.

Then, after helping the reader diagnose the type of change and its challenges, the book should provide some guidance on what to do about change. The reader may use the material for direct action—determining the techniques and approaches, given the situation. The book also describes approaches to guide change in different parts and elements of the organization landscape. For example, the sections on managing culture, reengineering, or architecture may provide ideas for specific efforts under way in an organization.

Finally, the book should help the reader diagnose an organization's current change leadership capability and identify ways of building the required leadership capability.

Organization of This Book

Part One provides a framework for looking at the different types of change and the action strategies for dealing with them. Chapter One, by David Nadler and Robert Shaw, positions our point of view about change: what's changing about change, what we're seeing in large organizations, and the need for change management as a core competency. In Chapter Two, David Nadler and Michael Tushman differentiate the two types of change (what we call *incremental* and *discontinuous*) and then outline approaches for managing these differences types of change. Chapter Three, also by David Nadler and Michael Tushman, describes the phenomena we increasingly see in our clients. Nadler and Tushman outline the key challenges of discontinuous change: recognition, strategic choice, and managing the change process.

Part Two begins with a look at the key areas in leading discontinuous change. Chapter Four reviews the fundamentals of change management—motivating change, planning for the transition state, and so on. This chapter, by Kathleen Morris and Charles Raben, adds two important features to past writings on transition management. First, it reviews the challenge of resistance, which is fundamental to all change. Second, it looks at the model for managing change from the perspective of ten years of experience. Thus, it provides examples and reflects on the power of the different intervention strategies. Chapter Five, by Robert Shaw, outlines the three main action areas addressed in discontinuous change: leadership, corporate identity, and organizational architecture. In Chapter Six, Elise Walton looks at a process of executive-led change. Taking an overview of the five phases of change, she identifies the challenges and opportunities executives face during a discontinuous change process. This chapter outlines both pragmatic techniques and potential pitfalls and explains when they are likely to arise. In Chapter Seven, on organizational renewal, Mitchell Lee Marks and Robert Shaw discuss how organizations can heal and revitalize after significant traumatic change.

Part Three looks at change in the specific elements of an organization and, specifically, how these elements are affected under conditions of discontinuous change. In Chapter Eight, Elise Walton presents an emergent approach called generative strategy. She discusses the role of strategy and organization as levers for change in the case of environmental discontinuity. Chapter Nine, by David Nadler, is an overview of organizational architecture and looks at the organization specifically as a mechanism and medium for managing discontinuous change. In Chapter Ten, Elise Walton reviews approaches and challenges of culture change. Chapter Eleven, by Robert Shaw and Mark Maletz, discusses the role of redefining how work is done and points out some of the strengths and weaknesses of the reengineering approach. Chapter Twelve, by Richard Ketterer and Michael Chayes, discusses the competencies that change leaders require and mechanisms for selecting and developing new leaders.

In Part Four, we turn to leadership and its role in creating and sustaining a change-capable organization. In Chapter Thirteen, David Nadler looks at the types of leadership needed to work through radical organizational change. Jeffrey Heilpern, in Chapter Fourteen, examines the changing role of CEOs as leaders of change. In Chapter Fifteen, Elise Walton and Robert Shaw interview some leading change authorities—leaders who have brought their organizations through dramatic, discontinuous changes. These change-capable leaders comment on their role in change, key challenges, and core beliefs about change. As leading practitioners, they offer valuable insight into theories of change and firsthand reports of live change efforts. Chapter Sixteen, by Robert Shaw and Elise Walton, concludes the book with a summary of key lessons learned.

Designing, creating, and implementing a change agenda is a key part of the leader's job and will become more so in the future, as demands on organizations increase. Our goal, then, is to provide the leader and manager with tools, ideas, concepts, and perhaps even inspiration to do things differently, to develop and test new approaches to change in complex organizations. *Discontinuous Change* is intended to contribute to ongoing dialogue around the leadership of change.

Acknowledgments

Invention in our domain of action doesn't occur in a laboratory, an academic office, or a library. Insight occurs through experimentation and reflection. Therefore, our clients have not only been customers; they have been co-producers of knowledge. Every one of the chapters in this book is the result of some client who became concerned about a particular issue, problem, or question. Our clients invited us to learn and discover along with them. Thus, in many ways, they are collaborators in the creation of this book.

We would like to express our appreciation to a number of our client organizations that have been particularly supportive of our efforts to break new ground. These include American Express, AT&T, Corning, Ford, KPMG, Lever, Pacific Bell, PepsiCo, Pfizer, Weyerhaeuser, and Xerox. We are deeply indebted to these companies and their leaders. While we recognize and thank the individuals and organizations who have helped us in this project, we, of course, take responsibility for the content and the opinions expressed here.

While each chapter has one or more authors identified with it, the thoughts expressed in the book are very much the reflection of the collaborative work that goes on at Delta. Many of our colleagues whose names are not listed as authors have indeed been collaborators. Finally, the operations staff at Delta has had a major role in producing this book. Stacey Beiter, Kate Linnihan, Debbie Schwartz, and Antoinette Zelig did a tremendous job of managing the production of the final manuscript.

New York, New York   David A. Nadler
September 1994   Robert B. Shaw
                                                                    A. Elise Walton

The Authors

Michael M. Chayes, of Delta Consulting Group, works in the areas of organizational diagnosis, strategy formulation, change management, executive leadership development, and organizational design. He formerly worked in management assessment and the design and implementation of management development programs. He received his Ph.D. degree in clinical psychology from The Institute of Advanced Psychological Studies, Adelphi University.

Jeffrey D. Heilpern, of Delta Consulting Group, specializes in helping CEOs and their senior management teams enhance leadership effectiveness in building and implementing an integrated change agenda that includes vision and mission, strategy and milestones, values and culture, architecture and design, and work process improvement initiatives. He formerly served as vice president of human resources and organizational development at Yankelovich,

Skelly & White. He received his B.A. degree in political science from Tufts University and his M.B.A. degree from Harvard University.

Richard F. Ketterer, of Delta Consulting Group, works in the areas of large-scale organizational change, executive leadership, senior team effectiveness, and strategic human resources management. Prior to joining Delta, he was director of executive and management development at Unisys Corporation, where he held diverse human resources positions, and served as director of Action Research Associates, a management consulting firm he cofounded in Ann Arbor, Michigan. He received his B.A. degree in political science from Wesleyan University and his Ph.D. degree in psychology from the University of Michigan.

Mark C. Maletz, of Business Process Design Associates, is associate professor of business process improvement at Babson College and a Perot Systems Corporation Fellow. His consulting activities focus on helping clients create the organizational capability to achieve dramatic improvement in business processes. Previously, he was managing director at American Airlines and adjunct associate professor at the Amos Tuck School of Business at Dartmouth College. He also served as chief executive of Enterprise Design Group, was director of the Xerox Work Systems Design Group and Knowledge-Based Systems Competency Center, and was national director for Coopers & Lybrand. He received his Ph.D. degree in cognitive and computer science from the University of Michigan and the Industrial Technology Institute.

Mitchell Lee Marks, of Delta Consulting Group, specializes in transition management, strategic choice, team building, and leadership development. He works extensively with organizations planning, implementing, and recovering from mergers, restructurings, downsizings, and other transitions. His experience spans the financial services, manufacturing, telecommunications, entertainment, health care, and high-technology industry sectors. He is author of *From Turmoil to Triumph: New Life After Corporate Mergers, Acquisitions, and Downsizing* (1994) and coauthor of *Managing the Merger* (1992). He has also written numerous articles for management and academic journals. Marks received his B.A. degree from the University

of California, Santa Cruz, and his M.A. and Ph.D. degrees in organizational psychology from the University of Michigan. He is the
recipient of the Outstanding Scholarly Contribution Award from the
Organizational Behavior Division of the Academy of Management.

Kathleen F. Morris, of Delta Consulting Group, works in the areas
of organizational change, strategic design, senior team development, transition management, and strategic human resources management. A seasoned practitioner, she brings close to twenty years
of corporate experience in the energy and chemical industries in a
variety of organizational effectiveness, human resource, and management development roles. She has worked on numerous change
issues—ranging from downsizing and renewal to culture and leadership change—and has extensive experience working with senior
managers and their teams worldwide. She received her B.S. degree
in behavior sciences from Drexel University and her M.S. degree in
organization behavior from Goddard College. She has authored several articles on the subject of organizational change.

David A. Nadler, of Delta Consulting Group, works with senior
management on organizational change, organizational design, senior team development, management succession, and leadership.
He formerly served on the faculty of the Graduate School of Business at Columbia University and on the staff of the Survey Research
Center at the University of Michigan Institute for Social Research.
He received his B.A. degree in political science and international
affairs from George Washington University, his M.B.A. degree from
Harvard University, his M.A. degree in psychology from the University of Michigan, and his Ph.D. degree in psychology from the
University of Michigan. He is author of numerous articles and ten
books on organizational behavior and change, including *Prophets
in the Dark: How Xerox Reinvented Itself and Beat Back the Japanese* (with David Kearns) and *Organizational Architecture: Designs for Changing Organizations* (with Marc S. Gerstein and
Robert B. Shaw).

Charles S. Raben, of Delta Consulting Group, works in the areas
of large-scale organizational change, organizational architecture
and design, business restructuring, senior team development, and

executive leadership. He formerly served as director of organizational planning and development at the ARCO Oil and Gas Company and served on the faculties of the University of California, Berkeley, and the University of Maryland. He received his B.S. degree in psychology from Farleigh Dickinson University and his M.A. and Ph.D. degrees in industrial and organizational psychology from The Ohio State University.

Robert B. Shaw, of Delta Consulting Group, works with corporate leaders on managing large-scale change, creating innovative organizational architectures, and enhancing senior team effectiveness. He is coauthor of *Organizational Architecture: Designs for Changing Organizations* (with David A. Nadler and Marc S. Gerstein), as well as author of numerous articles in management and academic journals. He received his B.A. degree from the University of California, Santa Cruz, and his M.S. and Ph.D. degrees in organizational behavior from the Yale University School of Organization and Management.

Michael L. Tushman, an affiliate of Delta Consulting Group, is Hettleman Professor of Management and director of the Research Center in Entrepreneurship and Innovation at the Columbia University Graduate School of Business, where he specializes in organizational design and management of innovation and strategic change in organizations. He received his Ph.D. degree in organizational studies from the Sloan School of Management at the Massachusetts Institute of Technology.

A. Elise Walton, of Delta Consulting Group, works in the areas of change management, globalization, strategy, organizational design, and quality. She previously worked at Citibank/Citicorp and at the Foreign Trade Research Institute in Belgrade, Yugoslavia. She also has experience in Russia and Eastern European countries and participated in a joint venture between Harvard Business School and the Soviet Institute for International Economics. Walton received her B.A. degree from Bowdoin College, her M.A. degree from Columbia University, and her Ph.D. degree from Harvard University.

PART ONE

The Changing Nature of Change

Change Leadership:
Core Competency for
the Twenty-First Century

David A. Nadler
Robert B. Shaw

Business leaders of the 1990s face a rapidly moving and unforgiving global marketplace that forces them to use every possible tool to sustain competitiveness. The days of effortless dominance by a few firms have passed. Recent turmoil in some of the largest and historically most successful businesses, such as IBM, illustrates the potential for rapid decline in even the most prosperous organizations. Sustainable profitability has become an elusive goal.

The companies that survive in the coming decades will be those that are able to respond quickly and effectively to changing environmental conditions. This puts a premium on certain capabilities—adaptiveness, flexibility, and responsiveness. Successful firms will learn and act at a faster rate than the competition, and their leaders will have no choice but to be effective anticipators and managers of large-scale change. This simple premise is easy to understand, but difficult to put into practice—as illustrated in the many examples of organizational dinosaurs that failed to adapt.

Part of the difficulty in adapting to change may be that many aspects of organizational life reinforce stability—that is, they are designed to ensure that any variations are modulated over time, eventually returning to the status quo, especially to policies and practices that worked in the past. In this respect, most organizations, like individuals, are resistant to change. As the business environment becomes more complex and competitive, the consequences of resisting change, or managing it badly, will become ever more serious.

Forces for Change

In broad terms, large-scale change is usually triggered by some kind of destabilizing event, an event of sufficient scope and magnitude to create significant disequilibrium in the organization. These destabilizing events vary quite a bit among industries, but in general they fall within six categories:

1. *Shifts in industry structure or product class life cycle.* Throughout the life cycle of a class of products, there are changes in patterns of demand and users, in the nature of required innovation, and in competition. In the emergence phase, competition is based on product innovation and performance; in the mature stage, competition centers on cost, volume, and efficiency. In particular, the emergence of industry standards or dominant designs (such as the DC-3 or the IBM 360) present major challenges. When an industry moves from one stage to another, it almost always involves a period of disequilibrium for companies in that industry.

2. *Technological innovation.* Whether it creates new products, such as jet engines, electronic typewriters, and microprocessors, or new processes, such as the planar process in semiconductors or float glass in glass manufacturing, technological innovation can change the basis of competition within an industry. When the basis of competition changes, great uncertainty is introduced. Firms that had sustainable competitive advantage suddenly find that their advantage is gone, or worse, that they are at a disadvantage. The core competencies of the organization are called into question.

3. *Macroeconomic trends and crises.* Significant shifts in

national and world economies can change the basis of competition
or present challenges to current ways of organizing. Oil crises, trade
barriers, foreign currency valuation, inflation, changes in exchange
rates, trade balances, consumption patterns, capital formation—any
of these factors can suddenly alter the situation in which an enterprise finds itself, thus necessitating significant change. A clear example is the fluctuating value of the yen in the early 1990s and the
changes it forced on Japanese automobile makers.

    4. *Regulatory and legal changes.* Changes in the legal en-
vironment or regulatory changes, such as the deregulation of telecommunications, trucking, airlines, and banking, can create major
modifications in the competitive environment. Such changes modify the "rules of engagement" for enterprises and therefore require
new approaches and strategies. Perhaps the most dramatic single
example in recent times was the deregulation of the telephone industry in the United States and the subsequent divestiture of the Bell
operating companies by AT&T. All the companies involved were
forced to make discontinuous changes to deal with the radically new
environment.

    5. *Market and competitive forces.* The entrance of new
competitors into a market may present new strategic threats if they
choose to compete in ways different from historical industry practices, such as the Japanese did in the 1980s with automobiles, consumer electronics, and copiers. The result is competition that is
more intensive, more aggressive, and simply better than in the past.
Apple's PowerBook was one of the most successful product
launches in U.S. history, yet competitive products surpassed it just
one year later.

    6. *Growth.* A final force contributing to strategic change is
a result of success in the competitive environment—growth. As organizations get larger, their competitive strategies and their organizing principles may bump into the limitations of size (Greiner,
1972). Successful niche players (for example, regional airlines) may
find themselves under attack as they get bigger. Companies with
distinctive organizing approaches may encounter problems as they
try to continue that approach with many more people performing
more complex and specialized tasks. The classic case of PeopleEx-
press illustrates a company that failed to cope with the problems of

Figure 1.1. Precursors of Organizational Change.

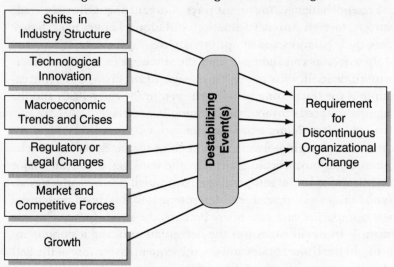

growth, while Microsoft exemplifies a company reshaping itself successfully in the face of such growth.

All these factors, as shown in Figure 1.1, call into question the company's most basic strategic issues: who are our customers, what are our offerings, and what are our sources of sustainable competitive advantage? As it addresses these issues, the enterprise frequently finds that it must make fundamental changes in vision, mission, and strategy, and those changes in turn necessitate basic changes in all of the elements of organization.

Key Challenges and Organizational Capacity

In this kind of destabilized environment, organizations face several key challenges. To respond effectively, they must:

• *Increase quality and customer value.* They must continually improve the features, performance, reliability, and functionality of their offerings (products and services) to meet increasing customer expectations.

- *Decrease the costs of internal coordination.* To compete in the price arena, but still make returns that satisfy owners, organizations must radically decrease the costs associated with producing their offerings and managing themselves.

- *Enhance competitive innovation.* A key source of value is innovation, the effective development of new products and services that will meet customers' expectations, either current or latent. Organizations will have to become much more effective at innovation, increasing the "hit rate" of new initiatives and investments.

- *Reduce market-response time.* Increasing evidence indicates that time can be a competitive advantage (Stalk and Hout, 1990). In a faster-changing environment, enterprises that can both anticipate and respond more quickly to market shifts will be privileged.

- *Motivate effective member contributions.* As the work force becomes more diverse and the fundamental conditions of work change because of competition, a key challenge will be to figure out how to leverage the talents and abilities of their work forces by engaging their employees and motivating them to contribute in the most productive manner. Increasingly, contributions will also be needed from people with varying degrees of membership (from core members to those loosely connected to the organization in part-time or affiliative roles).

- *Create scale without mass.* Global markets and competitors require broad scale and scope of operations, but at the same time, cost pressures argue against adding to size. Effective enterprises will be those that figure out how to create scale without adding to mass.

- *Manage change at a faster rate.* Given the reality of change and the apparent fact that periods of disequilibrium seem to come more quickly and last longer, organizations will have to develop the capacity to manage change more effectively, and manage it at an ever-increasing rate.

- *Find true competitive advantage.* All of this leads to the conclusion that organizations will have to work intensively to identify and then develop those capacities that yield true competitive advantage. Specifically, they will need to identify factors that are not easily replicable by others and that enable success in the marketplace.

This last point is indeed the bottom line. The ultimate question is how to identify and nurture sources of competitive advantage. Here, an important observation needs to be made: The new global competitive environment has negated many of the traditional sources of competitive advantage. For some time, competitive advantage was seen as arising from unique access to capital, technology, people, or markets. The organization that could gain control of one or more of these factors could hope to have sustainable and nonimitable advantage. The changes in the global economy, however, have created a situation where all major competitors have equal access to capital, technology, people, and markets. In the face of this equal access, where are the remaining sources of potential advantage?

Change Management as a Core Organizational Competency

We have begun to realize that a fundamental source of sustainable advantage is organizational capability (Ulrich and Lake, 1991). An organization's unique capacities provide an advantage that is not easily replicated by others. Capabilities are the specific skills, abilities, and competencies that are characteristics of the enterprise as a system, as opposed to the capabilities of an individual. For example, the ability to develop and quickly commercialize technology is an organizational capability. These capabilities are the result of experience, knowledge, individual skills and abilities, relationships, structures, and most of all, shared learning. They form the core of an organization's intellectual capital. Because they are a characteristic of the entire system rather than individuals, and because they are the result of shared learning, it is difficult for other organizations to create such capabilities.

In stable environments, organizational capability has a long shelf life. But as environmental uncertainty and the rate of change increase, the rate of depreciation of an organization's intellectual capital also decreases. The divisional structures and processes developed by Alfred Sloan at General Motors (Drucker, 1964) served the company well for decades in a relatively stable market environment. When faced with turbulence, change, and disequilibrium in the industry, those same capabilities that had been sources of success became root causes of problems. This implies that in periods of disequilibrium, enterprises will need to find new ways of organizing to generate and nurture new types of capabilities that are more relevant to the new environment.

If we carry this thinking through to its logical conclusion, we end up with a set of propositions about organizational effectiveness in the environment of the late 1990s:

- *A qualitatively new environment for enterprises is developing.* The rates of change and the volatility of outside forces are placing new, unique, and unabating demands on organizations.

- *Organizational capability is a key source of sustainable competitive advantage.* The ability of an enterprise to perform certain types of behaviors, resulting from shared learning, appears to be one of the few remaining points of leverage for enterprises that seek to fundamentally better their competitive positions.

- *Traditional concepts of organization are increasingly less effective.* The concepts of organization that have driven the design and construction of enterprises for the past 100 years are increasingly less effective in the face of increasing rates of change. Basic machine-bureaucracy theory, based on the concepts of Taylor and Weber, was designed to create stability in organizations; the new environments demand speed, innovation, and flexibility—the very opposite of stability. The new environment will therefore demand the development and implementation of new concepts of organization.

- *Enterprises that develop and apply new concepts of organization will gain competitive advantage.* If capabilities derive from the modes of organizing, and capabilities are a source of competitive advantage, then those companies that can take advantage of new concepts of organization in a way that enables shared learning and the development of new needed capabilities will be the companies that win.

Each of these realities poses considerable challenges in itself. Many companies, however, are experiencing the effects of several at the same time. The result is that they find themselves facing the reality of rapid rates of change as a fact of life. At times, the complexity of competing in the modern business climate can seem overwhelming, particularly to those accustomed to a more stable business environment. A turbulent business environment can also force those leading organizations to abandon—if not actively destroy—that which worked for them in the past. It is not surprising that some executive teams attempt to minimize or deny the changes going on about them. Others mistakenly believe their organizations and people are better equipped than they actually are to deal with the complexities of the new competitive environment. In most cases, our largest organizations are being led by people whose past has provided only limited experience in dealing with the new business realities.

The Particular Problem of Success

One of the paradoxes of organizational life is that success usually sets the stage for failure. Organizations tend to become locked in behavior patterns as they institutionalize the practices that produced the original success. This kind of rigidity can create the illusion of safety, even arrogance. If nothing changes in the environment, the danger may go unnoticed. But during times of disequilibrium, successful organizations are especially vulnerable because they are less likely to perceive destabilizing events. Paradoxically, the enterprises that are most exposed are those with a history of sustained success. Companies like General Motors, IBM, Kodak, Westinghouse, and Sears, for example, found themselves unable to deal with the change that was thrust upon them. There is no safe haven when firms as large and powerful as General Motors begin to stumble. While some of these companies are showing signs of recovery, they illustrate the fact that enterprises with success over time may be at greatest risk, given the recent acceleration in rates of changes.

These companies have fallen into what we call the trap of success (see Figure 1.2). Over time, sustained success appears to lead to certain patterns of organizational behavior and functioning that we refer to as the success syndrome. Practices and activities that were associated with success in the past become part of the standard operating procedure, even though the relationship between those practices and past successes may have been spurious or conditions

Figure 1.2. The Trap of Success.

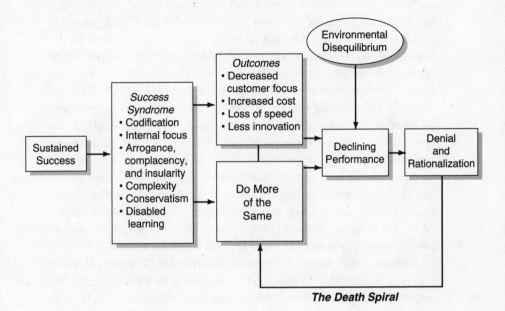

The Death Spiral

may have changed. Sustained success tends to lead to an internal focus, the perception that knowledge, insight, and ideas are found inside the organization rather than outside. Over time, this engenders a view of the world that can best be characterized as arrogant, insular, and complacent. Members of the organization believe in their own infallibility.

As organizations are successful, they grow, and as they grow, they become more complex and differentiated. This in turn causes people to focus on the relationships inside the organization between the various parts, rather than on relationships outside. As a successful organization matures, it literally has more to lose. Therefore, it may become risk averse. Finally, as a consequence of these factors, successful organizations become learning disabled. They are incapable of looking outside, reflecting on success and failure, accepting new ideas, and developing new insights.

The success syndrome leads to several outcomes. At the most basic level, it creates an assumption that future success will be produced by the same set of actions that produced success in the past, or "more of the same." When faced with new challenges, the organization falls back on the strategies, methodologies, and processes that have worked for it in the past. An example can be seen in the actions of one computer equipment maker that had long relied on its large direct sales force to distribute its products. In the past, that sales force had been seen as one of the "crown jewels" of the company. In fact, during periods when the product line was perceived as inferior, it was the actions of the sales force that enabled the company to weather these problems. However, as the industry environment changed, it became apparent to many that the future lay in other channels of distribution (dealers, distributors, direct mail). Yet the company continued to pour resources into its direct sales force. The response, when threatened, was to do more of the same.

Over time, the success syndrome leads to some immediate performance outcomes. There is less customer focus, and costs tend to increase while speed or response deteriorates. The organization becomes less capable of effectively innovating in ways that contribute to marketplace success. When companies dominate their markets or occupy commanding positions, they can continue to perform reasonably well (at least in some dimensions) for some time, riding on the inherent advantages of large market share, established channels of distribution, or customer purchasing patterns. However, when change in the environment is introduced, when disequilibrium enters the picture, this success-driven pattern of operating runs into big problems. Performance begins to decline and is evidenced by decreasing market share, customer attrition, limited or nonexistent growth, and declining earnings.

All of this would be bad enough. Remember, however, that the successful firm can become learning disabled. So in the face of declining performance, it cannot reflect and comprehend why performance has declined. Leaders become defensive. They blame their problems on external factors (government regulation or the Japanese), deny that their problems are real, or tell themselves that the situation is just temporary. Denial leads these organizations to respond in their traditional ways, to do more of the same. In turn, this leads to continued performance problems, which lead to denial, and so forth. This cycle of repetition, problems, and denials is called the death spiral—if companies are not able to break out of this pattern, they are doomed to die.

An organization that is not yet into the death spiral still has a chance to build on its prior success with a program of careful, deliberate change. An organization that is deep into the death spiral needs a dramatic shock to break itself out of its denial and rationalization. That shock requires much more immediate and drastic action. Frequently, those who have been part of the organization, part of its history and traditions and part of the web of relationships, are not capable of administering the needed shock. That is why most of the cases of successful re-creation start with the replacement of the CEO and much of the senior team.

Conclusion

One of the hallmarks of American business in the past decade has been the attempts by huge organizations to manage large-scale change. Some cases, such as AT&T, Chrysler, and GE, have been dramatic and have captured the public's attention. Others, such as Corning, Lever, PepsiCo, and Xerox, have received less attention, but the changes have been no less profound. This most recent generation of organizational changes is somewhat different from the more confined cases that received attention in the past. First, the most visible of them arise in response to, or in anticipation of, pressing—perhaps life-threatening—business issues (not just questions of organizational work life or corporate climate). Second, most of these changes can be traced directly to external factors, such as new sources of competition, new technology, deregulation, maturation of product sets, changes in ownership, shifts in fundamental market structure, or rapid growth opportunities. Third, these changes affect the entire organization, rather than individual parts or subsystems. They usually alter the core of what the organization represents to its customers and members.

Organizational effectiveness requires that organizations recognize the need for different types of change and manage them accordingly. In some cases, the type of changes required are incremental in nature. Managing ongoing incremental change is an essential and demanding task. Corporate leaders would be foolish to do anything more than incremental change when that is what's needed. In other cases, the type of change required is discontinuous, and to respond any differently is to risk organizational ruin. These are situations when incremental change is not enough and more dramatic actions are required. There are situations where the placing of "big bets" is the only reasonable course of action. We will describe the differences between these two types of change and, in particular, focus on the demands of managing discontinuous change. Organizational vitality and growth depend on the ability of leaders to craft sustainable competitive strategies, while effectively building the organization's capacity to deliver on those strategies (and in so doing, balancing the need for both incremental and discontinuous change).

Types of Organizational Change: From Incremental Improvement to Discontinuous Transformation

David A. Nadler
Michael L. Tushman

During the late 1970s, the New York division of Citibank initiated a major change in consumer banking technology. In a bold move, they leapfrogged other banks by installing automated teller machines (ATMs) in more than 300 branches. The Citibank approach was different from that of the other banks on several dimensions. First, the machines were designed and produced by a Citibank subsidiary and were more versatile and easier to use. Second, the machines were installed inside branch vestibules, rather than outside on the street, giving customers increased privacy and security. Third, each branch got at least two machines, so that even if one machine was under repair or having problems, customers could be reasonably sure of having access to a working machine. The project took almost two years and cost more than one billion dollars. When completed, it appeared to provide the bank with both cost and competitive advantages over other New York banks.

In May 1988, Robert E. Allen suddenly found himself the new chairman and CEO of AT&T, following the unexpected death of CEO Jim Olson. As Allen surveyed his new domain, he found a company still reeling from the traumas of divestiture, deregulation, and competitive attacks. He also saw a company caught up in its past, internally oriented, and slow to act. During the next four years, he initiated a series of actions that affected virtually every element of the company. He restructured the company into business units and pushed decision making down several levels, changed the mission and strategy of the firm, made several major acquisitions (NCR, McCaw), and initiated a major push into global markets. He articulated and implemented a new set of values called "Our Common Bond." He brought new people into senior management, replacing eight of the thirteen people directly reporting to him. By mid-1993, the press was hailing Allen for having reshaped the company.

Both of these cases illustrate significant change involving a lot of people and many resources. But they are quite different. The AT&T change was companywide; the Citibank change was focused on one business unit. The Citibank change did not involve a fundamental shift of its business; the bank continued to provide traditional banking services, but did it better. AT&T, on the other hand, created new services, entered new industries, found new customers, and changed its business proposition. The Citibank change was built around one innovation; the AT&T story involved shifts in strategy, products, people, and processes.

These two cases illustrate that organizational change includes a wide range of events, activities, and processes. The two cases obviously do not describe the same kind of change. Clearly something is different about them, and that implies that they might need to be managed differently.

The fact of these differences, or that "a change is not a change," demonstrates that if we are to understand and manage change, then we need a language system that will help us to comprehend some of the different types of changes facing organizations. We use the term *incremental* to refer to changes like the Citibank introduction of ATMs, and *discontinuous* to refer to broad-based

organizational changes like the AT&T transformation since deregulation. Such a language system would also help us to grasp how
different approaches to change management are appropriate to different types of change. Each type of change poses different demands
and requires different kinds of managerial strategies and techniques.

In our efforts to comprehend the nature of organizational
change, we've found it useful to step back from looking at the
individual enterprise or company. Rather, we begin by looking at
the patterns of changes in sets of companies within an industry over
time. By understanding the larger system in which the organization
sits, we can better understand the patterns of behavior of the individual firm. We can then return to the individual company and look
at the patterns of change in context.

The Organization as a Transformation Process

There are many different ways of thinking about what makes up an
organization. The challenge is to find useful approaches for describing organizations, for simplifying complex phenomena, and for
identifying patterns in what may at first seem to be random activity.
We have developed a model that views four major components of
organizations: the work, the people, the formal organizational arrangements, and the informal organization.

Organizational Components

The first component is the organization's *work*—the basic and inherent tasks to be done by the organization and its units, or the
activity in which the organization is engaged, particularly in light
of its strategy. The emphasis is on the specific work activities or
functions that need to be done and their inherent characteristics—
for example, the knowledge or skills demanded by the work, the
kinds of rewards it provides, its degree of uncertainty, and its inherent constraints, such as critical time demands and cost constraints.
Since it is assumed that a primary (although clearly not the only)
reason for the organization's existence is to perform the work consistent with strategy, the work is the starting point for analysis.
Assessing other components depends to a large degree on under-

standing the nature of the tasks to be performed and the inherent work processes that must be managed.

A second component of organizations involves the *people* who perform tasks. The most critical aspects to consider include the nature of individual knowledge and skills; the different needs or preferences of individuals; the perceptions or expectancies that they develop; background and demographic factors, such as age or sex, that potentially influence individual behavior.

The third component is the *formal organizational arrangements*—the structures, systems, processes, methods, and procedures that are explicitly and formally developed to get individuals to perform tasks consistent with organizational strategy. This includes the way functions are grouped and units are structured, the mechanisms for control and coordination throughout the organization, the human resources management systems, reward systems, the physical location, and structures that determine job design and the work environment.

The final component is the *informal organization*. In addition to the set of formal arrangements that exists in any organization, another set tends to emerge over time. They are usually implicit and unwritten, but they can exert considerable influence on behavior. The informal organization (also known as "organizational culture") sometimes complements formal organizational arrangements by providing structures to aid work accomplishment. In other situations, it may emerge in reaction to the formal structure, to protect individuals from it. Informal arrangements may either aid or hinder organizational performance.

The behavior of leaders, as opposed to the formal creation of leader jobs/roles/positions, is an important feature of the informal organization, as are common values and beliefs and the relationships that develop within and between groups. In addition, various types of informal working arrangements develop. Finally, various communication, influence, and political patterns combine to create an informal organization. All these can have a critical effect on behavior.

To summarize, an organization can be thought of as a set of components: the work, the people, the organizational arrangements, and the informal organization. In any system, however, the critical question is not what the components are but how they interact.

The Concept of Congruence

Congruence is defined as the degree to which the needs, demands, goals, objectives, or structures of one component are consistent with and complementary to the needs, demands, goals, objectives, or structures of another component. In other words, congruence is a measure of how well pairs of components fit together.

Consider, for example, work and people. At the simplest level, the work presents skill and knowledge demands on people who would perform it. At the same time, the people available to do the work have certain levels of skill and knowledge. Obviously, if an individual's characteristics match the demands of the task, the performance will be more effective. Obviously, too, the congruence relationship between people and work encompasses more factors than just knowledge and skill.

Similarly, each congruence relationship in the model has its own specific characteristics.

Patterns in the Life and Death of Enterprises

Starting in the late 1970s, Michael Tushman and his colleagues at Columbia University began to study whole sets of companies in several industries to understand some of the patterns of birth, development, change, and death (Tushman and Romanelli, 1985; Tushman, Newman, and Romanelli, 1986). A number of interesting patterns emerged.

For instance, different industries seemed to follow similar patterns of development. During the early phases of a particular industry, there is experimentation and slow growth. Then, as the product becomes accepted and dominant designs emerge, a large amount of rapid growth occurs. Later on, the product class begins to mature, and growth reduces and ultimately levels off. This leads to decline or to the emergence of a new product class that replaces the existing one (for example, jet airliners replacing piston craft or transistors replacing vacuum tubes), and the pattern starts all over again. This pattern of industry emergence is well known and is frequently referred to as the S Curve. There has been a good deal of research supporting the existence of such patterns.

The Tushman research, however, went beyond typical S Curve analysis and examined change. Documents, periodicals, and company data were examined to determine the amount of change that was going on in different companies within an industry during the various periods of evolution. The pattern that emerged from the research is shown in Figure 2.1. The wavy line superimposed over the S Curve in Figure 2.1 indicates the degree of change in firms in a certain class. Small oscillations indicate minor amounts of uncertainty and change, while large oscillations indicate large amounts of change in most of the companies in the class.

What the data indicate is that the amount of change in a set of companies is not random; it exhibits a pattern or regularity. Whole industries go through periods of relatively minor change or equilibrium, punctuated by intervals of major disequilibrium when the entire industry is shaken by some destabilizing event. This pattern of

Figure 2.1. Intensity of Change over Time.

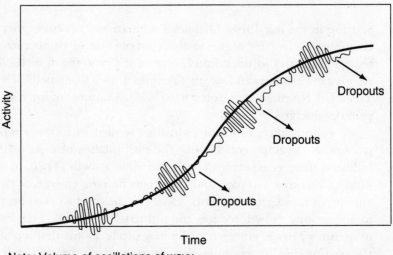

Note: Volume of oscillations of wavy
       line indicates amount of change in
       the industry at that point of time.

equilibrium, punctuated by destabilizing events and major industry-wide change, appears consistently in widely different industries.

Almost all companies undergo major changes during these periods of disequilibrium. They change strategy, they change structure, they change processes, and they change people. Those that do not change end up dropping out, either through exit, liquidation, or acquisition. Of those that do change, some succeed and some do not.

One of the factors that appears to be related to success is timing. Companies that move earlier during the period of disequilibrium tend to be more successful than those that move later. There are a number of reasons why early changers may have an advantage. First, they can experiment and even fail, and still have time to make second attempts. Second, companies that wait until later in the period of disequilibrium experience the stress of dealing with new environments, and therefore frequently find themselves running out of the resources (capital, people, time, reputation) needed to make the change. Third, those who move early may be able to influence the direction of either market or technology shifts. Fourth, those who act early learn and develop the skills to function effectively in the new environment.

A final point from the research concerns the rates of change. Every industry seems to go through periods of disequilibrium with some degree of regularity. However, the length of time between disequilibrium periods can vary greatly from industry to industry. In the cement industry, the periods are separated by thirty years, while in mini-computers, the periods occur every six years. In almost all industries, the rates of change appear to be increasing as underlying rates of change in markets, knowledge, and technology increase.

A Typology of Change

The research and the patterns that have been observed in industries and product classes suggest a way of thinking about change. At the broadest level, there are two types of change. First, there are the smaller changes that occur during periods of equilibrium; remember the small waves of oscillation in Figure 2.1. Then there are the changes that occur during periods of disequilibrium, represented by deep oscillations.

Even during periods of relative equilibrium, however, organizations do not stand still. Effective organizations are always implementing some form of improvement or modification: changing structure, modifying strategy, making improvements in culture, and so on. These changes are aimed at continuing to improve the fit among the components of the organization.

This type of change involves relatively focused and bounded improvements. Each step or change is part of a process of constant tinkering, adaptation, and modification as the organization attempts to solve problems and run itself more effectively. Each initiative attempts to build on the work that has already been accomplished and improves the functioning of the enterprise in relatively small increments. For these reasons, we call this type *incremental change*. Note that they are not necessarily small; they can be large in terms of resources needed or impact on people. But there is continuity to the pattern of ongoing change.

The second type of change occurs during periods of disequilibrium. The demands of a radically changing environment require equally radical changes in the organization. The organization is not trying to improve fit but rather to build a whole new configuration, with a new strategy, new work, new formal organization arrangements, and so forth. Ultimately, this new configuration should display high fit and become somewhat more stable, but only after a period of tremendous turbulence. Rather than a series of incremental changes on a continual basis, a continuation of a pattern already established, this type of change involves a complete break with the past and a major reconstruction of almost every element of the organization. Thus we refer to this type as *discontinuous change*. Figure 2.2 illustrates the two different patterns.

Discontinuous change is linked to major changes in the overall industry environment. For example, the challenges that Bob Allen faced at AT&T were the result of a number of different factors in the communications industry, including massive regulatory change, the emergence of new competitors, the development of significant new technologies, and the growth of new global players in the industry. All of these factors combined to necessitate a funda-

Figure 2.2. Incremental and Discontinuous Change.

Incremental Change   Discontinuous Change

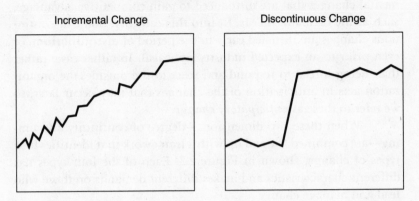

mental change in the industry, and therefore created an imperative for players in the industry to also make a fundamental change. Discontinuous change, therefore, is more traumatic, painful, and demanding on the organization. By its very nature, discontinuous change means that a certain degree of shock will be administered to the organization. It is often a radical departure from the past, and therefore carries with it all of the challenges associated with discontinuity. People, groups, and whole organizations not only have to learn new ways of thinking, working, and acting, but they also have to "unlearn" the habits, orientations, assumptions, and routines that have been baked into the enterprise over time. This unlearning can be difficult and even confusing for individuals.

Therefore, one way to think about change is that it is either incremental or discontinuous. However, there is a second factor to consider—the dimension of time. As we discussed earlier, timing affects success rates. Again, we can think of organizational change in two dimensions. In the first, an organization is forced to respond to changes in the environment, and forced to respond immediately. These are changes necessitated by some environmental event (in the incremental changes) or initiated late in the period of disequilibrium (in the discontinuous changes), but in either case initiated in reaction to a clear and present requirement. Therefore we refer to them as *reactive change*.

The other type of change, from a timing standpoint, is initiated without a clear and present environmental demand. Incremental changes that are introduced to gain competitive advantage, such as the Citibank ATMs, fit into this category. Some discontinuous changes are initiated early in the period of disequilibrium, or even prior to an expected industry upheaval. In either case, rather than being forced to respond and react to the outside, the organization acts in anticipation of the changes that may occur later, so we refer to these as *anticipatory change.*

When these two dimensions—degree of continuity and timing—are combined, we end up with a framework that identifies four types of change, shown in Figure 2.3. Each of the four types has different characteristics and makes different demands on those who lead and manage change.

The underlying hypothesis is that all significant change in organizations ultimately originates from the environment. Changes that occur in response to destabilizing events and periods of major disequilibrium must be, of necessity, discontinuous. Those that occur in the course of relatively calmer periods of industry development are usually incremental. Timing is the other dimension. Change happens in direct reaction to an environmental event or in anticipation of such events. Action in anticipation of change might

Figure 2.3. Types of Organizational Changes.

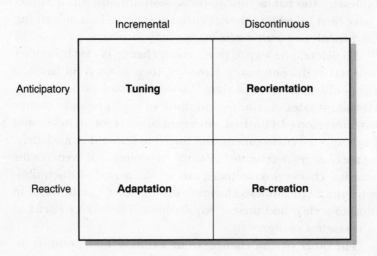

	Incremental	Discontinuous
Anticipatory	**Tuning**	**Reorientation**
Reactive	**Adaptation**	**Re-creation**

occur because someone either foresees a major destabilizing event occurring, or sees an opportunity to create a destabilizing event, which will in turn necessitate competitive reactions by others.

Tuning

When an organization initiates incremental change in anticipation of environmental events or in search of improved efficiency or effectiveness, but there is no immediate requirement to change, we call this *tuning*. Even well-run companies with relatively high congruence constantly seek better ways of achieving and defending their strategic visions. They may decide to:

1. Improve policies, methods, and procedures
2. Introduce new technologies
3. Redesign processes to lower cost, reduce time to market, and improve productivity
4. Initiate programs to improve quality and customer responsiveness
5. Enhance coordination and controls between units to increase organizational efficiency
6. Develop personnel especially suited to the present strategy through improved selection and training and by tailoring rewards to match strategic goals
7. Foster individual and group commitments to the company mission and to the excellence of individual department
8. Promote confidence in the accepted values, beliefs, norms, and organizational myths

Tuning maintains or enhances the fit between strategy and organization, and maintains or improves the internal congruence among organizational elements: work, formal organization, informal organization, and people. These incremental changes help maintain an organizational system that is more congruent and therefore more effective, efficient, and stable. Organizational change in these situations amounts to tinkering with a proven system in hopes of greater efficiencies or minor gains. Incremental changes occur over a finite period of time, usually weeks or months.

At the same time, these tuning changes can be sizable. The

Citibank ATM example is an illustration of large-scale tuning. ATMs were introduced both to gain competitive and cost advantage and in anticipation of some of the changes that new technology might create in the marketplace. It did not fundamentally change the concept of the bank's business (and that's what makes it incremental), but it did help fulfill the existing mission more effectively.

Adaptation

Tuning, as a rule, is initiated internally. But many incremental changes result from external conditions in the environment that require some response. That kind of change is called *adaptation;* it is incremental but reactive. In most cases, the enterprise is faced with an imperative to either change or suffer negative consequences. These consequences are not necessarily life-threatening, but they can be major.

Let's return again to our earlier example of automated teller machines. In New York City, following the Citibank actions, other banks found themselves in a tough position. As the marketplace responded positively to the Citibank move, customers began to demand access to ATMs. Other banks recognized that they would lose customers unless they, too, provided ATMs. One by one, they also installed the new technology, often at great cost. They were adapting to a reality of the external environment. While these changes were big, they were not fundamental modifications of the character, strategy, or identity of the institutions. The changes were incremental.

Reorientation

Change that is discontinuous but initiated in advance of or early in the cycle of industry change is called *reorientation.* It involves a fundamental redefinition of the enterprise—its identity, vision, strategy, and even its values. To maintain fit, it must also change the definition of its work, the capabilities and attitudes of its people, the formal structures and processes, and ultimately its culture. However, in reorientation, this is done before the change imperative has hit. An enterprise initiates a reorientation because an emerging environmental shift is perceived, or because it believes that by doing so, it can impact the industry in a way that will play to its favor as an early mover.

The changes that occurred at AT&T between 1988 and 1994 are an example of a major enterprisewide reorientation. The company that emerged in 1994 had a different identity, strategy, mission, and set of values. Its people had changed (by late 1993, eight of the original thirteen members of the senior team had departed), the organizational structure had been completely redesigned, and a new culture had been created.

An important feature of reorientations is that their anticipatory nature allows time for relatively gradual change, sometimes giving the outward appearance of incremental rather than discontinuous change. These transformations can be introduced initially in peripheral areas of the firm (Beer, Eisenstat, and Spector, 1990). The executive team can then manage the diffusion of these systemwide changes through transferring executives, building coalitions in support of the changes, and promoting and rewarding desired behaviors. The entire process might take anywhere from three to seven years.

The luxury of time also allows leaders to avoid disruptive departures from their organization's core values. Rather than being explicitly revoked, these values, which hold the organization together, are modified or "pruned" over time. At the same time, reorientations pose a unique challenge, since the need for change may not be as clear to people throughout the organization as it might be in a fight for survival. One of the key executive challenges in reorientation, then, is to create a sense of urgency about the change, despite the lack of an obvious crisis.

Re-creation

Unfortunately, not all organizations are blessed with visionary leaders who can anticipate environmental shifts, develop appropriate strategies and organizational approaches, and effectively implement these changes. Consequently, successful reorientations are relatively rare. More frequently, senior managers must bring about discontinuous change because an organization faces a fundamental crisis or because external conditions demand such a change.

A well-known example is Chrysler. During the 1970s, the

automobile industry went through a period of disequilibrium. The key destabilizing event was the emergence of the Japanese automobile industry and its successful entry into the U.S. market. This event created major shifts in the U.S. market, with customers expecting both lower prices and much higher quality in automobiles. Chrysler was late to perceive these changes and also lacked the resources to respond adequately. The response that it ultimately made was in reaction to the marketplace changes that caused a very real threat to the survival of the corporation. It recruited a new CEO, Lee Iacocca, who replaced almost all of the senior management team. It significantly redefined its scope, backing off from its goal of being a full-line car producer, eliminating its full-size cars, and divesting its foreign operations. Changes were made in virtually every aspect of how the company functioned. Iacocca had no choice; he was forced by the external events and the state of the company.

In situations such as Chrysler's, incremental change is not sufficient to allow the company to survive and prosper, yet there is not the luxury of time and opportunity to carefully craft a reorientation. The company must literally re-create itself if it is to survive. It does not have the luxury of time, resources, and reputation that the company in reorientation enjoys. The action must be swift, decisive, and all encompassing, and even then, the chances of survival are low. *Re-creation* involves the fast and simultaneous change of all the basic elements of the organizational system, usually in a matter of months. In particular, it differs from a reorientation in that it usually requires drastic shifts in the organization's core values.

Why all at once? Part of the timing imperative comes from the traumatic nature of this change. Rather than working within the present strategic and organizational context, re-creation requires a departure from core identity and values. It involves, of necessity, the destruction of certain elements of the organization, frequently elements that have been key to success in the past. A piecemeal approach gets bogged down in politics, individual resistance, and organizational inertia.

• Synergy can be a powerful force among the new elements of the organization. New executives with a fresh mission, working in a redesigned organization with revised norms and values, and bolstered by power and status, provide strong reinforcement for one another. During piecemeal change, on the other hand, portions of the new organization are typically out of sync with the old organization.

• Slow change gives pockets of resistance a chance to grow and spread. Such resistance is a natural response to fundamental changes that upset familiar routines and precedent. If strategic change is implemented slowly, individuals have a greater opportunity to undermine the changes, thus strengthening the organizational inertia that works to stifle fundamental change.

• In most organizations, there is usually a pent-up need for change. During stable periods of high congruence, basic adjustments are postponed. Boat rocking is discouraged. Once normal constraints are relaxed, a host of improvements press for attention. The exhilaration and momentum of a fresh effort (and a new team) make difficult moves more acceptable. Change is now in fashion.

• Re-creation is inherently risky. The longer the implementation period, the greater the period of uncertainty and instability. The most effective strategic changes are those that swiftly initiate the new strategy, structure, processes, and systems, and then embark on the next period of stability and congruent change. The sooner fundamental uncertainty is removed, the better the chances of organizational survival and growth.

Types of Change

Perhaps a metaphor can help us understand the differences among these types of change. Incremental changes are made within the context or frame of the current organization. The fundamental definition of the organization—its identity, values, and mission—does not change. These form the boundaries and borders of change. Incremental change happens within these borders, as indeed it should. Changing the frame is difficult and even dangerous, because it involves fighting against the forces of balance, fit, and congruence. So we think of these incremental changes as *changes within the frame*.

Discontinuous change is qualitatively different, since here the goal is to change the organizational frame itself. In reorientations, the goal is to modify the frame slowly (at least in relative terms), maintaining a degree of continuity with the past, building on the best of the past. The frame of the organization is changed, modified, and reshaped, but hopefully not broken. In reorientation, there is time to identify and build upon the existing strengths of the organization, including its history and traditions. Therefore, we refer to reorientations as *organizational frame bending*.

In re-creations, the changes are more sudden, more severe. Of necessity, they involve destruction of elements in the existing system. There is some breakage; there is no way to avoid it. We refer to this type of change as *organizational frame breaking*. The existing frame is deliberately broken and discarded, and a new frame is created. There is no time for any other course of action.

The four types of change are very different from one another. The first difference is the driving force of the change. While all change ultimately stems from the environment, the immediate driving force of incremental change is the search for internal efficiency, whether in anticipation of or response to external events. In reorientation, the driving force is the anticipation of future strategic shifts or periods of disequilibrium, while in re-creation the driving force is the need to respond to a very real and current strategic shift in the environment, frequently creating a performance crisis.

The focus of change is also different. In incremental change, the focus is on individual parts or subsystems of the organization, such as technology in the ATM example. In reorientation, the focus is on most, if not all, of the systems of the organization, including strategy, work, people, structure, and so on. In re-creation, there is a similar systemwide focus, but the immediacy of the change may not permit maintaining continuity with the past as can be achieved in reorientation. Re-creation often directly challenges, and even destroys, the existing core values.

The pacing is also different. Pacing will vary in incremental change; in reorientation, it will be relatively slow, with changes often starting in the periphery of the organization (in pilot units or distant operations), and then moving to the core. In re-creation, there is rapid, simultaneous, and systemwide change, usually during a short period of time.

The role of senior management is another point of difference. Incremental change requires support and effective delegation, while discontinuous change requires intimate, active leadership by the top of the organization. In reorientation, the senior management, including the CEO, are key drivers. They create a sense of urgency, and they are critical in keeping the organization focused. Persistence is key. In re-creation, they must also be key drivers, but it becomes particularly critical that they make the right strategic decisions, since the margin for error is small.

Different types of change also make different demands on the senior management. In incremental change, senior managers can continue to manage the way they have in the past; little replacement of individuals is required. In reorientation, many members of senior management may be unable to make the changes required in values, behavior, and thinking; almost all successful changes involve replacement of a significant number of senior executives. However, the pace provides the opportunity for people to learn and grow, and some of them will be able to change and function successfully in the new environment. In re-creation, this luxury does not exist; large numbers of senior managers are replaced, including, in almost all cases, the CEO and most of the senior team.

Finally, the reason that these differences are significant is that each type of change requires a different approach to change management. The senior-level change-management requirements in incremental change are relatively minor. Good implementation planning (in itself not a minor issue) is required. Reorientation demands that great effort be put into change management. In particular, reorientation poses a special problem. Since the enterprise is moving early in the period of disequilibrium, it may not be apparent to the organization why there is a need to engage in such major change. Therefore, the task of senior management is to create a sense of urgency and motivate people to change before there is a clear and present danger. In re-creation, the danger is already present, and the urgency may be apparent, so that management's task becomes one of creating a vision, providing confidence, and dealing with resistance to change.

Implications for Change Management

The different requirements of change management form the foundation of this book. A basic hypothesis is that different types of change require different types of change management strategies, approaches, and methods.

A starting point for change management is to consider the different degrees of intensity—the stress, trauma, dislocation, and even pain caused by the change. Discontinuous change is more intense than incremental change, and reactive change is more intense than anticipatory change. During reactive change, all are aware that failure may threaten survival. Time pressure is great, and resources may be short. In relative ranking, tuning is the least intense change, followed by adaptation. Reorientation brings a jump in intensity, and re-creation has the highest level of intensity.

If we take the idea of intensity and add another factor, we can better understand different change requirements. Organizations vary in complexity—the number and variety of different pieces that make up the organization, whether they be functions, units, people, or processes. As an organization becomes more complex, the task of managing change becomes more difficult.

When considering possible situations where change management is required, we can combine the two dimensions of intensity and complexity. This is shown graphically in Figure 2.4. At the lower left, where complexity is low and intensity is low, changes can be managed through normal management processes. Enterprises that are reasonably competent in project management and other forms of basic implementation can manage changes through the normal systems and processes of accountability.

However, as change becomes more intense or the organizational setting becomes more complex, the task of change management grows significantly, to the point where it cannot be handled by those normal processes. The preferred approach here is change through delegation. The senior management creates special structures and roles to facilitate the management of change. This approach is frequently referred to as transition management, and involves mechanisms specially created for the purpose of managing a specific change. In transition management, however, the senior team plays a supporting role, and the organization continues to be run as it was before. If the change is intense enough, it may appear on the senior team's agenda as one of a number of important items to be reviewed and managed over time.

Figure 2.4. Types of Change Management.

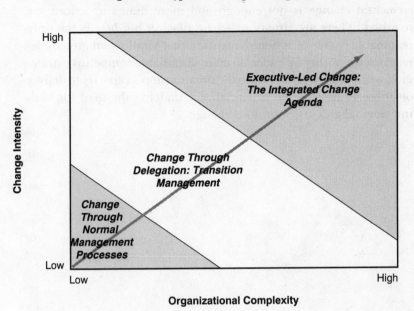

As intensity and complexity increase, the processes used to run the organization are themselves the subject of change. In those situations, delegation can no longer be employed; change management becomes a primary executive task. In these situations of high intensity and high complexity, the primary job of senior management becomes to lead the company through discontinuous change. Change is not merely one of the issues on the CEO's agenda, it *is* the CEO's agenda.

Conclusion

Organizational effectiveness requires that organizations recognize the need for different types of change and take steps to manage them accordingly. In some cases, the type of changes required are incremental in nature. Managing ongoing incremental change is a demanding task. Corporate leaders would be foolish to do anything more than incremental change when that is what's needed. In other cases, discontinuous change is required, and to respond any differently is to risk organizational ruin. These are situations when incremental change is not enough and more dramatic actions are required. There are situations where placing big bets is the only reasonable course of action. Organizational vitality and growth depend on the ability of leaders to craft sustainable competitive strategies, while effectively building the organization's capacity to deliver on those strategies, and in so doing, balancing the need for both incremental and discontinuous change.

The Challenge of
Discontinuous Change

David A. Nadler
Michael L. Tushman

In 1983, James R. "Jamie" Houghton was named chairman and CEO of the Corning Glass Works. He should have been elated at finally reaching the top of the prestigious firm that his family had run for five generations, but he was actually deeply disturbed by what he saw around him. The operating margins of the company had slipped to a mere 2 percent. Whole sets of businesses appeared to be mired in what was, at best, mediocre performance. Other businesses were facing tough new competition from new players in Europe and Japan. The quality of products and services had deteriorated, and customers were unhappy. In the face of all this, the company's "country club" atmosphere conveyed a sense of detachment, complacency, and lack of aggressiveness.

Early on, Houghton realized that the company would have to undergo very profound and far-reaching changes if it were to survive, much less prosper. Starting with a dramatic speech to a group of his senior managers, and under the banner of performance and total quality, he began a whole series of initiatives. He created a new senior team called the management committee and announced a new, more collegial style of leadership. Along with this new team, he set high performance goals, calling for a return to a minimum of 10 percent operating margins. He instituted a companywide, intensive program of quality improvement. He created a new strategic vision called "the wheel" and divested divisions that chronically underperformed or did not fit the vision. He then shocked many by removing a member of his new senior team for failure to meet performance objectives. The management committee worked on the development and implementation of a new set of corporate values. Compensation programs were changed to increase variable compensation and tie rewards to corporate or unit performance.

Over time, the changes began to pay off and pay off big. By 1992, the company had regained and even surpassed its historical performance levels. The market value of the company more than tripled, and Corning was rated twelfth on the *Fortune* most admired list.

Jamie Houghton's success at Corning is an example of effective management of discontinuous change. While the firm was threatened and performance had declined, he and his colleagues were still far enough ahead of the game to approach the change as a reorientation. They could build continuity with the past and take several years to bring about the change. At the same time, the changes were deep and profound. The very identity of the company changed—indeed, about halfway through the process, the company changed its name from Corning Glass Works to Corning Inc.

Corning's return from near death is a remarkable story of vision, leadership, and change. Fortunately, there are similar stories about other companies, such as British Air, Chrysler, Hewlett Packard, and Xerox. These companies have demonstrated that it is possible to successfully anticipate or react to environmental disequilibrium. In each case, however, the leadership recognized that the challenges facing their enterprises required a vastly different kind of change. They realized that major discontinuous change was the only way out of a cycle of despair and failure.

The Challenge of Discontinuous Change

Discontinuous change is qualitatively different from incremental change. It requires a break with the past, perhaps even the deliberate destruction of certain elements of the current system. It raises fundamental issues of values and basic vision. It is frequently uncertain, incomplete, and headed toward a future that is unclear. It is traumatic, painful, and demanding on the organization and its people.

Given all that, why would an organization undertake such a task? Because failure to do so has calamitous consequences.

There are a number of key differences between discontinuous and incremental change:

• *The role of organizational fit.* During periods of equilibrium, the goal of those leading and shaping the organizational system is to promote congruence or fit. In the short term, fit leads to effectiveness. The challenge is to identify those elements that display poor fit and take corrective action. In the face of discontinuous change, fit ironically ceases to become a facilitator and becomes an obstacle. It is because of fit that organizations display inertia or are impervious to outside influence. In fact, good fit helps create stability, which is useful in times of equilibrium. This very inertia creates problems when major change is attempted. Discontinuous change frequently requires the destruction of some elements in the current system that are in fit with each other so that change will be possible in all of the parts of the organization.

• *Strategy and vision.* While incremental changes may involve any number of components within an organizational system, discontinuous change always involves major shifts in enterprise strategy and vision. Because of this, it raises questions of purpose, identity, and meaning of the enterprise, and it therefore may raise fundamental issues of values and basic questions such as, "Who are we?" or "Why does this enterprise exist?" It also calls into question the core competencies of the enterprise. Industry disequilibrium and change can destroy the value of certain competencies. If, for example, one has strong competencies in optically based reprographics (as did Xerox), and the industry undergoes a technological

shift to digital scanning and printing, the value of those competencies depreciates to almost zero very quickly. On the other hand,
industry change may increase the value of other competencies.
Change in competency value strikes at the heart of what an organization is, what it does well, who it values, and how it competes.

• *Multiple and concurrent changes.* Discontinuous change
involves change in all elements of the organization—strategy, work,
formal organization, informal organization, and people. It leaves
very few points of stability and requires simultaneous management
of multiple initiatives, investments, and programs. As a result, it
places great stress on the core management processes of the organization at the very time that those same processes are being challenged and changed. Multiple streams also raise the potential
problem of overload. People find that they can only handle so many
initiatives, programs, or changes at once. When overloaded, they
may disengage from the changes at hand.

• *Incomplete transitions.* In incremental change, the expectation is that the move to the future state will be completed.
Given the environmentally driven uncertainty resulting from disequilibrium, many of the individual transitions initiated during
discontinuous change may not get completed as events occur and
new issues gain priority. This creates the need for managers of
change to be ready and able to readjust their initiatives and recal-
ibrate their objectives during the process of change.

• *Unclear future state.* The incremental change model is
based on the concept of a current state, a future state, and a transition state. This perspective is useful for incremental change since
it is usually possible to describe and specify what the future state
is. In discontinuous change, the future state is unclear. In fact, since
it is not certain when the transition period ends (or at least abates),
the whole concept of moving toward a specific desired future state
has little meaning, and may even be misleading. A discontinuous
change entails multiple transition states heading toward an uncertain future state that itself may be a transition state of some form.

• *Change time span.* Incremental changes occur over a finite period of time, usually ranging from weeks to months. Discontinuous change, because of its depth and scope, usually takes more
time. Reorientations of enterprises of any size appear to require

anywhere from three to seven years, depending upon the nature of the change and the size and complexity of the organization. Recreations appear to take less time because the initial actions usually take place during a short period of time. The replacement of management, changes of strategy, and restructuring of the enterprise all might happen in a matter of months. Upon closer examination, these initial dramatic and often shocking events are generally followed by other changes that may take years.

• *Leadership.* Incremental change can be delegated. While the most senior levels of management may need to encourage, monitor, and support such change, they need not be intimately involved. Discontinuous change, because of its scope and depth, must be led by the CEO and his or her senior team. It cannot be delegated. Leadership becomes a necessary and critical element for success.

Given these differences, it is important to understand the nature of discontinuous organizational change—be it frame bending or frame breaking—if we are to develop approaches for the effective leadership and management of these transformations.

Discontinuous change poses three basic challenges to enterprise leaders. First, there is the challenge of *recognition.* Disequilibrium—major turbulence in the environment, exacerbated by a destabilizing event—creates a change imperative, and the early-moving frame benders have a greater chance at success than the later-moving frame breakers. The ability to recognize the building conditions is critical. Second, there is the challenge of *strategic choice.* Disequilibrium calls into question the basic strategies, directions, mission, and core competencies of the organization. The effective response to disequilibrium must of necessity be a strategic response—a repositioning of offerings, the development of new offerings, change of the portfolio, new types of innovation, improvements in quality, and so forth. The internal changes should flow from the core strategic choices. The third challenge is *organizational change management.* Discontinuous change requires change in all of the components of organization and frequently all at once. The challenge is how to go about constructing an integrated change agenda, how to execute it, and what role institutional leaders should play.

The Challenge of Recognition

An enterprise can't anticipate or respond to disequilibrium if it can't see it. Therefore, it is absolutely critical that the leadership of organizations develop the capacity to recognize important environmental shifts and be capable of predicting ahead of time the need for discontinuous change. Several methods are available to help the senior team discern the need for change.

1. *Scanning the environment.* Recognition is more likely when leaders are engaged in frequent scanning of the environment. They should be searching for evidence of the precursors of discontinuous change identified in Chapter One: technological change, industry maturation, macroeconomic trends, regulatory changes, new competitive forces, and growth. More specifically, they should be on the lookout for leading indicators. For example, the emergence of new and nontraditional competitors may be a clue. The development of new offerings that serve as substitutes, rather than direct competition, for the products and services one provides, can also serve as a clue.

In particular, they should be especially vigilant for events that appear to change the rules of competition and the rules of engagement in an industry. For example, the emergence of CNN should have served as a warning to the U.S. television networks that the rules of industry competition were changing. Similarly, the invasion of Japanese automobiles in the late 1970s violated the long-held assumption that high-quality, low-cost cars were not possible; the death of that assumption should have signaled a fundamental change in the marketplace.

This environmental scanning needs to be more than a purely intellectual or academic exercise. The decision to initiate discontinuous change is ultimately a question of judgment, influenced by the feelings of the CEO and the senior team. That judgment needs the benefit of real experiences, rather than just distant and sanitized data displays.

2. *Make the senior team a learning device.* The CEO and the senior team can be a collective learning device. To accomplish this, the team must devote dedicated time to learning, and needs to

ensure that it has the processes in place to enable individuals to learn together. The goal is a team that is constantly engaged in scanning the environment and building and testing hypotheses about what is happening and how it might affect the enterprise.

Specifically, senior teams that are good learning mechanisms bring in outsiders (industry analysts, experts, consultants, academics) to share their views of the world, the industry, and the company. They also spend a lot of time engaging customers to understand firsthand and viscerally what is on the customers' minds and agendas. These teams engage in competitive benchmarking, visit other companies, and seek to learn from their best practices. They spend time examining and reflecting on both failures and successes to derive the maximum insight possible.

The need to learn goes beyond its value for recognition of disequilibrium. Senior teams and organizations at large develop unique knowledge over time that provides them with potential sustainable competitive advantage. We can think of this knowledge as the intellectual capital of the organization. Normally, this intellectual capital, like any other kind of capital, depreciates at a certain rate. New events negate the value of some older knowledge. During times of disequilibrium and discontinuous change, however, this becomes more acute. As the rate of change increases, intellectual capital depreciates at a faster rate. That means that the organization as a whole, and the senior team specifically, must invest more time and effort to learn in order to replenish its dwindling stock of conceptual equity.

3. *Experimentation.* So far we've talked about methods to scan and recognize the actions of others that may precipitate disequilibrium. The ultimate competitive advantage, however, comes when the enterprise is able to author a destabilizing event that reshapes the industry in a way that plays to its own competencies and advantages. That is made possible through experimentation and innovation. The senior team needs to encourage and then make room for sources of learning and invention. These may be market probes, new products, new ways of relating to customers, or new processes. The important point is to make sure that experiments and innovations that challenge the collective wisdom or traditions of the organization are protected and encouraged.

A classic example of the value of experimentation is seen in the early days of the IBM personal computer. The approach taken by those developing this product challenged many of the organization's commonly held truths. The open architecture, third-party chip and operating system, and distribution channels were all experiments with new ways of thinking and working. Despite later problems, the introduction of the IBM PC turned out to be a major destabilizing event that created a new period of disequilibrium in that part of the computer industry.

4. *Vigilance of success.* We know that success can create problems. To avoid the success trap (see Chapter One) senior teams need to be very vigilant. Corning's Houghton talks about this in his "contrarian leadership role." His view is that the role of the leader during troubled times is to be optimistic, upbeat, and future oriented. The leader's role during periods of great success is to be the skeptic, to question success, and to point out its potential problems and threats. The CEO and the senior team play an important role in preventing the success syndrome from settling in and in keeping the organization skeptical of its own success.

5. *Scenario development.* Another approach involves the development of hypothetical scenarios related to possible environmental changes. The senior team spends time identifying possible destabilizing events and working through either responses or implications for anticipation. A very graphic example of this is given in an account of Shell Oil's planning system (DeGeus, 1988). Building scenarios related to potential OPEC actions enabled the company to anticipate and then respond more effectively to major disequilibrium in that industry.

At the core of all these approaches is the need to spend "senior time" on the issue of environmental shifts. Leaders need to understand the nature and the dynamics of the system of which the enterprise is part. Only then can the precursors of discontinuous change be detected.

The Challenge of Strategic Choice

Once an environmental shift is recognized, the second challenge is to develop the appropriate strategic responses. Our purpose here is not to investigate the content issues of strategy; significant and valuable work has been done on this issue elsewhere. However, the *process* of strategy formulation in these periods is crucial to change management.

When faced with disequilibrium, successful companies had to address four major issues. First, they had to reconceptualize the environment. They had to spend time understanding the nature and implications of the destabilizing events. They also spent time creating hypotheses about where the strategic environment might lead. Second, they spent time examining and understanding their core competencies in light of the value-creation or value-destruction effects of the environmental change. They worked to understand which competencies they had that would be of value in the new environment, and in some cases they identified critical, but missing, competencies. Third, they developed a new core positioning, a rethinking of "what are the market needs we are responding to, what are our offerings, and what is our competitive advantage relative to other suppliers?" Fourth, they developed specific strategies, initiatives, programs, and investments to implement those new strategies.

The process that many have found useful is what we call *strategic choice* (Bliss, 1992). The bias of strategic choice is that the senior team, including the CEO, should be the ones who shape strategy, not specialized staffs. This is consistent with our view of the senior team as a critical learning system for the organization. Strategic choice advocates that the team work together to discuss multiple views of the environment, and then develop and debate alternative strategic models or prototypes, called integrated strategic alternatives. This is an ongoing process, with much "senior time" spent in team settings.

Strategic choice is not an event, it is actually a process. It's not a matter of making one key strategic choice and then implementing it. Particularly during times of disequilibrium, the strategy process is inherently iterative. The environment is analyzed, core competencies are assessed, and choices are made and executed. These actions have consequences in terms of impact on the environment. In light of those consequences, the environment and core competencies are then examined again and new choices are made. These choices are critical, since all the other organizational change activities are driven in one way or another by the strategic alternatives chosen.

The Challenge of Re-creation

The third challenge is how to effectively lead and manage discontinuous change. Once disequilibrium has been recognized and understood, and the initial strategic choices have been made, leaders then face the very major task of managing all other elements of organizational change (beyond strategy and vision), which make up the CEO's integrated change agenda.

The management of discontinuous change draws on the basic concepts of transition management presented in Part Two of this book, but it also goes beyond those concepts. Discontinuous change, like incremental change, poses issues of power, anxiety, and control. In fact, all of those issues are felt much more dramatically and intensively. In the following chapters, we will address this challenge and draw on our experiences to identify effective approaches and methods for managing discontinuous change.

PART TWO

The Practice of Discontinuous Change

The Fundamentals of Change Management

Kathleen F. Morris
Charles S. Raben

Managers leading organizations through a period of change encounter a number of potential obstacles that make the transition a complex and challenging process. This chapter looks at contemporary applications of fundamental principles. These principles apply to situations of incremental and discontinuous change and thus comprise a basic framework for change agents. Specifically, we see three keys to effectively managing the basics of organizational change: motivating people to act constructively by providing opportunities for ownership and empowerment; managing the transition to ensure sustained performance and control; and managing the political dynamics by building a critical mass of support for change.

Resistance to Change

Why should change leaders care about the top layer of managers? It is easy to assume that resistance is something that occurs among the rank and file, and that managers are completely in agreement with the change. Yet resistance to change is part of the human condition, and senior managers are not immune.

An imposed change reduces a person's perceived autonomy or self-control. In addition, people typically develop patterns for coping with their current situation. Change means that they will have to find new, perhaps less successful, ways of managing their own environment. Many perceive that the change will cause them personal loss (reduced status, authority, pay), either directly or because of some eventual consequence not yet apparent.

People may also resist change for cognitive reasons; they truly believe, based on their best information and accumulated experience, that the desired future state is misdirected and that the current state or other alternatives are better. They may believe that the change itself, or unintended consequences of the change, will cause the organization to lose something valuable. They may also resist change for ideological reasons, believing the change violates an important principle or commitment that the organization must stand by.

Our experience suggests that an observable pattern of responses often emerges during periods of transition. Anxiety and political issues fuel a predictable set of behaviors that are generic to many change circumstances. Let's look more closely at this pattern of responses.

- *Change is fought with "rational" arguments.* An initial form of resistance is support for the status quo. Well-developed reasons that "explain" why the current situation exists are put forth. Things are the way they are for reasons that have been around for a long time and that everyone accepts as legitimate. In comparison, the proposed changes are often not as well developed; many questions are yet to be addressed. Consequently, the completeness of the argument for change will appear less strong than the one that supports the status quo. People will capitalize on this incompleteness by claiming the case for change is less "rational" than the case for not changing.
- *Targets of blame are sought.* Once a change has been

proposed, people will begin to look for someone to hold responsible. The usual targets are the individuals perceived as the decision makers, either senior management or the task force or committee that made the original recommendation.

- *"Hall talk" increases and productivity suffers.* During periods of change, people will begin to seek each other out to test various interpretations of what they hear and what it all could possibly mean. As a result, there is a lot of "hall talk" and speculation about the future. Individuals will spend a lot of time with others trying to piece together a complete story from what they are told. The consequence of all this is a predictable and dangerous dip in productivity. Less time is spent worrying about the job and more time worrying about the future. Why work if the job may not be there? People will often adopt an attitude of "wait and see" during periods of change.

- *Factions begin to form.* As the "hall talk" continues, factions begin to form. People seek out those who share their point of view about the proposed changes. These groups serve to comfort those who belong to them and to reinforce their beliefs about the change. Under threat of a common enemy, these "vigilante groups" continue to oppose change while gaining strength in numbers and in the firmness of their beliefs.

- *Informal leaders emerge.* From the several groups and factions that form, informal leaders begin to emerge. The strength of their conviction tends to increase because of the added social dimension of representing a group that cheers them on. These leaders become more vocal and opposed to the change than they might originally have appeared.

- *Perceived decision makers are tested.* As the messages about change persist, people begin to test the conviction and support of the decision makers they view as responsible for the change. If the people behind the changes don't really believe in them or endorse them, how real could they be? This is an especially vulnerable point for senior teams. The lack of common support for change among members of a senior team will be viewed by the organization as a sure sign that the reality of the change may be less than it appears. On the other hand, a team strongly in support of change strengthens the perception and belief that change is real and very likely to occur.

• *Individuals begin to align with perceived power structure.* With the passage of time and persistent messages, the possibility of change becomes more real. As they come to accept the reality of change, people also begin to strategize about how to ensure they emerge on the winning team. Some people will go to great lengths to declare their support of the change. Others will seek out those who they see as responsible and try to get on their good side.

• *As a failsafe, people appeal to relationships.* In an effort to ensure their future, some people will ultimately appeal to their personal relationship with those they see as capable of taking care of them. This line of thinking goes something like this: "Friends take care of friends. If I have a good relationship with my manager, she will be sure that I'm not hurt when all of this is over. At the very least, guilt will prevent her from acting harshly toward me." To further this strategy, people begin to renew their relationships with people they haven't seen in a while, especially those who matter. Social invitations to lunch, dinner, or a weekend game of golf become increasingly common. Although direct discussion of the subject rarely occurs, expectations are clearly established.

Of course, many other dysfunctional behaviors arise during periods of change. The behaviors discussed here appear in diverse situations and circumstances, and they represent fairly common patterns that any organization should expect to see whenever major change is initiated.

One of the major difficulties in dealing with resistance to change is identifying the type of resistance and dealing with it appropriately. Often, change managers assume that cognitive resistance is actually disguised emotional resistance. We have found this to be true, but usually this occurs later in the process. Initially, much of the cognitive resistance is actually cognitive, and discussion, education, and sharing sessions do quite a bit to address it. However, there are some holdouts who continue to resist long after the majority have been convinced. Diagnosing their resistance and dealing with them is far more complex.

Motivating Change

To counter the forces of resistance, strategies for motivating constructive behavior are needed. When a broad and significant change occurs in the organization, the first question many people ask is "What's in it for me?" or "What's going to happen to me?" These are an indication of the anxiety that occurs when people are faced with the uncertainty associated with organizational change. The task of management will be to somehow relieve that anxiety and motivate constructive behavior. This is done through a variety of actions. Some actions are aimed at providing much-needed information: communicating the nature, extent, and impact of the change. Others are focused on building ownership, providing clear rewards for required behavior, and recognizing and dealing with some of the natural anxiety.

The first action step is to *identify and surface dissatisfaction with the current state.* Most people are psychologically attached to the current state, because it is comfortable and familiar. A critical factor, then, is to demonstrate how unrealistic it is to assume that the current state is and always will be good. The goal is to unfreeze people from their inertia and to create some willingness to explore the possibility of change. The greater the pain and dissatisfaction with the current state, the greater the motivation to change and the less the resistance to change.

More and more organizations are recognizing the need to design and manage a set of events that enable people to experience *for themselves* the need for change. Based on the premise that a "selling" strategy has limitations—while it may induce compliance, it does not necessarily engender commitment—thought must be given to how to help people build their own compelling story for change, and then enact it as part of their own reality.

Techniques for this involve providing specific information, such as educating people about what is occurring in the environment that is creating the need for change. In addition, it is useful to help people understand the economic and business consequences of not changing. It may be helpful to identify and emphasize the discrepancy between what the situation is and what it should be. In critical cases, it may be necessary to paint a disaster scenario in which people can see what would happen if the current state continued unchanged—the more graphic, the better. One manager spoke very dramatically about what would happen if the division did not become successful within eighteen months: "They'll pull buses up to the door, close the plant, and cart away the workers and the machinery."

A robust strategy also makes use of participation efforts, such as self-diagnostic or study teams, who collect customer information, engage in benchmarking efforts, or are tasked to help the organization improve. An important role of leadership, in this case, is to sponsor the collection of data and provide opportunities for organization members to understand the overall themes and associated actions needed to move the organization into the future.

The second action area for motivation is *participation in planning and implementing change.* One of the most consistent findings in the research on change is that participation in the change tends to increase excitement, reduce resistance, build ownership, and thus motivate people to make the change work (Coch and French, 1948; Vroom, 1964; Kotter and Schlesinger, 1979). Participation also facilitates communicating what the change will be and why it has come about. Participation may also lead to obtaining new information from those involved, information that may enhance the effectiveness of the change.

In one of the regional Bell operating companies, this strategy took the form of a set of transition teams made up of a diagonal slice of managers, supervisors, and craftspeople from all parts of the state. Their role was to function as change agents for their particular business units. Armed with a broad array of business information, quality tools, and an understanding of change, they acted as influencers, interpreters, and feedback loops to people at *their* own level of the business. The amount of candor, energy, and enthusiasm that these teams built over a period of two years was, in the word of their sponsoring executive vice president, "awesome." To him, this group offered the hope that, indeed, broad-scale participation in running the business was possible. He regularly sought them out to act as sounding boards for his policy and practice proposals. They, in turn, brought him unfiltered news of the organization's pulse.

Many change leaders struggle with participation. It takes time, involves giving up some control, and may create conflict and increase ambiguity. However, using some form of participation usually outweighs the costs of no involvement at all. The essential task, then, is to choose where, how, and when to build in participation. People may participate in the early diagnosis of problems, in the design or development of solutions, in implementation planning, or in the actual execution of the implementation. There are many options. Different individuals or groups may participate at different times, depending upon their skills and expertise, their information, and the need for their acceptance and ownership of the change. Participation can be direct and widespread, or indirect through representatives. Representatives may be chosen by position, level, or expertise. Many specific participation devices are available, ranging from large-scale data collection to sensing groups to questionnaires to cross-unit committees.

A third action step is to *build in rewards* for the desired behavior, both during the transition state and in the future state. People tend to do what they perceive they will be rewarded for doing. Both formal and informal rewards must be identified and tied to the needed behavior, both for the transition and for the future state. The most frequent problem is that organizations expect individuals to behave in certain ways, especially in a transition, while rewarding them for other conflicting behaviors (Kerr, 1975). A more subtle variant of this is that while leaders want people to behave differently, they often don't take the actions necessary at their level of the organization to demonstrate that rewards have changed.

In our experience, promotion decisions during transition are the most telling signal of whether "they're serious" about the change. When significant change in operating style or culture is required, new behaviors will be needed by leaders and managers. Typically, the promotion system continues to run as usual during the transition, resulting in promotions that send mixed signals at best, and all too often, the wrong signal. In addition, senior managers are sometimes unwilling to remove or demote managers who do not demonstrate the right behavior. Both of these actions undermine the organization's perception of the seriousness of the change.

Bonuses, pay systems, promotions, recognition, job assignments, and status symbols all need to be carefully examined during major organizational changes, and then restructured to support the direction of the transition. Change leaders should put into place immediate rewards that reinforce behavior consistent with the change (such as informal recognition and involvement in decision-making forums); they should also actively monitor promotions, both within their control and through their organizations. Over time, a key action step is revising other reward systems, such as financial compensation, that can pose more risk if handled improperly.

Finally, people need to be provided with the *time and opportunity to disengage from the present state.* People feel a natural attachment to the way things are. Change frequently creates feelings of loss, not unlike a death. People need to mourn for the old system or familiar way of doing things. This is frequently manifested in the emergence of stories or myths about the "good old days," even when those days weren't so good. Dealing with a loss takes time, and those managing change should take this into account.

Management, knowing this is essential, can greatly help it along. A number of specific techniques are possible. One is to provide the appropriate time for letting go, while giving people enough information and preparation to help them detach from the current state. Another technique may be to provide the opportunity to vent emotions through something similar to a wake. This can be done in small group sessions or discussions, in which people are encouraged to talk about their feelings. While this may seem at first to promote resistance, it can have the opposite effect if facilitated with a focus on moving toward the future. It may also be useful to create ceremony, ritual, or symbols (such as farewell or closing-day ceremonies) to help give people some psychological closure on the old organization.

Managing the Transition

The transition is that time period between the current and the future state, when the change process is under way. It is a time of high uncertainty, because the current state is being disassembled before the future state is fully operational. Problems of control are the most critical here. Change leaders need to manage the transition with the same degree of care, the same resources, and the same skills as any other major project.

One of the first and most critical steps for managing the transition state is to *develop and communicate a clear image of the future*. Resistance and confusion frequently develop because people are unclear about what the future state will be like. The goals and purposes of the change become blurred, and individual expectations are formed on the basis of information that is frequently erroneous. In the absence of a clear image of the future, rumors develop, and people design their own fantasies to act upon. One senior manager refers to this as "MSU"—making stuff up.

A clear image of the future state should be developed to serve as a guideline, target, or goal. The image does not need to specify every aspect of the new organization, but should describe what the new key principles will be and how they will look in operation. In a financial services organization, the CEO described the future state this way: "We will be a client-focused, market-segmented business where there will be clear line of sight to our clients. This will mean a variety of things—for example, our product organizations will provide offerings based on what our new segment managers tell us their customers need."

This is one area where the alignment of the senior management group is a critical success factor. The challenge lies in taking the image of the future state to various parts of the organization and making it *real* to them in terms of how it may look in their segment of the organization. The CEO cannot, and should not, do this alone, since another litmus test is the degree to which other members of the senior group are on board with the change and able to describe it in consistent and appealing terms.

Building alignment around the future state image requires an investment of time by senior groups to discuss, debate, and construct their collective view. A written description may help clarify the image. It also may be useful to construct an impact statement that identifies the effect the change will have on different parts of the organization and on people.

It is also important to maintain a stable vision, and to avoid unnecessary or extreme modifications or conflicting views of that vision during the transition. Similarly, it is important to communicate information to everyone involved in the change, including what the future state will be like, how the transition will come about, why the change is being implemented, and how people will be affected by the change. This can be accomplished in a variety of ways, such as written communications, small group meetings, large briefing sessions, videotaped presentations, and so forth. In fact, what is needed is *over*communication. Anxiety impairs normal functioning; people may be unable to truly hear and integrate messages they receive the first time around. It may be necessary to repeat key messages two, three, four, and even five times, using different media and methods. When senior managers reflect on their leadership of change efforts, inevitably they believe that they underestimated the amount of communication needed, particularly at the outset.

A second action step for managing the transition involves the use of *multiple and consistent leverage points.* An organization, remember, is a system made up of four interdependent components: work, people, and formal and informal arrangements. Changes in all areas are needed to bring about significant and lasting changes in organizational behavior. Changes targeted at individuals and social relations (such as training and group intervention) tend to fade out quickly with few lasting effects when done in isolation (Porter, Lawler, and Hackman, 1975). On the other hand, work and structural changes alone, while powerful and enduring, frequently produce unintended and dysfunctional consequences (Lawler and Rhode, 1976).

Lasting change in the intended direction requires multiple leverage points to modify more than a single component. And the changes must be structured so that they are consistent; the training of individuals, for example, should dovetail with new job descriptions, reward systems, or reporting relationships. Otherwise, changes run the risk of creating new poor fits among organizational components. The result is either an abortive change or a decrease in organizational performance.

In any transition, there is the question of how much change the organization can absorb. In two recent cases, sequencing the leverage points became an interesting challenge. Both companies had significantly altered their structure, created new general management positions, and asked each unit to develop business strategies and plans for its new piece of the business, staff the new organizations, take on profit and loss responsibility, develop new measures of performance, and get access to new information on business operations—all in a period of nine months.

Not surprisingly, the new managers were trying to do all of this using the same behaviors and competencies they had before taking the new positions. A major aspect of the change focused on teamwork and empowerment, and yet these managers were exhibiting serious turf-guarding and backbiting. Clearly, the operating style of the future state hadn't taken hold, but where was the share of mind to influence it? In hindsight, the obvious lesson is that there are limits not only to the amount of change organizations can handle but also to the amount that should be initiated. Multi-year transition strategies need to be developed and communicated so that managers know how much they need to absorb and change.

The next action area involves using *transition devices*. Since the transition state is different from the current and future states, some kind of structure is needed to manage it (Beckhard and Harris, 1977). Ideally the structure should incorporate four elements: a transition manager; specific transition resources, including budget, time, and staff; specific transition structures, such as dual management systems with steering committees, design teams, transition teams, and backup support; and a transition plan.

1.   *Transition manager.* This person should have the power and authority needed to facilitate the transition, and should be appropriately linked to the CEO, probably a key senior manager. This person should also be capable of dealing with the extreme stress that comes with the role, and be able to act constructively in the face of pressure. This individual needs extensive support resources, however, since it is virtually impossible for one person to handle all of the details inherent in major transitions.

The transition manager is often supported by a transition team. We are seeing the increased use of transition steering groups, made up of line managers and key managers from corporate resources, including human resources, planning, quality, communication, and information systems, because so much of the organization needs to be redesigned.

2. *Transition resources.* Major transitions involve potentially large risks for organizations. Given this, they are worth doing well, and worth the needed resources to make them happen effectively. Resources such as personnel, financing, training, and consultative expertise must be provided for the transition manager to be effective.

3. *Transition structures.* It is difficult for a hierarchy to manage the process of change, and so it is usually necessary to develop other structures outside the regular organizational arrangement during the transition period, such as special task forces or design teams, pilot projects and experimental units (see Beckhard and Harris, 1977, for a discussion of these different devices). Existing networks and roundtables on quality, communication, and diversity are also useful as transition structures.

A word of caution is necessary: organizations frequently underestimate what it takes to design and implement a change. The downside of pilots or experiments, especially in companies anxious for early "wins" or evidence that the change is happening, is that they are exported too quickly into operation without the necessary check step of learning and generalizing to larger applications.

4. *Transition plan.* A transition is a movement from one state to another. To have that occur effectively, and to measure and control performance, a plan is needed with clear benchmarks, standards of performance, and similar features. Implicit in such a plan is a specification of the responsibilities of key individuals and groups.

The final action step involves *developing feedback mechanisms* to provide information on the effectiveness of the transition and areas requiring additional attention or action. There is a huge amount of anecdotal data about senior leaders ordering changes and assuming those changes had been made, only to find out to their horror that they never occurred. These situations develop because leaders lack feedback devices to tell them whether actions have been effective or not.

During stable periods, effective managers tend to develop

various ways of eliciting feedback. But during the transition state, these mechanisms often break down because of the turbulence of the change or because people are hesitant to deliver bad news. The transition is a time when managers particularly need to know what is going on, and, given the additional complexity that comes with change, there is more information than usual to be absorbed. Thus it becomes important for transition managers to develop multiple, redundant, and sensitive mechanisms for generating transition feedback. Formal methods may include individual interviews, various types of focus group data collection, surveys used globally or with select samples, or feedback gathered during normal business meetings. Informal channels include meetings between senior managers and individuals, group breakfasts, informal contacts, and field trips. Finally, feedback may be promoted through direct participation by representatives of key groups in planning, monitoring, and implementing the change.

Managing the Political Dynamics

Any significant change usually involves some modification of the political system, thus raising issues of power. This disruption may be in the formal status and power within an organization or, just as important, in the informal power that develops among individuals and groups. There is a need to shape and manage the political dynamics prior to and throughout the transition, to build and sustain a critical mass of support for the change.

The first task involves *obtaining the support of key power groups*. The organization is a political system with competing groups, cliques, coalitions, and interests, each with varying views on any particular change. Some oppose it. Some may be disinterested. But the change cannot succeed unless there is a critical mass of support, and building that support is a key problem. For a change to occur successfully, power groups must be assembled and mobilized in support of the change.

Sometimes, this strategy must start with the senior team. A number of CEOs have told us that the decision to reshape their team is one that they ultimately stepped up to but, in hindsight, wished they had acted on sooner. Replacing members who represent major and chronic resistance to the CEO's agenda is often the very thing that mobilizes the team and the organization. It's as if "the frozen brakes on the car had been released, and we were finally able to do seventy miles an hour," as one CEO expressed it.

This task usually begins with identifying the key players or stakeholders in the organization—the people who have a positive, negative, or neutral stake in the change. Frequently, drawing a diagram or creating a stakeholder or influence map may be useful in thinking about and conceptualizing these relationships. This map should include not only the various stakeholders, but their relationships to each other, as well as who influences whom and what the stakes are for each individual. Asking the question "What's in it for this individual?" is a way to understand what needs to happen to build support.

There are several possible methods for building support. The obvious one is *participation*, which has long been recognized as a tool for reducing resistance to change and gaining support. As individuals or groups become involved in the change, they tend to see it as *their* change, rather than one imposed upon them. However, participation, while desirable, might not be feasible or wise in all situations. In some cases, it merely increases the power of opposing individuals or groups to forestall the change. Another approach may be *bargaining with individuals or groups*. Those favoring the change get the support of others by providing some incentive. The incentive may be the promise of a position or the responsibility for additional functions. Since each situation is different, this often becomes a critical, yet sensitive, role for the senior human resource person to play on behalf of the CEO.

For those who resist participation or bargaining, and who persist in attempting to undermine the change, a third possibility is *isolation*. The goal here is to minimize their impact on the organization by assigning them to a position outside the mainstream. Tactics include executive development programs, business development work, regulatory or government liaison, or international assignments. The final step, in the extreme case, is removal. Individuals who cannot be isolated or brought into constructive roles may have to be removed from the scene through transfer to another organization or by outplacement. Obviously, participation and bargaining are more desirable and leave a more positive aftermath. However, it would be naive to assume that they will be successful in all cases.

Beyond the senior team, the next group of managers to influence are the top management group, the people who manage major segments of the business and whose influence is needed if change is to occur. Resistance can be used effectively to surface potential problems, so their participation in work sessions to identify implementation pitfalls is one way to build support. Teaching is another influence tactic. Most change efforts require new learning about customers and changes in processes and culture, as well as competency development. Successful companies already use their senior groups in management development efforts; a natural extension is to employ them in the service of the change. This not only builds commitment, but also models the desired behavior. Xerox Corporation coined the phrase "Learn, Use, Teach, Inspect (LUTI)" for its quality efforts, and now uses it as part of its change technology.

Another major factor affecting the political terrain of an organization is the behavior of powerful key leaders. Thus, a second major action step involves *using leader behavior to generate energy in support of the change.* Leaders need to think about using their own behavior to generate energy (see House, 1977, on charismatic leadership), as well as to build on the support and behavior of other leaders (both formal and informal) within the organization. Leaders can mobilize groups, generate energy, provide models, manipulate major rewards, and do many other things that can affect the dynamics of the informal organization. Sets of leaders working in coordination can have a tremendously powerful impact on the informal organization—hence the reason for alignment among the top managers.

There are a number of specific things that leaders can do. First, they can serve as models. Through their behavior, they can provide a vision of the future state and a source of identification for different groups within the organization. Second, leaders can serve an important role in articulating the vision of the future state. Third, they can play a crucial role in rewarding key individuals and specific types of behavior. Fourth, they can provide support through political influence and needed resources. Similarly, leaders can remove

roadblocks and maintain momentum through their public statements. Finally, leaders can send important signals through the informal organization.

During times of uncertainty and change, people throughout
the organization tend to look to leaders for signals. Frequently,
potent messages are sent through minor acts, such as patterns of
attendance at meetings or the phrases and words used in public
statements. By careful attention to these subtle actions, leaders can
greatly influence the perceptions of others. This was brought home
to one organization when its CEO left in the middle of an event
recognizing teams for quality improvement. Hall talk went something like this: "He says TQM is important when it results in things
he values, but where is he when it really matters to us?"

The third action step involves *using symbols and language
to create energy.* By providing language and symbols to describe the
change with emotional impact, it is possible to create new power
centers or bring together power centers under a common banner.
Language is also important in defining an ambiguous reality. If a
change is declared a success, then it may actually become a success
in the perception of others. Social movements know the value of
symbols for building unity; organizations can also use them to benefit when dealing with the political system. A variety of devices can
be used, such as names and related graphics that clearly identify
events, activities, or organizational units.

Language is another type of symbol; it can communicate a
different way of doing business. During a recent change in a functional organization, a new linking mechanism emerged to enable
senior managers from various parts of the business to deal with
critical parts of the value chain—customer acquisition, product development, and service. The term "gearbox" was used to express the
new way of thinking and working together. People in the gearbox
knew that they had to develop ways to mesh their individual actions
(or gears) as smoothly as possible to ensure effective motion or
direction. This one word captured the differences of the parts, yet
the need for unity of the whole if movement was to occur.

Symbolic acts are also important. To reinforce a change in
operating style, one senior team moved off its executive floor and
onto the floors where their organizations resided. There were at least

two immediate benefits to this action: they were closer to the action and were able to do things more easily and quickly, and giving up their executive-floor status sent a powerful message of intent to downplay the hierarchy.

Finally, there is the need to *build in stability*. Organizations and individuals can stand only so much uncertainty and turbulence. The issue today is how can we all best manage when, as some have said, change is an inevitable state—"permanent whitewater." We know that an overload of uncertainty may create dysfunctional effects: people may begin to panic, engage in extreme defensive behavior, and become irrationally resistant to any new change proposed. The increase of anxiety created by constant change does have its costs. People need sources of stability—structures, people, physical locations—that serve as anchors to hold onto and provide a means for self-definition in the midst of turbulence. A well-articulated vision, which captures both the business direction and the noble, human aspirations of the organization, can be a profound source of balance.

A number of steps can help, such as preparing people for the change by providing information in advance. This buffers them, to a degree, against the impending uncertainty. Second, some stability can be preserved, even in the face of change, if leaders make sure their messages are consistent throughout the period of change. Nothing creates more instability than inconsistent or conflicting messages. Third, it may be important to maintain certain visible aspects of the business, such as preserving certain units, organizational names, management processes, staffing patterns, or physical locations. Finally, it may help to communicate specifically what will *not* be different—to ameliorate the fear that everything is changing, or that the change will be much greater than what is actually planned.

Summary

Any change will encounter three universal problems: resistance, control, and power. To counter those problems, change leaders need to motivate change, manage the transition, and shape the political dynamics of change. Specific action steps are summarized in Figure 4.1.

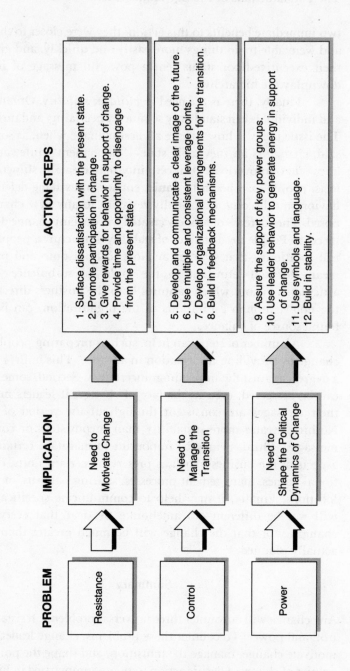

Figure 4.1. An Overview of Large-Scale Change.

PROBLEM	IMPLICATION	ACTION STEPS
Resistance	Need to Motivate Change	1. Surface dissatisfaction with the present state. 2. Promote participation in change. 3. Give rewards for behavior in support of change. 4. Provide time and opportunity to disengage from the present state.
Control	Need to Manage the Transition	5. Develop and communicate a clear image of the future. 6. Use multiple and consistent leverage points. 7. Develop organizational arrangements for the transition. 8. Build in feedback mechanisms.
Power	Need to Shape the Political Dynamics of Change	9. Assure the support of key power groups. 10. Use leader behavior to generate energy in support of change. 11. Use symbols and language. 12. Build in stability.

All these actions will be more or less critical—and more or less feasible—in different organizational situations. While general principles can help those leading change, there is no handbook for transforming organizations. Each situation, while reflecting broad patterns, has unique characteristics based on differences among individuals, the history of an organization, and the competitive environment in which the organization operates. Thus, leaders need to be diagnostic in their approach to the problems of managing large-scale change; otherwise, they run the risk of "malpractice." Specifically, leaders must "scale" their change efforts to meet the requirements of the situation. In the following chapters, we examine approaches to the unique challenges of discontinuous change.

The Essence of Discontinuous Change: Leadership, Identity, and Architecture

Robert B. Shaw

Discontinuous change occurs when an organization fundamentally alters its core business strategy and transforms itself to execute that strategy. Most transition management approaches draw on models of incremental change. Those managing corporate change, for example, often stress the need to solicit the views of organizational members in an attempt to create more ownership for the change agenda. While participation is useful, discontinuous change almost always requires more extreme measures. The composition of a senior executive team, for example, may need to be altered given the pressures facing the corporation (Nadler and Ancona, 1992; Nadler and Gerstein, 1992b; Nadler and Tushman, 1988). Involvement, by itself, is not enough when a committed, skilled, and collaborative leadership team is needed to guide a corporation through a difficult period of change. Similarly, advocates of change often suggest that a detailed vision of the future be developed before altering an organization's structures and management processes. However, in situations of discontinuous change, fundamental modifications in an organization's current structure *may* be needed before a clear vision for the future can be developed (see Chapter Three). This may be necessary when the current organizational structure is convoluted to the point that the information needed to develop a future vision is unavailable (information such as profitability by product line, competitive comparisons, clear customer expectations, and so on). The prescription for initial clarity of vision may not be possible in the initial stages of discontinuous organizational change. These examples suggest that discontinuous change requires techniques that go beyond the more common approaches used to manage organizational transitions.

No simple road map exists to guide change leaders. Each organization faces unique challenges and exhibits particular strengths and limitations as a result of its history. The process combines broad strategic direction with specific organizational changes, leading to ongoing experimentation and learning. New change initiatives alleviate some problems but also result in new issues and opportunities.

Those leading discontinuous change often "soak" in the problems facing them, observe the results of their ongoing efforts, and then make changes as needed on a real-time basis. Those taking their organizations through this type of change learn to balance the need for forceful leadership with the need to let large-scale change evolve at its own pace. In many cases, organizational leaders lay track for changes that will not occur for years to come. These early efforts are important in setting the stage for later shifts in organizational behavior.

We believe a few fundamental ideas can help those leading organizations through periods of discontinuous change. In our work with senior executives, we have developed a model of key dimensions that need to be addressed:

• *Leadership.* The degree to which the CEO and senior team are willing and able to lead an integrated and prolonged effort to fundamentally alter the way their organization operates.

- *Corporate identity.* The essence of the new organization, including its future vision, mission, general business strategy, and basic operating philosophy.
- *Organizational architecture.* The overall form of the new organization, including its formal structures and management processes, informal culture, work processes, and people.
- *Change agenda.* The key themes that will be at the heart of the change effort. These "vital few" themes are those that will provide a foundation, or reference point, for all change activities and a way to evaluate progress over time. Also included in the change agenda are the key streams of activity that will lead the organization from its current state to the future state.
- *Change interventions.* The specific initiatives that will change the organization. Of particular importance are changes to an organization's business strategy, organization structure, and work processes (what we call the "hardware" of change). Equally important are changes to the informal operating style and culture (the "software") and changes in the people who make up the organization.

The relationship among these elements is portrayed in Figure 5.1. The remainder of this chapter describes each area in more detail.

Figure 5.1. Leading Discontinuous Change.

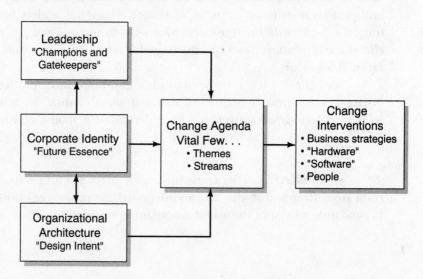

Leadership—The CEO

The CEO is the single most important factor in managing discontinuous change. Recent events in the United States underscore the impact that one individual can have, successfully leading an organization through a demanding period of transformation (as have Bob Allen at AT&T and Jack Welch at GE) or failing in that objective (as we saw with Bob Stempel at GM and John Akers at IBM). Those that fail are often superb managers who rose through their organizations based on their accomplishments and, in less turbulent times, would be considered superior executives. In conditions requiring radical change, however, a different set of skills is necessary. An initial step in launching a major change initiative is for CEOs to assess their own capabilities to lead the change and the level of support they need from the executive team. The need for leadership in situations of discontinuous change cannot be underestimated— and in most cases requires some difficult decisions about the composition of the executive team and the skill set required to guide the transition.

The CEO needs to embrace the need for radical change and be willing to drive the organization to a new corporate identity. The will of the CEO in driving the change is critical in moving the organization through the difficult challenges of large-scale change. We know of no case where discontinuous change occurred with only a marginal commitment or involvement on the part of the CEO. Commitment must also be combined with a hard-edged awareness of the CEO's own strengths and limitations in leading the transition. Conviction alone, without necessary leadership skills, is simply not enough.

There are CEOs with only a limited ability to think creatively about new organizational possibilities; thus, while they may see the need for change, they have difficulty creating the specific agenda to make it happen. Other CEOs may have difficulty building support for a change agenda; they are able to develop a change agenda but cannot foster enthusiasm and alignment around its implementation. We also see CEOs who lack the forcefulness needed to replace those who will not or cannot support the new direction.

In total, each leader brings certain strengths and limitations to a change effort. Serious self-assessment is an important part of the early work in setting the stage for what is to follow. In some cases, the leader can strive to develop the necessary skills; in other situations, others with the requisite skill sets need to be involved to compensate for the CEO's shortcomings.

Managing an organization through a period of transformation can be one of the most challenging and personally draining tasks undertaken by a CEO. Most who have led their organizations through a period of radical change believe in retrospect that the process was more difficult and more emotionally draining than they anticipated. The CEO needs to be honest about the depth of personal commitment; a deep conviction that the change must occur is essential if the CEO is to persist through the inevitable problems and setbacks.

Leadership—The Executive Team

The qualities needed in the CEO and the executive team will vary across organizations but a few attributes are essential in almost all cases.

Right People on the Team

A CEO cannot lead a large-scale change effort alone; those who try will inevitably fail. The executive team at the top needs to support the change and collectively assume responsibility for its success. In discontinuous change, the CEO should be comfortable with the executive team before moving forward. The key question for the CEO is: "Can I trust this group of people to work with me to lead the organization through a complex and risky period of change?"

Clearly, the CEO needs time to work with the team to build a collective understanding of the need for change and potential plans of action. The natural inclination, however, is to assume that individuals who initially resist the change will over time become more supportive. Our experience suggests that a safer assumption is that senior executives have great difficulty changing their core beliefs, which could potentially threaten the CEO's vision. In particular, a CEO contemplating discontinuous change may need to quickly determine which individuals are willing to experiment with a new approach and which are not. Often, change in the make-up of the senior team is needed before a large-scale change initiative can move forward.

Bringing outsiders onto the executive team can help by pro-viding a new perspective on the business, while sending a powerful signal that the need for change is real and will affect all members of the organization. Including outsiders on the senior team also underscores the need to remain open to new ideas in the spirit of enhanced learning. New people, carefully selected, can help the CEO "think out of the box" in developing a new corporate identity and support aggressive action in implementing the emerging change agenda. In many cases, new members are not bound, practically or emotionally, by past decisions or the network of personal relation-ships. "Inside outsiders"—those who have come up through the organization but have remained on the periphery of the dominant power coalition—can have a similar impact.

The CEO needs to beware of bringing a single outsider onto the team as a change agent. One individual runs the risk of being rejected by the team or being assimilated to the point of losing the unique perspective that originally made him or her attractive. The CEO should look at the team as a whole and assess the overall "band width" of differences—too narrow a perspective among team members means that dramatic changes are unlikely, while wide differences of perspective will most likely result in a divided or gridlocked group. The goal is to obtain diversity in looking at things differently while sustaining the team's ability to collaborate in driving toward a common organizational vision.

Right Work for the Team

Once the composition of the team is appropriate given the chal-lenge facing the organization, the CEO needs to assess the value-added work of the team as the organization moves forward. The key question is: "What is the most effective role this team can play in leading the effort?" For example, the team may need to interact with the organization differently than in the past where their contact was primarily in terms of individual functional responsibilities. Transforming an organization requires that the team be leveraged as a resource, which in most cases requires modification in the team's role.

Right Processes for the Team

After defining the value-added work of the team, the CEO must also address how the team should function in order to reach a high level of effectiveness. In particular, the CEO needs to assess if the team can deal with the conflicts that will arise during the lengthy period of transition and collaborate in leading the change (Nadler and Ancona, 1992). This is not to suggest that team members need to be close on an interpersonal level, but they do need to be able to work toward a common objective and not let interpersonal baggage get in the way.

Shortcomings in team effectiveness can be addressed through planned interventions that, in most cases, begin with the team's formal work processes. For example, the team's ongoing agenda may not include scheduled time to evaluate progress or the actions needed to ensure momentum. Later, after addressing the formal work processes, the CEO can address as needed the interactions and interpersonal relationships of those on the team. For instance, the transition may require a level of team collaboration and collective institutional leadership that is far beyond past requirements. The goal is to develop a team that can perform under the pressure of discontinuous change and sustain itself through the difficult times that will surely follow.

Another critical role for leaders is the ability to address resistance at various organizational levels as it arises. Early in the effort, the CEO must assess the degree of support he or she will need in leading the change and the current level of support within the organization. Using the broad themes outlined in the emerging new corporate identity, he or she can assess to what extent others will support the transition. In particular, the CEO should identify a critical mass of people who will be active sponsors of the change and those who must allow the change to occur.

In discontinuous change, the potential for political turmoil is high. To counter this, a significant number of "thought leaders" in the company must believe in the CEO and what he or she is striving to accomplish. Those who are capable of supporting the change can be built into the change process and encouraged in a variety of ways to assume ownership of it. If they strongly oppose the change—and from what the CEO can determine will not be capable of evolving over time to support the effort—they should be removed from their positions of influence or repositioned in a way that minimizes the potential threat they pose. Of course, this is done with a full awareness of the political and perhaps even legal constraints that may limit how quickly the CEO can make such moves. We have found, however, that it is essential to build support for the change before developing a detailed change agenda.

The CEO also needs to build support on the part of external constituencies including members of the board, institutional shareholders, and financial analysts. These key stakeholders need to be informed of the rationale for change, the overall direction, and the potential risks in implementing the new vision. The support of these groups is essential, particularly as we see more external involvement in the management of our largest firms.

Corporate Identity

Discontinuous change, by definition, involves a fundamental shift in an organization's vision and mission. The result is to change the essence, the identity, of the firm. In the simplest terms, corporate identity expresses why the firm and its products and services are important, and how the firm will compete over time.

Terminology can be confusing, as terms are used differently in each organization. The key is to make sure that the issues are addressed, and in a way that moves beyond slogans or broad statements. We have developed these working definitions for key elements of identity: *Vision* is broad qualitative statement of what the organization will be like in the future. It includes key assumptions about the marketplace, the organization, and its people. *Mission* is a description of the organization's customers and the product and service offerings provided to them. *Corporate strategy* contains, at the simplest level, the key ideas that will provide a sustainable competitive advantage for the enterprise and allow the enterprise to achieve its vision.

Most efforts to recast an organization's identity start with an "outside/in" assessment of the firm. It is helpful for companies to look at changes in the sociopolitical environment, industry and marketplace trends, and potential shifts in customer expectations and needs. This type of analysis eventually leads to an assessment of an organization's core competencies in relation to new and emerging competitors and marketplace trends. In particular, we have found that the executive team must exhibit an active distrust of the firm's "crown jewels"—the competencies that currently produce the majority of profits and are seen as areas of strength. In almost all cases requiring discontinuous change, there is a need to challenge, and to varying degrees modify, the current set of core competencies.

Shifts in strategy and direction usually threaten those who rose to their current positions because they mastered the firm's existing core competencies. For example, many of the senior executives in Xerox grew up in the world of light lens technology, but that industry is rapidly moving to digital technology. More generally, changes in a corporation's identity result in changes in individual responsibilities, and the power coalitions that exist within an organization. These political factors make the search for a new or even modified corporate identity all the more difficult and, if not actively managed, unlikely.

In most discontinuous change efforts, the executive team needs to spend time developing a general direction for the future. The goal is to produce a compelling and real vision of what the organization will become. The vision includes broad themes describing what the organization must accomplish over the next five to ten years. For example, "We survived through the '80s—now we want to build market share in our core business and revitalize the bottom line." The key is to determine how the company will create a sustainable competitive advantage in the future. Part of the challenge is to clearly describe those aspects of the current organization that are strengths, and will be sustained, and those that will necessarily be left behind in making the transition.

Organizational Architecture

A third element of the change process, after leadership and identity, is the articulation of a broad organizational architecture that will drive the organization. At this stage, the goal is to create a general blueprint for the organization of the future. For example, the new organizational architecture may revolve around decentralized business units that face off against customers, supported by centralized technology and manufacturing operations. The executive team need not go far beyond this type of general description of the future architecture. The team should also remain flexible; they may need to consider alternatives and new features to their initial blueprint as more in-depth design work is completed and the change unfolds.

Also included in the architecture overview is a description of the core values or operating principles that will guide the company. The goal is not to create a statement that addresses myriad values that people can rally around, but instead to come to terms with the few values that will be at the core of the enterprise. For example, PepsiCo values, above all else, performance and integrity. These broad themes are uniquely definined in that company's culture and drive PepsiCo's members in ways that have produced impressive results.

Potential points of leverage fall into three broad categories that we label hardware, software, and people. A first potential point of intervention involves the overall structure or design of the organization. In many cases, the current structure is out of sync with the new identity and strategic intent. Second, an organization's informal culture is also ripe for change, since cultures, like structures, are robust and typically lag changes in strategic direction. Third, changes in an organization's approach to its people—selection, training, and staffing—can also be modified to reinforce a new direction. Some key people will probably have to be moved, and those who remain will have to be exposed to new ideas.

Hardware. We use the term hardware to refer to the formal elements and structures of the organization. Two types of organizational restructuring are possible. The first occurs when the strategy is clear and the restructuring is done to execute that strategy; in other words, the new organizational structure is an expression of the strategy. In some cases, this restructuring focuses on core business processes and comes under the label of reengineering. A second type of restructuring occurs when the organization can't get the information needed for strategy without doing so. For instance, some large organizations don't know the true profit and loss of their groups or their competitive viability, given the way the different units are intermeshed organizationally. A business unit could be losing money and vulnerable to competition but these facts remain unknown until a larger restructuring occurs. In this respect, organizational design is one element of strategy and a restructuring can produce needed information in determining how to respond to marketplace. Chapter Nine provides an in-depth look at the development of new organizational architectures.

Software. We use the term *software* to describe the informal elements of organizational life. Often, discontinuous change efforts focus almost exclusively on the formal arrangements without sufficient attention to the softer aspects. This lack of attention reflects, in part, the difficulty in understanding and impacting culture. In this respect, the soft part is the hard part. The organizational software is the platform for the change and, in the long run, will probably make more difference than changes in structure and processes.

The informal organization is particularly important in sustaining changes begun with structural modifications. Change agents need to understand the leverage and risk points in the organization's culture. Otherwise, changes in an organization's structure run the risk of failing. One example of such a failure occurred at General Motors (GM) several years ago (Keller, 1989). GM reorganized in a way that fractured the informal organization that had developed over decades. While the new design made sense on paper, it severely disrupted the informal means that people had developed to get work done. The designers of change did not understand the power of the informal culture and consequently failed in their efforts to fundamentally change the way GM operates. Chapter Ten discusses how to change an organization's culture.

People. A final element of any change involves people. The staffing of the new organization involves some of the most important decisions the CEO will make—beginning with the senior team. Throughout the organization, a critical mass of executives is needed to implement the changes required to realize the new corporate identity. Often, massive change requires an infusion of new people not bound by the history of the current organization. While care must be taken to ensure outsiders can develop a power base needed to foster change, they are in some cases the primary means of moving from the current to the future state. The key is not to make isolated decisions about each executive but to look at the organization's ability to deliver the change agenda.

This portfolio management approach to change requires that a certain diversity be developed to push the organization to the future state. A group of key executives that think and act alike will, in most cases, be unable to lead a large organization through discontinuous change. Alignment on the end state and change agenda is needed; homogeneity of views and style is not. The apparent paradox is that differences, properly managed, can lead to the realization of a common agenda.

Discontinuous change also requires innovative approaches to the development of people. Innovative educational sessions can help people break from past approaches that may have served, intentionally or not, to reinforce the status quo (as in trying to teach executives about customer service without exposing them in any way to customers). For instance, some organizations will expose senior management to on-site visits to benchmark companies, innovative work sites within their own organization, or develop or hold focus groups with key customers or industry experts. Linking people's motivation and skill to the change agenda is discussed further in Chapter Twelve.

Integrated Change Agenda

To summarize, the first three phases of managing discontinuous change involve assessing senior leadership's capacity for change, creating a corporate identity for the future, and outlining an overall corporate architecture. These steps are "prework" for creating a more specific change agenda. The change agenda is a general map of the future organization and the means by which the transition to that future state will be achieved.

Parts of an agenda will surface in the preparatory stages, but they won't as yet have been coalesced into an integrated framework. The executive team must take these emerging elements and identify the key themes in moving the organization from the present to the future state. These themes should simply summarize the vital few topics that capture the core of the transition. In some respects, the change agenda is the "high concept" that outlines the "theme" of the change effort. It provides a map of the overall change effort and contains usually three or four key points.

Part of the artistry in developing the change agenda is crafting an approach that captures the hearts and minds of organizational members—including the CEOs. The agenda must be simple enough for people to remember, yet real enough to provide useful guidance in day-to-day activities. For example, Jamie Houghton at Corning continually talks about a few key initiatives that people have heard consistently over the years (quality, performance, and diversity). These points build on many of Corning's existing organizational strengths while charting a new direction for the future.

The change agenda also embodies key streams of activity. These are the essential steps that will produce the new corporate identity, and they delineate the course of action over the next twelve to twenty-four months. Developing a short list of possible change interventions depends on early diagnostic work that highlights the areas of greatest leverage and the potential for success in each of those areas. A large part of successfully managing discontinuous change is understanding which actions have the greatest potential to alter the organization and, of these, which have the greatest likelihood of success. Every possible lever is needed, given the tendency for behavior in organizations to reinforce the status quo.

The potential for conflicting initiatives in most large organizations is quite high in situations demanding discontinuous change, if proper precautions are not taken. Some firms get into trouble by failing to integrate the various initiatives they have launched. Change efforts should be integrated in such a manner that each leverages the others. Paul O'Neill of Alcoa, for example, emphasizes the importance of consistency and connectedness whenever he introduces change into the organization. He has found that disjoined initiatives confuse people and decrease the overall likelihood of success. For example, we have often seen companies institute broad quality change initiatives that are disconnected from ongoing reengineering efforts. The lack of connectedness results in confusion, potential redundancy, and less leverage.

Intervention Considerations

One consideration in determining appropriate intervention strategies is the senior executive group's willingness and ability to engage in different strategies. This is not to suggest that change should be completely focused on the predilections or talents of the executive team. However, efforts that fail to take into account their willingness to support a particular initiative have far less chance of success. This is one reason for assessing the CEO and senior team before developing a specific change agenda.

Many change efforts develop an agenda before doing the prework described above. We believe this is a mistake: the change agenda must evolve from these previous steps or run the risk of being ahead of itself—with potentially disastrous consequences. A change agenda sponsored by the CEO can be launched without the full support of the executive team, but this will result in mixed signals from the top or lukewarm sponsorship in key areas. The process requires balancing the extremes of acting prematurely and waiting too long.

A second consideration in developing an intervention strategy involves assessing which changes should be driven from the top of the organization and which should originate elsewhere. Some changes, such as the overall architecture of the new organization, must begin with the CEO and the executive team. Others, such as the redesign of work processes for high performance, can and in many cases should be owned locally. Each potential intervention needs to be evaluated. A common mistake is to assume that the headquarters staff must drive each initiative. Equally problematic is the other extreme, where change is decentralized, for there are some initiatives that must be driven from the senior team. The ownership of different leverage points differs in each organization; in general, ownership at the top should involve only the initiatives (such as the overall corporate strategy) that cannot be owned by others.

A third factor to consider is the degree to which changes are managed through detailed implementation plans versus being allowed to emerge on their own. In some situations, a great deal of detail and control is needed. However, it is also vital to allow the general change to emerge on its own terms within the broad guidelines set forth by those initiating the change. Some refer to these as "emergent designs" (Brown and Walton, 1993). The complexity of organizations precludes total understanding or control of all aspects of the change. Those responsible for the new organization must recognize the desirability of allowing some aspects of the design to emerge on their own terms.

Summary

Managing discontinuous change in large corporations begins with the CEO and the senior team—assessing the degree to which they can lead their organization through a difficult period of transition. Once those around the executive table are collectively equipped to lead, the critical work of clarifying the corporation's identity and overall architecture begins. This produces an articulation of what the organization will be in the future. These are the general characteristics or themes that point to where the organization is headed, including a broad strategic vision, organizational form, and core corporate competencies. This rough template of the future allows the executive team to then assess the political environment and intervene if necessary to ensure sufficient support throughout the organization for the change. In particular, it is important to identify champions for the change and organizational "gatekeepers," the key people whose support is essential for success.

These three factors—senior leadership capability, corporate identity, and architecture—provide the input for the change agenda. The overall change should rest on a foundation of a few vital change themes and activities, the "high-concept" ideas that will guide the change effort at every level of the organization. In most cases, the change agenda can be summarized on one page and understood by everyone in the organization. A detailed change plan follows from the change agenda, and includes interventions that over time will change an organization's formal structures and systems, informal culture, and people.

Staging Discontinuous Change

A. Elise Walton

We view the management of discontinuous change as consisting of five fundamental phases: diagnosis, clarifying and coalition building, action, consolidation and refinement, and sustaining. Each phase tends to have its own climate, its own key challenges and hurdles. The stages outlined in this chapter go beyond the fundamentals of change management to assess the specific challenges facing those leading discontinuous change.

Diagnosis

The first phase in any major transition must be diagnosis, a thoughtful assessment of the current state—its strengths, weaknesses, and embedded aspirations. Diagnosis can be made in a range of ways. Diagnosis should not be complex or cumbersome; its primary purpose is to identify the resources available for developing the new organization. Therefore, the focus is on clarity, simplicity, and communicability.

Diagnosis typically focuses on three broad areas: leadership, corporate identity, and organizational architecture. As these three areas were presented fully in Chapter Four, here we will only summarize the key issues. The leadership question to be answered is whether the CEO and the senior team have the commitment, conviction, and competencies they will need to sustain themselves and the organization through this enormously difficult process.

The first leadership objective is to begin building the change agenda. The CEO must create the case for change—why it is needed and what it entails. The CEO will have to talk about the change agenda with conviction and clarity for several years, and therefore needs to have a clear commitment to stay with the agenda that period of time. The change agenda must achieve the critical objective of proving that the pain of *not* changing will be greater than the pain of changing. This can be handled by identifying the potential costs of change (layoffs, power realignment, and customer disruptions) and pairing them off against the same costs given no change (continuing on the current path may lead to more layoffs, more power realignment to competitors, or the inability to meet customer needs). The objective is convincing all audiences that it is in the organization's best interest, and in their own best interests, to change.

Leaders who have been at the helm for a time will find that leading discontinuous change often requires a drastic change in style. The change is so dramatic that when one individual plays both roles, his credibility may suffer. This may be one reason so many reinventions and reorientations are led by new leaders, either outsiders or "inside" outsiders. In addition, it is often hard for insiders to relentlessly challenge the system that made them.

Normal Leadership Role	*Leadership Role in Major Change*
Build clarity	Build tolerance for ambiguity
Build confidence in and support for status quo	Build confidence in the advantages of change

Normal Leadership Role	*Leadership Role in Major Change*
Support solid performers	Question the value of historical performance; support renegades
Improve existing information systems and databases	Question or redesign information systems and databases

Some leaders have found it helpful to start support teams at this point. This may be an informal "kitchen cabinet," or a more formal structure such as a transition team, a strategy team, or a customer team. The CEO cultivates a close relationship with this team and their work, using these individuals as key change agents.

Another major activity during diagnosis is shaping a new corporate identity. The challenge is to keep what is currently good while adding what is possible and required for the future. This begins with a realistic appraisal of what strategies are possible. This is the time for strategic leaps, for identifying new markets, new customers, new services, and new ways of providing offerings. Clarifying the new identity can be a challenging process, for there are no formulaic answers. It must be built both on the past history, on current market data, on future predictions, and, most important, on the gut feelings, values, and commitments of the senior team.

Reviewing corporate identity provides the frame for the future organizational architecture; it sets forth the few principles that will guide the operational plans. Thus the diagnosis phase must look at the organization in place and assess both its current strengths and weaknesses and its capability for change. Realistic self-appraisal is critically important. Too often, an assessment identifies a wish list of current competencies that has no credibility at all.

One of the key challenges of this first phase is actually recognizing the need for diagnosis and assessment. Often, executives are ready to launch, or have already launched, changes designed to move toward a new organization. Diagnosis and self-assessment seem unnecessary, like backtracking and delay. However, plunging ahead without some common understanding of the current baseline creates substantial rework later on. Even worse, the rush to action creates an impression of impulsive leadership and, consequently, the change enlists few supporters.

A second key challenge is to have an energizing, persuasive, and compelling change agenda. To enlist the senior management of the organization, the change agenda must convince them that there is no alternative to change. Senior management can be the toughest to convince; they are the ones who see the big picture, see what is at risk, and have the most opinions about what should be done. They tend to challenge the change the most heartily and be the most adept at overt compliance but covert resistance.

At the end of this phase, the CEO and the senior team should feel that they are headed in roughly the right direction. They must manage the dilemma of seeking alignment, clear direction, and deeply felt agreement while embracing ambiguity, open issues, and unanswered questions. There should be an outline for a broad new identity and the guiding principles for a new organizational architecture. The plans for enlisting broader support should be in place.

Clarifying and Coalition Building

With the main diagnosis accomplished, the change effort moves to the second phase: clarifying and coalition building. The objectives are to refine and clarify the vision of the future state, to recruit key change agents and advocates, and to optimally plan the organizational changes and interventions. Here, activity picks up; staff are involved in articulating the future state and describing the specific changes to take place.

This is a time for building senior team capability. If the diagnosis phase has been passed successfully, the team will already be composed of the right people using the right processes. Although they may be hand picked and may have worked together in the past, the change invariably places new demands on them. Change itself is stressful, so even those with good teamwork skills may revert to a protective, individualistic stance. Change implies new roles and relationships, requiring unusual effort. Finally, the team has to work in a high-performance mode—this means they must communicate frequently, with integrity, and the messages must be consistent. They must think through the moves in depth and even rehearse them, anticipate possible problems, and be prepared for them.

Teams that will define the future state are formed during this phase. Working closely with the CEO and the senior team, design teams further design the change agenda and the future organizational architecture. The structure of these change teams varies widely, from a small senior team, a large diagonal slice of the organization, several teams with an overseeing board, or a team that "shadows" the future organization.

Meanwhile, another team may be planning the transition organization that will bridge the gap between old and new. The old organization, complete with reporting relationships, accountabilities, activities, and outputs, continues to exist. The future state of the organization is being formally designed. However, the transition organization also includes reporting relationships, accountabilities, activities, and outputs. For a period of time there are actually dual organizations running side by side. Many key employees are working two or more jobs, with usually well over half their attention devoted to the new transition job.

The dual organizations create opportunities for leadership to expand its understanding of the organization, particularly if the change teams have representatives from other parts of the company. These teams give leaders regular exposure to perspectives and ideas that they wouldn't otherwise hear. In addition, this is a testing time for new people. Junior and high potential people may be brought in and exposed to senior-level challenges. These people are subsequently given key roles in the new organization, refreshing the senior management cadre in a way that traditional promotion and development schemes don't allow.

This exposure is also important because this broader group is the first to test whether the intent to change is genuine. Posed as innocuous hallway questions, employees find indirect ways of ascertaining the commitment level of the CEO and the senior team, the degree to which they have thought the change through, and how integral the effort seems to how the CEO plans to lead the business. One key indicator is the time and attention senior leadership is giving to the effort. Does the transition team have access to the CEO, or has he delegated authority?

At this phase too, coalitions begin to take shape. During discontinuous change, everyone has an agenda. First, all members of the organization see the change as the chance to "set things right"—from their point of view. Certainly, the change cannot incorporate everyone's opinions. Those whose opinions do not ultimately prevail become resistant. Others will view the change as the new gospel—the only possibility of saving the company. Still others may see change as a threat to the very things that got the company as far as it is today. Some see personal opportunity in the change, others see danger. All in all, a number of different coping responses emerge: grudging compliance, conversion, withdrawal, denial, resistance, and so on.

Another place to look for coalitions to form is around historical conflicts in the organization. Often the issues, the weapons, and the arguments, are new but the players are the same. Coalitions also emerge around the pace and degree of change—how fast and how much to change. During this phase, it can be useful to build a customized strategy for dealing with different segments.

Also during this phase corporate identity—vision, mission, strategy, and values—is solidly built. Needless to say, the senior executives have spent a great deal of time on this already, but the thoughts and additions of a broader group often refine and improve the vision. This is essentially the first real test of the vision—is it realistic, can people connect to it, is it credible given other available information? This first exposure—usually with a friendly, but tough, audience—provides useful insights for improving the concept, communication, and marketing of the change.

It is this activity that shapes the new identity as it relates to the old identity. There are elements that will stay the same, but they are reinterpreted and their relationships to each other change. Certainly there are radical breaks from the past, but the challenge is to reconstruct past strengths in innovative ways, not to try to deny or avoid them. In one very interesting such reshaping, a helicopter company, seeing the decline in defense spending, unlinked and relinked two of its deep competencies. It reapplied its expertise in precision woodworking and amplification and resonance technologies to building guitars. Kamen Helicopter thus began producing Ovation guitars.

During this phase, major interventions are planned and sequenced. These interventions form the core of the communicated and enacted change. They may include quality initiatives, restructuring, cultural redirection, people moves, and so forth. Often the executive team has been planning and discussing the big moves and the senior team now reaches a conclusion. Sometimes they are prodded to action and decision by growing pressure from the transition teams. This may be the time that the senior team agrees on a percentage cut and a restructuring charge, or begins to consider wildly divergent new business units and opportunities. This is the time for big bets.

This is also when the organizational architecture moves from strategic principles to operational design. During the diagnosis phase, the CEO and the senior team have laid out the principles of the design, but now the work moves to a more operational level and plans specific changes in hardware, software, and people. What will be the primary units? How will they work together? How will we inculcate new values and a new culture in the organization? (Part Three describes specific interventions and changes in these areas.)

At this time too, the transition team specifies the sequencing of interventions. Will training and customer action teams come first, and then a restructuring, or will we restructure first and then focus on education? Will we have new people in the same positions, the same people in new positions, or new people in new positions? Will we do cost reduction and restructuring at the same time as we introduce a new values statement, or will we do cost reduction first and then introduce the values statement?

Different sequences have different outcomes. For example, changing structure is a fast, high-impact intervention, but new people in the new structure immerse themselves in their new jobs and give little attention to software aspects—education, training, learning, and reflection. Alternately, starting with a process of software enrollment (with forums, training, and on-the-job assignments) gets more attention and energy focused on the desired attitudinal and behavioral changes, but often runs up against an organizational structure that doesn't support the new way or isn't capable of processing new ideas and efforts. These tradeoffs must be thoughtfully discussed, debated, decided, and acted on. In any case, the change strategy must focus on both supply-push interventions, which increase the "supply" of new behavior by building new capabilities, and demand-pull interventions, which create environmental pressures and rewards for new behaviors.

The change effort must now struggle with the tradeoffs between simplicity and clear and specific direction. The horns of this dilemma are on the one hand underdirection and on the other hand, overspecification. First, without some clear guidelines and answers about the future, leadership is failing to lead and to provide direction. But the second problem, overspecification, is far more common—particularly when structural change is involved. As people begin to contend with the momentousness of the change, they begin to crave specific, formal clarity. Further study and further specification then become delay tactics. A common concern is that all of the new organization's details haven't been worked out. There may be many causes behind this—anxiety, credibility tests, special interest pleading, or a very rational concern: If there is no one to load the truck, the product won't be delivered. Underlying agendas are often masked by requests for greater specificity. For example:

When you hear . . .	*It can mean . . .*
"How will marketing know when to order more inventory?"	"Let's see if these guys really have their act together."
- - -	- - -
"Shouldn't we design a process in which marketing has a build sheet so they can tell the plant when to build more of a certain product?"	"We have to make sure the marketing guys stay in control of supply and demand."
- - -	- - -
"We don't even know where most of the inventory will be held: in the manufacturing company or the marketing company?"	"I'm totally lost—this will never work."

In response to these pressures, many groups overspecify—they build in too much specificity, formality, and mass. Simplicity is important for several reasons: it makes the new organization easier to learn about, it avoids the error of presuming that the design team sees far into the future, and it empowers the heirs of the change to create change themselves. It is far better to have the design emerge based on a basic set of principles.

The clarifying and coalition-building phase is replete with challenges. The vision—both the corporate identity and the organizational architecture—should be clear enough to direct action. Leadership must have passed early credibility tests. The planned changes must be simple but powerful. Informal leaders and laggards should be identified and the effort must target key audiences for the change messages. When this stage is completed, a vision of the change and commitment to it should be institutionalized.

Action

Action is the phase that often receives the most attention—publicly. It is also the time of greatest activity throughout the organization, even though the earlier phases were just as active for the senior team. The sequencing issues have been resolved and the first wave of action begins. The major changes are launched, and the organizational identity and architecture are communicated. At the end of this phase, the major pillars of the new organization should be in place.

This phase places new demands on leadership, but it also offers many rewards. Often, CEOs bloom during this time. Having spent time debating and developing the vision, they now become increasingly articulate and passionate about it. They are often involved in giving speeches, having town meetings, making videos, and a range of other very public communications efforts. The leader champions and sells the change, but at the same time must appear open to concerns and questions.

Managing the political process becomes crucial during this phase. This is when coalitions can gain power—which may be either helpful or dysfunctional. As people hear the new plans, they experience confusion and anxiety. They turn to trusted colleagues to help them construct meaning from the information. By shaping the interpretations of the change, coalitions enlist new members. At the same time, resistance is building to a peak now.

Much of the change is communicated and interpreted locally. It may be through coalition leaders, or through the direct manager. For this reason, there is often a formally planned enrollment or deployment process. The managers or supervisors must explain the change to their direct reports, who in turn must communicate about the change to their direct reports, and so on. This is one mechanism for managing the grapevine.

The CEO and the senior team now face late credibility tests. People will be testing to see if they have the commitment to follow through, what are the payoffs for getting on board, and what is the cost of noncompliance. They are concerned with the fairness of the process, and the placement of people is one key signal used to evaluate fairness. Credibility tests often come in questions such as these:

"My boss isn't doing this. What are you going to do about him?"

"This won't affect the corporate staff, will it?"

"Are you prepared to take action on those [marketing, research, manufacturing] guys? I'm sure they're not buying this!"

In the action phase, the early majority has been enrolled (see Figure 6.1). This phase is completed when the organizational architecture is implemented, and the new organization is running. There may be a period of overlap in which the old organization backs up the new one, but this is typically as brief as possible.

The challenge in this phase is how to do a lot quickly, while keeping energy positive. The potential for burnout is high. Most people are faced with doing new and unfamiliar tasks and behaving in new and unfamiliar ways. The provoked anxiety spreads rapidly

Figure 6.1. Enrolling the Organization.

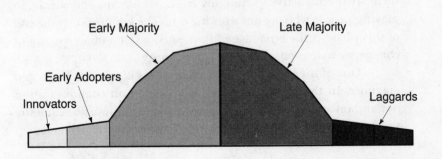

from one person to the next, and groups may convince themselves that the change is impossible. In the soup of ambiguity and anxiety, one group looks to another group for answers and information; the other group, still struggling with startup, provides no answers. Distrust and anxiety feed each other, and many false and dangerous assumptions are made.

Handling resistance, overload, and stress is another challenge in the action phase. Many members become immersed in the changes and will often say directly, "Tell me what to do." This is the time of greatest uncertainty for most, and "working on how to work" becomes an anxiety-provoking effort. There are serious listening blocks, and people often do not learn or internalize the message until after it has been repeated several times.

Another part of the challenge is to keep energy high among the early participants, particularly the senior team. Often, they fall prey to the fallacy that the work is finished when the plan is launched—but in fact *most* of the work remains to be done. It is in these later phases of action and implementation that the ideal is realized.

Finally, it is important to keep a focus on the business. The hoopla and excitement of the change often distract people from the fundamentals. It is important to repeat the message that the change is all about being more competitive in the market, and to ensure that close customer contact is maintained.

Consolidation and Refinement

The consolidation period follows directly after action and addresses the need to solidify and learn from the change. During this phase, there are several activities, ranging from assessments and checks, to moving people who are not working out. The key output at the end of this phase is the broad-based implementation and acceptance of change, as well as enrolling the late majority.

One of the leadership tasks during this phase is to listen and diagnose. In the action phase, leaders focused on communicating out and on selling the message. Now, leadership must be honestly reflective, assess how the communications were received, and step out and assess whether the new organization meets requirements. One helpful tool is a communications audit: focus groups or interviews that determine what messages have been received and how they have been interpreted. Essentially, the task is to close the communications loop and find out if what was meant is the same as what was heard. Another helpful tool is CEO "office visit interviews," where the CEO goes out to other people's offices to talk frankly about how the change is going—but mostly to listen.

One of the key assessments involves the performance of key people. Are they supporting the change in word and action? The leader does not have the luxury of tolerating poor performance, but also does not have the luxury of mistaking organizational failure for individual failure. It is very difficult to evaluate managers' performance from secondhand information, because most people offering that information have an agenda. If the senior team has become a learning device, the leader will rely on them heavily in making difficult assessments such as these.

In the listening role, the leadership is also well positioned to coach—to observe the players and give them constructive advice. Perhaps most important is the need to *unlearn* the past. Strategies that worked in the past—increasing advertising spending to boost sales, dropping price to win back customers, and attracting buyers with new styling—may not work in the new organization. However, when faced with trouble, organization decision makers often revert to form and rely on the old truths once again. The challenge is to pull attention away from its natural home, the well-understood solutions. A coach can be watchful for the old truths sneaking into the new organization.

Another aspect of the leadership challenge is to maintain support for the change intent, but also to be flexible enough to make further changes if required. Undoubtedly, the organization will need further changes as new information emerges, and certain people will need to be removed. This must be done quickly and in a way consistent with the original intent. These follow-on changes must be carefully communicated to avoid perceptions of retrenchment.

At this point, coalition management becomes tougher. Resistance among nonsupporters is now at its peak, and if the change is going well, the nonsupporters have gone underground. If they have not been penalized or moved out of key positions, it must be done now, or the change is at serious risk.

In one case of a poorly managed consolidation phase, many nonsupporters were still in place. Their behavior was at odds with the intent and aspirations of the new organization. This created a disastrous credibility gap, particularly for the CEO. As the CEO went on the road with new speeches underscoring the importance of the change and the senior-level commitment to it, two or three key lieutenants were flagrantly defecting. In the hallways, one employee summed it up by saying, "Well, we don't listen to what comes out of their [senior management's] mouths any more; we just watch what they do."

The moves at this point should not only take out individual nonperformers and nonsupporters but also break up and reconstruct the political webs. As change occurs, the "old boy" networks interpret the change—what it means, and just how much personal change is required—often in ways that undermine the intent of the change. Yet, if challenged, the members support each other; George says John really is cooperating, John says George is, but in fact neither one is. What is needed is a way to replace these old social networks unfavorable to the change with new networks. One positive way of accomplishing this is to build learning forums around specific problems. Typically, a majority of people with pro-change views are invited, but selected recalcitrants are also included. The groups are intended to process the ambiguous, unresolved issues of the change in order to reach understanding and positive action. By forcing exposure and discussion, certain relationships and interpretations can be nurtured, hopefully in place of the old groupings.

This connects to another challenge of the consolidation phase—managing information troughs. Usually, the new organization seems data-poor by comparison to the data-rich environment of the past. The old systems may have been useless in the past and are certainly useless in the new organization, but there was comfort in having hard numbers to debate, reports to read, and forms to fill out. Now managers must think their way through decisions with simpler data, unfamiliar data, or no data at all.

In this phase, the critical challenge is synergy. The change should now be moving toward an organization architecture with high fit. The change should be firmly entrenched and highly credible. Issues raised by a communications audit in an earlier phase must have been addressed. Leadership will now be judged by its actions; the new organization will be judged by its performance. Presumably the "dip" associated with startup has passed, and the system must now work.

While pushing for synergy, the leadership team must look for new information about how the change is working. What insights have emerged? What is not working? The team must concentrate on foresight and identifying necessary mid-course corrections. This may mean a modification of the culture, or a change in the structure. Again, it requires listening, synthesizing, and being open to change. Failures of the new organization, such as information troughs, should be considered opportunities. Information troughs can provide the impetus to manage faster with less and to substitute roughly right reasoning for excessive data crunching. The challenge is to capitalize on the opportunities presented by the evolution of change.

Sustaining

During this phase, the challenge is to reflect on how the organization is working and what refinements, if any, are required to achieve the original design intent. Typically, the executive team collects data and uses it to evaluate the new organization's strengths and weaknesses. In fact, one of the outputs of this phase may be to launch incremental change—refinements to the now-current state. The purpose is to build the new organization into a high-performance mode.

Leadership must continue to listen and keep information flowing up, down, and across the organization. One of the important things to look for at this stage is the emergence of rigidity in the new system. Leadership often relaxes its vigilance and assumes that life returns to normal. In so doing, important issues and required refinements may be missed. One of the clear requirements of this stage is that an active process of direction and change must be instituted around identity and strategy. That is, while the current organization addresses these issues, new information and learning will undoubtedly call for further changes. The point is that the system should ensure organizational fluidity (techniques for creating fluidity are discussed in Chapter Eight).

At this stage, one challenge is emotional climate. Because people feel that the change is "over," many employees experience a mild depression, a postbattle fatigue. The mundane, steady state can pale in comparison to the excitement of designing the future. So interventions that maintain and enhance interest and challenge are often vital.

This stage focuses on building a sustainable, high-performance organization. Now is the time to harvest the accomplishments and success of the organizational change. Leaders must resolve the challenges of maintaining fluidity and excitement. This final stage may never be completed per se, but often ends when the organization requires another major change.

Conclusion

An underlying premise about planning change is that not all problems can be solved in advance. Often we cannot see solutions until events unfold and more information emerges. It is a bit like trying to untangle a twisted rope: sometimes you need to try certain moves before solving the puzzle. The clear implication is that designers must avoid trying to solve problems too far in advance. They must forsake rational planning for opportunistic evolution.

The challenges are twofold. The designers must be excellent at defining the framing principles, the few key thoughts that will shape future actions. They must also have the courage to act quickly, moving through problem identification, definition, solution, and action once enough information is available. The leaders must play god, identifying which new forms survive, and which should be killed off.

Sustaining Change: Creating the Resilient Organization

Mitchell Lee Marks
Robert B. Shaw

Participants in a recent workshop on organizational renewal introduced themselves:

> "I'm from Sears and we've had five restructurings in five years."
>
> "I'm from Nynex and we've had *nine* in *four* years."
>
> "I'm from Citibank, and I've had seven bosses in four years."

Increasingly, people in organizations are being exposed to multiple waves of transition, often with one transition overlapping another. Many remain cynical about the payoff of going through the pain of significant transitions. Even successful large-scale change can result in a work force that is "change weary." The magnitude of the change places people in stressful conditions that can cause mental and physical fatigue and undermine the ability of the organization to sustain change over time.

After a period of significant change, organizations often need to be revitalized—both in the emotional realities and business imperatives. Organizational renewal recognizes the need to drive business success by minimizing the unintended effects of transition, by gearing people up for their new roles and responsibilities, and by reviving motivation for addressing critical business challenges.

The Emotional Impact of Change

Sources of Stress

From the field of psychology we have learned that the stress of an event is determined by the amount of change it implies, not necessarily whether the change will be beneficial or detrimental. Most transformations are seen as a mixed bag of costs and benefits. A downsizing may be painful, but may also lay the foundation for enhanced business results. A culture change in a historically paternalistic organization may distort people's hopes for security, but may shake them into action to begin taking responsibility for managing their own career development. The arrival of a new CEO may inject enthusiasm and inspire greatness in an underperforming organization, but may also produce many changes in protocol and processes.

Those involved with major change are faced with several sources of stress. The *loss* of someone or something to which people are attached is painful, and it necessitates a period of mourning, sadness, or depression while they make adjustments in their lives. The potential for loss abounds throughout discontinuous change— people may lose jobs, co-workers, title, status, or perks. They also may lose the opportunity to realize their career aspirations, achievement of their personal goals, and their sense of personal competence.

The amount of stress people perceive is based upon their subjective perceptions of an objective reality that is constantly shifting. It's important for change managers to understand that the *threat* of loss is as debilitating as the actual loss. The threat of job insecurity, for example, is experienced like job loss. Worrying about the unknown—will I fit into the new culture, do I have to prove myself all over again, what will happen to my long-term career goals—can produce as much stress as any actual specific change.

Another source of stress is the *frustration* experienced when people feel something is preventing them from meeting basic needs or getting what they want—or they feel helpless to do anything about it. Frustration is at its worst when people have little perceived control over their work situation. This is why long hours of work during transition do not necessarily create higher levels of stress, but a high degree of pressure, when coupled with a lack of control, will create stress.

Finally, the critical mass of *uncertainty and ambiguity* is a source of stress. The announcement of a broad change initiative usually raises more questions than it provides answers. People don't know what to expect and, in today's environment, generally anticipate the worst. Some may have new duties to master, a new superior and peers to adjust to, and new policies and procedures that alter established ways of going about the job. For others, there is the more palpable threat to job security.

The Positive Potential

In the best of situations, people can rally around the notion that the change is not only a necessary response to business realities but an opportunity to make things better for all. A transition holds the potential to unfreeze the organization and its people, and provides a rare chance to dramatically improve corporate culture and reinforce a new way of doing things (Marks, 1994). Managers and supervisors can use the transition as an opportunity to enhance teamwork, increase effectiveness, and identify and correct impediments to productivity and quality.

Individuals also can experience a personal form of renewal. The most successful actively search out ways to gain from the transition. They share three key characteristics. First, they feel in control of things that matter to them. They recognize that they cannot manage what is beyond their control and do not try. Instead, they assess the situation at hand and act in the areas they can influence. Second, they feel involved in what they are doing. They see themselves as architects of change, rather than its victims. Third, they seek challenges, take risks, and look upon their work with a fresh perspective. They recognize that the rules of the game have changed, that there is no "business as usual." They see transition as an opportunity to learn new skills, to stretch and grow both personally and professionally.

Over time, as people recover from the transition, they eventually settle into a pattern of behavior. If nothing is done to manage this process, odds are that people will return to their old ways of doing things, hold onto their old perceptions, and retain their old expectations. Alternatively, if the post-transition period is managed to take advantage of this opportunity, then people will settle into new behaviors. We have found four keys to realizing the potential in large-scale change: restoring individual faith and confidence; building effective and supportive work teams; enhancing organizational dialogue; and creating a culture of innovation and learning. These points of leverage encompass both a look back at the unintended consequences of transition and a look forward to the essential building blocks for sustaining desired change.

Restoring Individual Faith and Confidence

Executives can renew their organizations and people after transition by restoring faith in leadership and creating more confidence in where that leadership is taking the company. To do that, leaders must get people to see that the old order is inadequate for dealing with current and future business realities while inspiring confidence in the new order. Forces for the status quo and forces for change are constantly operating, and effective leadership of organizational renewal requires weakening the former and strengthening the latter.

Restoring Faith

Embracing the Future. People will not set their sights on new business challenges and opportunities until they have actively rejected the perceptions, expectations, and behaviors that predominated in the "old" organization. A small but growing number of executives recognize that people must let go of the old before they accept the new, but also that this inevitable process can be accelerated. In organizations ranging from entertainment conglomerates to manufacturing firms, special forums have been conducted to provide organizational members with an opportunity to vent their anger and anxiety about the past. Talking about what they have been through and what they are currently experiencing helps people bring their feelings to a conscious level. This is an emotional and highly charged process, yet it helps employees accept that negative emotions, while once valid reactions to perceived past injustices, will not serve them or their organization well today or in the future.

Executives must remember not to take what they hear in these sessions as a personal attack. Instead, they realize that, over time, people will recognize that their leaders were sensitive to their need to vent and willing to deal with the tough issues of transition.

To truly let go of the past, people have to believe that it no longer serves them or their organization well, that there are personal advantages in accepting change, and that a sound vision exists for where the organization is headed. Today's organizational leaders must share a clear sense of the marketplace and the forces that are acting so powerfully on their companies. Said another way, they must make the case for change.

Sometimes CEOs take an intellectual tack, laying out the financial, strategic, or technological imperative for ongoing change. Other times, an emotional approach is required. In a telecommunications firm, for example, an external expert was brought in to give a dire prediction of how firms that did not continue to radically revise their most basic ideas of business would become the first corporate dinosaurs of the twenty-first century. In a financial services company, managers at a transition management workshop were asked to write a hypothetical newspaper article ten years after the call for additional change went unheeded. This proved a highly effective way to corral attention and energy toward the need for embracing change.

Seeing an Opportunity for Influence. Unless people feel some degree of ownership over the new organizational order, their actions in reinforcing it are usually half-hearted. Change programs are constantly being derailed by individuals and groups who, having no personal investment, refuse to "get with the program." If senior leaders dictate authoritarian, "one-size-fits-all" prescriptions for change, and if managers merely comply with passive obedience, employees will quickly recognize that the managers' behavior is not based on a strong personal commitment. It's the difference between creating a work of art and coloring by the numbers. When stress or controversy develops in the organization, the program is easily abandoned, and managers and workers alike revert back to their traditional way of operating (Lawler, 1989). If people are to maintain faith in the new organizational order, they need to feel that they have some influence over their work. The best plans are blueprints to guide the local efforts of teams and their leaders, rather than rigid mandates.

Seeing an Opportunity for Reward. People will accept the new organizational order if they see the promise of an eventual reward. This could be extrinsic rewards of pay and benefits, opportunity rewards of learning new skills or moving into new positions, status rewards like perks and promotions, and other intrinsic rewards such as increased self-esteem or feeling part of an achieving team—or any combination. If, over time, people come to associate receiving desired rewards with accepting change, this will confirm their faith in the new organizational order as a source of advantage for both the organization and themselves.

Companies must design a fair reward system that reinforces values and behaviors congruent with the new organizational order, and that is sufficiently flexible to respond to rapid changes. The rewards should also be consistent with business strategy, management philosophy, employee needs, and, of course, financial realities. Ultimately, a reward system should attract, motivate, and retain good organizational members at all levels.

Some basic questions need to be addressed. Can new values and behaviors be rewarded and recognized adequately through existing compensation practices? If not, what kind of changes are needed? How can the desired values and behaviors be quantified and measured? If they cannot, would recognition programs be a better alternative than financial incentives? What distinction is to be made, if any, between producing desired results at any cost versus getting the job done in line with the new organizational order?

What respective weightings will individual, team, and organizational performance receive in compensation equations?

Building Confidence

Interviews with organizational members soon after major transitions indicate that they want to *understand* how life in the new organizational order will be better and, in particular, how they can approach their work in a way that will allow them to *realize* benefits. In the short run, people need to discern how they can align their work with the new organizational order. A supervisor in the nursing department of a health care organization that had grown rapidly wondered what direction she was expected to take her unit. "How does administration want us to prioritize cost cutting, service quality, and retention of nurses in a competitive job market? I have ideas, but I need some sense of which way we are going, because I want to make sure what I am building is coordinated with the goals of the organization." In a manufacturing concern decimated by continual waves of downsizing and restructuring, a machine operator looked forward to finding new and better ways of approaching work: "I get a sense that the worst is behind us now, but we have got to make some improvements in how we get the job done. There's been a lot of talk about quality improvement and increasing productivity; that's good, but now we have to take the time and do it instead of just talking about it."

People also want to know what it takes to achieve personal success from performing their jobs in line with expectations. A middle-level manager in a consumer products firm reported, "Look, I've given up on the idea that pay raises and promotions will come automatically around here. Those days are gone. But what do I have to do to protect my job and maybe get a shot at what new openings are available?" Another manager from the same company wondered, "What is going to distinguish the successful from the mediocre managers around here? I don't mind giving my all and working hard, but I want to know I'm doing the right thing. Give me a clue what [my business unit head] wants from me."

Then, over time, people want to gain the benefits of doing their jobs in line with expectations. They cite three specific personal benefits in particular. First, they want fairness to prevail as the fruits of organizational success are shared. Fairness here refers to a hybrid of two dimensions: a reasonable chance for growth in pay, and equitable distribution across groups and levels. "No more of these fat bonuses for the guys upstairs while we get paltry 3 percent pay raises," demanded one manager. "I understand there is a shift in our industry from base pay to greater at-risk pay," observed another; "I'll play by those rules, but I want a fair shot at getting the prize if I hit the target."

The second benefit people look for during recovery from change is the opportunity to gain new skills and experiences. People who have made it past transition and into recovery accept that from this point forward, staffing needs are rapidly changing and the individual employee must increasingly be responsible for training and development. A middle manager in a computer manufacturer observed, "It's been a rough road [living through the transition], but I've learned a lot about myself and about working in organizations today. I want assignments that will broaden my skills and increase my chances to be of value here or, if necessary, at another employer." A colleague noted, "With fewer people around after the cuts, I'm expecting to get a wider variety of assignments and experiences as time goes by."

A third benefit transition survivors look for is enhanced career development opportunities. Interestingly, most managers distinguish between career "development" and career "advancement." They recognize that the mergers, delayerings, and other restructurings that have flattened organizations have blocked upward mobility. Instead, they look to lateral moves as recognition of their contribution and to participation on special committees or task forces as opportunities to learn new skills or get exposed to new information. A trading manager in a U.S. financial services institution that was acquired by a European-based bank commented on his hopes to "be transferred to newly emerging product areas or foreign locations. With the globalization of business today, this could be a real boon to my career." And the manager of a mature business line at a consumer products company put it succinctly: "Our product has seen its day, and I have demonstrated that I can produce for this company. Let's see what they do—if they just let me waste away here, or transfer me where the action is."

Training during recovery also provides some essential benefits in restoring confidence. First, it helps the organization bolster prevailing perceptions of the link between effort and performance. An organization may have identified attractive rewards and have every intention of paying off for a job well done, but employees who feel they do not have the information or skills necessary to get the job done will only grow increasingly demotivated. Second, skills training provides knowledge and tools to help people align their work with the new order. Third, awareness training conditions people for ongoing change and disruption in their work settings—organizations need to develop a work force that can change several times, not just once.

Like never before, individuals today share the responsibility—and the rewards—for acquiring new skills and capabilities. Lifelong learning increasingly will be the rule, not the exception. People who have training and experience in a variety of areas will be all the more valuable to current or alternative employers. And those who can document transition-management skills, team-building behaviors, and other process skills will distinguish themselves when looking for jobs in the future. In total, training raises people's self-esteem and self-confidence by equipping them with the skills and ideas to contend with new organizational realities.

Forming Supportive Teams

The work team is also a focal point for revitalization during periods of significant transition. First, teams are the link between the individual and the organization. The team level is where most people assess whether the new organizational order truly works or is nothing more than just another round of executive lip service. People either see that their work team is embracing experimentation, adopting new and improved work methods, and as a result achieving short- and long-term goals, or that time for learning is not allowed, new and better ways are not emerging, and goals are not being met.

While success elsewhere in the organization helps influence

people's sentiments about life after transition, evidence from their own work teams matters most. People are more firmly and mutually committed to team goals, and are more readily able to influence their attainment, than widespread company goals beyond their reach. They are much more likely to be able to make a difference— and to receive relatively immediate feedback as to success or failure during recovery—in local team performance than in overall organizational results.

A second important way in which the work team operates during revitalization is similar to the way a family responds when a loved one goes through a difficult time: the team amplifies the small victories and offers support during the setbacks. The tone set within the work team influences the extent to which successes are celebrated and built upon, experimentation and innovation are nurtured and parlayed into even greater earnings and returns, and ultimately, faith and hope come to replace cynicism and distrust. It also forms the foundation for social support by reducing levels of occupational stress and buffering individuals from the physical or psychological consequences of stress that result (House, 1981). A work team with a high level of social support is not as susceptible to stressful dynamics that tend to accompany life during and after transition.

Finally, teams are important to organizational renewal because of their potential to produce results far greater than the sum of individual contributions or, conversely, to stifle the contributions of even the most talented individuals. Depending on how well members develop shared goals and operating procedures, team dynamics can either stimulate creativity and enhance productivity or restrict innovation and hinder performance.

The work team is the focal point for achieving quick wins in recovering after transition, and provides the concrete evidence people seek to prove that life after transition will not just be different, but holds the potential to be better. When asked what it would take to make him feel optimistic about being part of the post-transition organization, a manufacturing supervisor in a computer company stated, "Truly coming up with better ways of getting the job done. We all know that the old ways of doing things are what got us in trouble. Me and my team are the ones who know this work best; put us to work on thinking about improvements and that will get us excited."

As time moves ahead, transition survivors need to feel that they are part of a team that achieves its goals. "I cannot influence our overall corporate results," one manager commented, "but I can make a difference in [our department]. Being part of a team that makes its contribution to the bigger scheme is all I can ask for."

Fostering Organizational Dialogue

A new organizational order—and with it, new and better ways of approaching work—cannot be built without the exchange of accurate, timely, and complete information. Organizational members will not know how to align their tasks with the new vision unless they understand what that vision is and how they are expected to behave on the job. Teams will not be able to coordinate and convey knowledge within and across their boundaries unless information flows freely in multiple directions. And organizations will not receive reliable feedback about critical matters unless a climate is established that invites input in a relatively uninhibited and uncensored manner.

Rebuilding Trust Through Dialogue

Communicating to revitalize after transition is much more than conveying information, however. The goal is to create an environment where productive dialogue at all levels is encouraged. It is a yardstick by which the predominating values and behaviors of the organizational order that is *truly emerging*—as opposed to what is being espoused—are measured. The content and frequency of communication vehicles, for example, indicate the degree of trust and concern between parties. The accuracy and genuineness of communications measure the extent to which spirit, teamwork, and effectiveness have developed. And the proactiveness and multidirectional nature of communications gauge commitment and consideration to and from employees in the organization. The impact of communication on revitalizing an organization cannot be overstated; when a national sample of 3,000 wage and salaried workers were asked why they decided to take their current job, "open communication" topped the list of reasons.

Even in the best of times, there is static on the communication lines in most organizations, and it only gets worse during times of change and crisis. Organizational members do not trust the messages they hear and are cynical about their management's intentions. Ironically, these same organizational members crave information; they want a clear and convincing picture that the transition makes sense for the company and its future, signs that the transition will be well managed and lead to a new and better organization, signals that people matter in the transition, and answers as to what all of this means for them personally.

Senior management, in turn, is wary of saying too much when so little is known. They are legitimately afraid of saying something that later could be proved wrong or be used against the company in a wrongful-discharge suit. Some executives feel they have to have a tangible plan before communicating with their people. Others say they are too busy to communicate. Still others fantasize that by not communicating about the transition, they are "buffering" people from stress. Employees, of course, will tell you that no news is bad news.

Constricted communication during transition is the basis for anger, distrust, and cynicism that linger afterward. It creates a precedent and becomes ingrained in the organizational culture. Most important, it is difficult for top executives to create a new organizational order when they are out of touch with employees' current perceptions of everything from how to improve operations to what motivates them. One recent survey found that only about half of all employees feel it is safe to say what they truly think or that managers seek out or listen to their opinions ("A Survey of Employee Communication Practices," 1993). Just one-third of employees say their ideas are acted on or that they are given the reason why their ideas are not used. And only one in four employees reports that management takes employee interests into consideration when making important decisions.

Sharing information has traditionally followed the need-to-know philosophy in most organizations. Management tells employees only what they need to know to do a specific job, and then only when it is "safe" to reveal the information. Managers who communicate this way are sending a message that they do not think employees would understand more information, they feel employees cannot be trusted with sensitive data, and that time spent on communication is not productive, so why bother?

If these messages are congruent with the values underlying the new organizational order, then managers need not bother changing their communication styles. But if the new organization calls for a more respectful, trusting, and open relationship across levels, then managers at all levels must become aware of the inadvertent messages that these standard communication practices send. Moreover, too many managers fail to consider how much time is being wasted on second guessing other people's intentions because they have not built effective lines of communication, or how much time and effort is lost because of gamesmanship, politics, and maneuvering.

Trust is rebuilt following transition by communicating honestly the facts about the organization, its actions, and its points of view. This must include problems and controversies as well as attributes and achievements. Open and honest communication helps people gain a feeling of personal control—something they have sorely missed during transition. One major multinational corporation installed a toll-free telephone number so the media could have daily recorded updates of company news. Much to their surprise, company executives discovered that most of the calls were from their own managers anxious to learn what was going on in the corporation.

Revitalizing communication during recovery takes more than simply committing to telling the same story in more and different ways. Rather, it requires a commitment to assessing and understanding the fundamental role of communication within an organization. This, in turn, requires an understanding of the communications needs of the intended audience and the values that shaped them (Cooper, Morgan, Foley, and Kaplan, 1979). Then management must identify and talk about the organizational issues that most closely match people's needs. And in the process, it must identify, define, and articulate those issues that are the product of management's own perspective from the top of the organization. But for successful communication to happen, such issues must be couched in terms that are important to the employee audience.

The Value of Proactive Communication

During recovery, a proactive communication process offers some
important advantages over the reactive process. First, it tends to
identify the organization's concerns and priorities and to indicate
what management intends to do about them. This is reassuring to
employees. If they do not hear the organization's problems, which
they experience on a day-to-day basis, discussed and possible solutions considered, they become anxious. Second, it focuses on the
significance of events, rather than their mere occurrence. To help
them make sense of the new organizational order, people want to
know "what this event means."

Third, the proactive communication process provides a
frame of reference within which particular events may be placed and
explained: "Yes, this may be a setback, but it is no disaster. Remember, we told you that we anticipated one of the toughest issues
confronting us this year would be . . ." A fourth advantage of the
process is that it can be used to foreshadow subsequent change and
provide justification for it. Organizations in recovery may have to
take actions that look poorly conceived when viewed in isolation.
But when explained in the broader context of where the organization is headed and why, they can begin to make very good sense.
Fifth, proactive communication pressures leaders to match their
words with actions, as changes made are linked to previously discussed issues. Finally, proactive communication encourages hope
and optimism among organizational members, who understand
and see more fully where their organization is headed, why it is
going in that direction, and how it will get there.

Leadership must set the tone of communications during recovery. Their hands-on involvement demonstrates that keeping
people in the know and keeping in touch with employees' issues are
important components of the new order. Managers and supervisors
must play an active role in the communication process also, to
ensure that messages are heard and to reinforce the role of communications in the new organizational order. The proactive communication process highlights particular issues that the organization
must address if it is to be successful. In addition to these issues are
a set of content areas that must be communicated in revitalizing

after transition. Many of these areas, such as communicating vision and mission, have already been discussed, but some warrant fuller attention.

Organizational Goals. An important step in helping organizational members understand what is happening around them is to make them fully aware of what the new organization expects to accomplish. This includes not only the reasons for an action but also the specific results the organization expects. For example: "We eliminated layers to push decision making closer to the customer. Account representatives now have authority to grant discounts of up to 20 percent on customer orders without needing management approval. Here is how criteria for granting a discount should be set . . . "

Additionally, people are more willing to accept what they perceive as immediate injustices if they can foresee long-term benefits for themselves and others. The communication goal is to provide people with a sense of how the organization's vision and guidelines eventually will lead to a more equitable situation for themselves and their co-workers. Knowing the organization's plan helps restore levels of personal security.

New Opportunities. Paths toward success as demarcated in the old organizational order are gone, and many transition survivors falsely conclude that there are no new opportunities at hand (Brockner, 1992). In reality, the new organizational order may provide many opportunities, but they may be quite different from the old ones. The organization's responsibility is to clearly articulate the new opportunities and the rewards for adopting new behaviors.

Areas of Uncertainty. Even as the new organizational order is being built, employees often assume that the leadership really know more than they are saying. Managers should communicate what they know and be clear about what they do not know. Acknowledging areas of uncertain or incomplete information staves off employee suspicions that important matters are being withheld from them. Obviously, there will be some information that is too sensitive to communicate on a general basis throughout the organization. Having established a norm of communicating on a full and timely basis, however, will enhance employee tolerance for these situations. Beyond merely imparting information, communication patterns and norms powerfully establish and reinforce the essence of the new organizational order. That is, the act of communicating sends a series of messages over and above the content of what is being conveyed.

Bad News. Communication consultant Dennis Ackley (1992) notes that organizations show their real values when they communicate bad news. "Not communicating" is not a choice. If there is bad news, it will find its way into the work force—generally in a form worse than reality. Think that communicating takes too much time? Add up all the hours spent standing around the water cooler or coffee machine, gossiping on the phone, and stopping in the hall to pass on the latest rumor. Executives and managers have a choice: control the formal communication channels or rely on the inevitably more dubious informal channels.

Good communications planning cannot occur at the last minute. Organizations that are good at communicating even the worst of news have contingency plans ready if they are needed. These plans include prototypes for direct communication with employees, along with timelines and materials to ensure that supervisors and managers have the information they need to reinforce the proper messages.

Calls for better communication between levels or teams in the new organizational order need to be backed up with some actions that break traditional barriers. Some organizations get key middle managers talking to one another at periodic meetings that create opportunities to exchange information on business challenges, operational results, and successful adoptions of new operating procedures. In addition to helping managers learn what is happening in other parts of the organization, these meetings raise opportunities for coordination and cooperation across previously entrenched teams.

Many organizations work hard to enhance upward communication during recovery. In some cases, executives rely on informal ways of keeping in touch with people's feelings. They spend unstructured time with employees, individually or in groups, to hear their views on the new order and the extent to which it is being realized. At first, the executives may have to reveal their own feelings to encourage employees to do the same. A sincere concern for the employee point of view will be reciprocated with an increased regard for the welfare of the organization.

Other organizations use more formal methods for upward communication. Employee attitude surveys are excellent vehicles for involving most or all employees in two-way communication. Nucor Steel conducts an all-employee survey every two years, asking them what they think of newly emerging programs and policies. Chemical Bank surveys a sample of employees every quarter, with a focus on what they need to best contribute to organizational results. The survey findings are reviewed by Chemical's top-level management committee, and then individual managers receive specific results to use for action planning.

It may take some time for communication behaviors to catch up with the new vision. Barriers built up through years of constrictive communication do not come tumbling down overnight. People may be shy about revealing their truest feelings, and managers may be cautious about exposing what is really happening in their work areas. Poor communication during transition mismanagement may have residual effects in the post-transition organization. To revitalize communication effectiveness, leaders in recovering organizations must model open, timely, and complete communication. And they must reward it when they see others doing the same.

Promoting Organizational Learning

Discontinuous change is an exercise in organizational learning, the essence of which is the ability to gain insight from experience. When learning-efficient companies try something new, be it a new technology, product offering, or management approach, they can comprehend what works, what doesn't, and why. These companies can examine their overall strategy in relation to what is learned and incorporate new learning into their day-to-day practices. And they do all this in a short period of time. The ability to learn quickly is particularly important during major transitions.

Learning begins with the beliefs that influence behavior in an organization. In the broadest sense, beliefs are a combination of values, knowledge, expertise, and information. Belief systems encompass core values, many of which are implicit and taken for granted, and more mundane assumptions about the way the world functions. Individuals see the world through the lenses of these belief systems and take action based on their belief systems. These actions in turn influence particular outcomes, such as success or failure in an endeavor.

Effective learning occurs when people reflect on the consequences of their actions and thereby gain insight, such as a richer and more accurate understanding of the key factors in their environment. This is particularly important in understanding cause and effect linkages. The relationship between actions and outcomes is complex and often subjective. Still, effective reflection can add to a person's existing knowledge base and result in a better understanding of the relationship between action and outcomes.

Group learning cycles are similar to those for individuals: belief promotes actions that influence outcomes. Effective reflection helps a group modify, if warranted, its existing belief system. A team chartered to develop a new product learns a great deal while completing its task. Successes and failures, if fully examined, result in a better understanding of what works and what doesn't. The group's learnings influence the strategies employed in completing the work. These insights occur at a group level, in that no single individual in the group embodies all the learnings of the group as a whole.

Diffusion of what is learned through reflection is more than a simple transmission or exchange of cold facts. Sharing information among organizational groups is critical in facilitating reflection and action. Effective learning systems surface differing perspectives in order to better interpret experience and spark innovation. Without exchange, effective reflection is more difficult because those engaging in reflection lack the information they need to interpret the consequences of their actions.

In total, learning is most likely to occur when:

- Individuals and groups effectively reflect on and interpret the outcomes of their actions.
- Individuals and groups disseminate new learning throughout an organization.
- Individuals and groups act on their beliefs and leverage new learning (their own and others) to produce the greatest benefit to their organization.

Open the Boundaries. A first step in promoting learning is to open the boundaries of the organization to new ideas and information. This can be done by sending out scouts, importing ideas through speakers or seminars, and by bringing in people from the outside. One of the most productive boundaries to open up is the one that exists between a company and its customers. Effective learners constantly listen to their suppliers and customers. They bring customers in to talk about their perceptions of the market, of competition, and of the company itself. Jack Welch of General Electric dreams of a "boundaryless" company free of the walls that separate companies from their customers and suppliers. Boundaries are opened by events like DEC World, an annual gathering drawing more than 50,000 people; activities such as Corning's management meetings, which feature outside speakers; or devices like Citibank's customer laboratory.

Motivate Experiments and Risk Taking. Learning cannot occur without experimentation. Effective organizations create an environment where people feel both motivated and free to try something new and different. This may come about by creating special funds for experiments (as is done at Xerox or 3M) or by telling people, as one company does, that 15 percent of their time is theirs to explore or do whatever they want. Most experiments do not result in successes. New approaches will occur only if people feel they have permission to fail productively and that experimentation for its own sake will be rewarded. They must also be able to look around them and see organizational heroes who are experimenters.

Structure Experiments for Learning. Learning-efficient companies recognize the value of productive failure and the shortcomings of unproductive success. A productive failure is one that leads to insight, and thus is an addition to the commonly held knowledge of the organization. An unproductive success occurs when something goes well but nobody quite knows how or why other than to say "We must be doing something right!" No one can generalize from or reproduce such a success, although attempts to do so can result in misguided efforts and significant financial losses. Productive failures, in contrast, provide the capacity to create productive successes—where organization members know what they're doing right, and where they can take the lessons of success and apply them elsewhere. Learning-effective organizations thoroughly examine their successes and failures to ensure that productive learning occurs in both cases.

Learning-efficient companies make an effort to set up experiments with clear objectives, ensure that experiments are executed well, and document the results along the way so that a contemporaneous record is available. This process replaces what is typically an after-the-fact justification of success or failure. Not coincidentally, many of these companies also have instituted major total quality processes throughout their organizations, and thus provide training in statistics, experimental design, and problem analysis.

Extract and Disseminate Learnings. Good experiments alone aren't enough. Learning requires an environment where the results of experiments are sought after, examined, and disseminated throughout the organization. Effective learners spend much time and effort holding meetings, off-site sessions, conferences, and training programs to disseminate learning. Procter & Gamble gathers thousands of its managers each year to exchange information; Xerox and Corning hold annual events linked to their quality efforts, where teams of employees present their projects, experiments, and innovations. Some companies have designed what might be called "inefficient off-sites"—meetings with agendas that are not packed with presentations and work sessions, but that provide the time and opportunity for managers to meet together, mingle, hold informal meetings, and share their experiences. Other companies write case studies about successes and failures, and use them in meetings and training programs.

More generally, norms are needed to encourage people to examine their own beliefs and, as needed, modify them. Letting go of existing beliefs and assumptions is difficult at best. Most of us would rather cling to that which we know than experience the discomfort of embracing a new paradigm. Those organizations and managers who have not experienced failure over their histories are particularly prone to defensive reasoning.

Encourage the Capacity to Act. Ultimately, the payoff for organizational learning is more effective action over time. It's not enough to hear about an experiment or what someone else learned; real leverage comes from applying that learning in hundreds of different places throughout the organization. This requires overcoming the "not-invented-here" syndrome, which resists ideas from elsewhere. To do this, organizations need to free up and motivate people to use what others have learned. Part of this comes from rewarding people who apply the insights of others, as opposed to rewarding only those who come up with new and bright ideas.

Conclusion

An effort to revitalize an organization can be more than a reactive response to overcoming the unintended human and business consequences of a transition. It can be a proactive opportunity to rebuild the organization, work teams, and individual contributors in a way that results in greater efficiency, desired cultural norms, and renewed zeal. Organizational recovery and revitalization can be a platform for clarifying organizational vision, work team mission, and individual responsibilities, and for unifying all these forces into a coordinated and successful effort to achieve the prize of desired business goals.

PART THREE

Key Leverage Points for Discontinuous Change

8

Generative Strategy: Crafting Competitive Advantage

A. Elise Walton

In the past five years, U.S. executives have come to realize that they are playing a new game with strategy. It is increasingly less a game of "competitive advantage," dominated by quasieconomic models, and less a field of managerial choice. Instead it is quickly moving toward a capability-based model.

Executives have come to recognize that it is truly sustainability that counts, at the same time realizing that no competitive advantage is sustainable. The traditional economic models strive for profit, yet these profits are typically nonsustainable. The old logic showed that high profits attract new entrants, who then compete on price and eliminate the advantaged position. In modern organizational life, few products are sustainable, and many firms actively cannibalize their own products.

Recent experience and evidence have called into question much of the logic that drove earlier strategic models, including profitability drivers, such as market share or industry (Schwalbach, 1991; Rumelt 1991; Loomis, 1993). Even the idea of executive vision has been questioned as a strategic driver (Evans, 1992; Lavin, 1993). The rational, data-based approaches to strategy have not proved fruitful in shaping administrative or organizational behavior, and executives have increasingly looked to alternative approaches to bring strategic thinking to life (Hitt and Tyler, 1991; Mintzberg, 1978). Finally, and most important, in a high-speed, fast-changing economic environment, data and analysis no longer provide answers, and lengthy study is a luxury executive decision makers can seldom afford.

What we are seeing in innovative companies is an approach we call generative strategy. The objective is *organizational* sustainability, not market or product sustainability. It differs from traditional strategy in that it focuses heavily on organization and processes, team learning, and choices. It relies less on market or economic analysis and traditional competitive analysis per se. Generative strategy is not the search for long-lasting economic competitive advantage, but the design of an organization that will perpetually regenerate competitive advantage. To do this, a firm must continually reinvent itself, must continually test itself and its thinking. The organization, by generating new information, new perspectives, and new frames, *generates* new strategy naturally. Firms that practice generative strategy rarely find themselves blindsided by possibilities they never considered.

In some cases, it is the new form that gives birth to the new strategy: new strategy could not even be envisioned before the form existed. In other words, form itself is strategy. Form creates the ability to see and interpret information differently and therefore the enlightened ability to act differently. Structure works together with strategy to co-produce new knowledge and new strategies. The process is illustrated in Figure 8.1.

In contrast, many firms find themselves locked in a strategic doom loop (see Figure 8.2). New information cannot get enough management attention to warrant action. Standard paradigms continue to dominate the enacted reality. Trapped in such a cycle, companies can't change the strategy unless they change the organization, and they can't change the organization unless they change

Figure 8.1. The Generative Strategy Cycle.

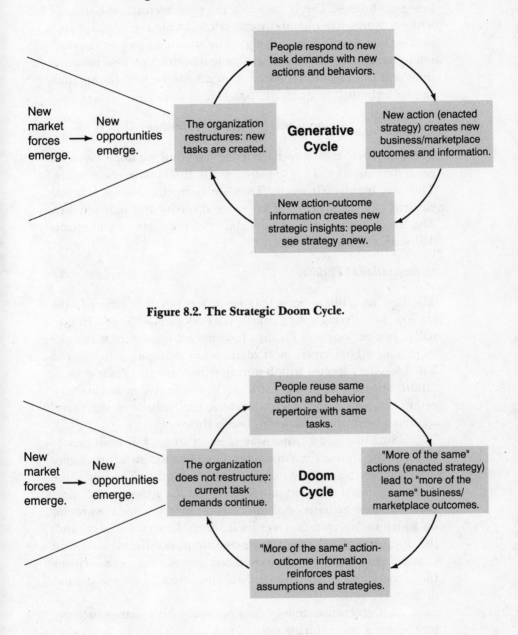

Figure 8.2. The Strategic Doom Cycle.

the people. The perceptions of the people limit their ability to see
new possibilities. The behavior of the people creates the strategy
while it works like organizational gridlock: the organization isn't
flexible and doesn't admit divergent information; people, responding to the internal organizational demands, don't see new information; and the capabilities required to act on the new information
cannot be built. The quandary is, where to start?

Components of Generative Strategy

There are some common characteristics among organizations with
generative strategy. They are structurally fluid and ever-changing.
They are highly self-aware. They see competition as a valuable
element of the landscape. They value diversity and individuality.
And they focus on netware—the ability of people to communicate,
dialogue, and learn together.

Organizational Fluidity

The first recognition in generative strategy is that strategy—the
choices, the offerings, the markets, the customers—changes continually. Just as Sony and Phillips have moved from records to tapes
to CDs to digital tapes, most markets are changing rapidly. The
half-life—the expected length during which any particular organization, business, or product strategy stays effective or profitable—
of any strategy is shrinking; therefore, the half-life of any corresponding organizational design is also shrinking.

Structure is the major way to enact strategy; it leads people
to "see" the strategic environment. Organization structure frames
information: creating a set of units, accountabilities, and jobs, the
structure directs employees' attention to specific activities and information. These activities and information then become the ground
on which the organization sees itself acting. However, this ground,
the competitive landscape, can be seen in quite different ways, and
changes in structure are the most direct way executives can refocus
the activity and perspective of their employees to see the ground
differently.

But generative strategy does not end with a change in structure. Once a restructuring occurs, executives pursuing generative

strategy look quickly for what new information emerges. Take the example of a high-technology company moving toward globalization. Initially, the challenge was stated as a financial goal: increasing nondomestic revenues. Despite a lot of attention and specific financial targets, progress was slow and inadequate. Executives concluded that the strategy could not be enacted with the current organizational structure (a traditional global organization with a domestic headquarters) and that the company needed to move to a transnational organization architecture. Restructuring by installing significant leadership around the world and empowering local managers was the implementation strategy.

Immediately after the change, new information about the business emerged. (In actuality, it was not *new* information, but information that had been unattended to in the previous structure.) The new information called for a different approach—including changes in pricing, cash management, and human resources—which was ultimately taken. And so the primary value of the new structure was what it brought to light. The old structure was unaware of, or filtered out, the regional limitations it had placed on people and market development.

In another example, an organization structured by regions changed to a business-unit structure. In the regional structure, strategy had been a corporate function, and products were looked at in terms of a few key features, particularly speed and technology features. When the business units were formed along product lines, unexpected information immediately emerged about customer perceptions of products previously classified as the same. Speed and new features were important to certain customers, but monumentally unimportant to others, for whom cost and product size were critical. Data that had once been ignored now took center stage.

Restructures may increase organizational fluidity, but other information frames also create rigidity. There are other ways in which organizations frame information so as to *restrict* the range of what is perceived and considered. For example:

- *History*. History is one of the biggest contributors to setting up expectations, resources, and activities.

- *Financial Parameters.* Financial success parameters clearly affect how information is presented and how it is interpreted.
- *Market Parameters.* The way the market is seen affects what is seen and what is identified for action.
- *Customer Parameters.* Customer parameters also frame decisions. First, the definition of the customer can limit choices involuntarily. Second, one-dimensional, inflexible definitions of what the customer wants are also limiting. Third, product categories often constrain the ability to see opportunities.
- *Employee Parameters.* Often, executives make assumptions about the motivations and abilities of their people. Frequently these assumptions limit the organization's ability to use resources differently.

Structuring invariably changes these frames and how they are attended to. Restructuring forces executives to rethink the organization's capabilities and opportunities. In a certain sense, restructuring, like zero-based budgeting, sets the organizational assumptions at zero. Everything becomes a clean slate.

Fluidity deals with the issues of recognition and choice—two components of discontinuous change—by expressly building in alternative views of the organization. Restructuring is one way to increase fluidity, but there are also other techniques. One is the assignment of issues to senior managers. That is, executives are being held accountable for a Total Quality program or a key cross-unit strategic initiative. The accountability goes away as soon as the issue is resolved. Other organizational practices, discussed later, also support a continually fluid organization.

Identity and Self-Awareness

The second characteristic of a generative-strategy approach is the priority placed on identity and self-awareness. Generative strategy places importance on knowing what you don't do well and saying no. Doing this provides the all-important ability to reject options and choices that are poor fits and to free up attention and resources for key priorities. A clear, realistic sense of identity enables the firm to act on its decisions, to choose what it will do, and to reject what it cannot do. This becomes the sustaining logic that allows people to survive in a highly fluid organization.

Rather than looking at identity as a constraint or limitation, self-awareness looks at identity as an *opportunity*. Identity can be a positive force that wins over employees, customers, and shareholders. For example, since its inception, 3M has seen itself as an innovative company. Executives still repeat the saying of the founder: "If an employee wants to do it his own way, and it doesn't interfere with the overall good, let him do it." Innovation has borne 3M through many industry transitions and enabled it to achieve its goal of 25 percent of its revenue from new products.

There are different ways that this self-awareness can come into play. First is the recognition and building of core competencies. The Sony Walkman is a prime example. Sony, combining its expertise in miniaturization and recording, came up with the idea of a listening device small enough to walk with. And 3M, building on its capability in adhesives, invented the Post-it—a brand-new product, once unthought of—and created a market worth several million dollars.

Second, self-awareness can be helpful in building organizational capabilities or routines. Walmart built up horizontal ordering and inventory processes that allowed it to surpass its rival, K mart, handily. Xerox, with its deep understanding and commitment to quality, was able to put teams together to solve problems rapidly and efficiently.

Third, self-awareness provides credible, durable direction—expounding on organizational values, routines, and identity. The third factor is perhaps the most abstract but also the most sustainable. Specific offerings have short lives as markets change, and the organization has to be able to identify higher-order values to guide decisions. That is, AT&T can be a communications company in 1901 and also in 1991, but "communication" now includes cellular telephones, videophones, electronic messaging, and document transfer. The guiding principle of being a communications company survives product, market, and customer changes.

Finally, identity and self-awareness allow organizations to build alignment in the context of fluidity. Organizations have three mechanisms for achieving alignment: hierarchy, formalization, and

socialization (Hickson, Pugh, and Pheysey, 1969; Mintzberg, 1978;
Ouchi, 1981). When conflicts and differences arise, they may be
resolved by a common boss (hierarchy), by formal rules or procedures (formalization), or by a common set of beliefs, values, and
goals (socialization)—that is, identity. In highly fluid organizations, structure (hierarchy) and process (formalization) change frequently. As units reconfigure themselves and reporting relationships change, it is often unclear who approves what and how the
old processes need to change to reflect the new accountabilities.
Therefore, fluid organizations are less capable of using the chain of
command or routine processes to ensure coordination and alignment. A clear and common identity—values and norms that guide
practice, behavior, and choice—enables organization members to
make decisions that achieve synergy and alignment fluidly.

Each mechanism has its weaknesses. Hierarchy creates
bottlenecks and engenders rebellion. Formal systems are time-
consuming. Shared identity, or socialization, has to compete against
individual identities. Yet there is evidence that, of the three methods, "soft" influence strategies work best as a mode of alignment
(Falbe and Yukl, 1992).

Organizations are increasingly looking to identity to provide
direction and alignment among its members. Using a process it
called strategic choice, Xerox worked through an identity crisis in
the 1980s. Recognizing that the corporation was involved with
many markets and needed some strategic alignment, Xerox outlined
the available options, using analogies of well-known companies
with recognizable identities:

- *BMW:* Xerox would select the high-margin businesses and
  pursue only those, harvesting or divesting some of its main
  products.
- *Sears:* Xerox would focus on distribution and providing a full
  line of products. This implied continued build-up of sales and
  distribution capability, along with the outsourcing of products
  and components.
- *Boeing Wide:* Xerox would use a stick-to-the-knitting approach,
  focusing on its primary business: copiers.
- *Chrysler:* Xerox would focus on being a second player in the

computer market, keeping many of its existing products and being a close follower of IBM.

Subsequently, Xerox chose an intermediate option. Choosing its terminology with care, Xerox called itself The Document Company. The new identity built on the existing identity (The Document Processing Company) but matured and refined it. A critical insight was recognizing that the ability to print or copy had become a commodity and that part of Xerox's capability was understanding how documents work—how words on paper facilitate or hinder business processes. This self-assessment, coupled with an environmental assessment, allowed Xerox to build a new identity, which led to new strategies, new structures, new investments, and ultimately a new culture.

The Competition

A third principle of generative strategy is *coopetition*. There is growing recognition that business relationships are extremely complex and dominated by both cooperative and competitive aspects. Partners are competitors, suppliers are partners, competitors are suppliers, and so on. Firms are increasingly linked with others via electronic inventory management, supplier quality control, joint product development and launches, co-advertising, and many other activities. Organizations are not merely passive recipients of market changes, but are often key actors in creating new market paradigms. Some firms continually reinvent their markets by introducing new products, even at the expense of their own older products. And organizations evolve in concert with their markets. For example, the success of digital tapes depends not only on hardware but also on changes in distributors. Electric cars, even if built to desirable specifications, will suffer low adoption rates unless there is an infrastructure to support them. The success of the more powerful RISC microchip depends on the availability of new software, because CISC software runs more slowly on this chip.

The key point is that competitors, markets, and market relationships are highly interdependent, and these relationships have themselves emerged to a "high-fit" situation. Generative strategy

embraces this by recognizing that *no one can play the game alone.*
It values all other players—including the competitor.

The old "kill-the-competitor" mindset is no longer appropriate; in fact, it has become a competitive blind spot for many firms
(Zahra and Chaples, 1993). Coke and Pepsi battled over market
share and one-to-one comparisons while Snapple and others redefined the beverage market. Xerox, focusing on Kodak, missed the
Japanese threat. A singular focus on one enemy often distorts the
organization's perspective of the overall market and market opportunities. Even worse, it detracts from a creative focus on how to serve
the customer better, since "better" becomes a measure relevant only
to the competitor's wares. Furthermore, the failure of market leaders
such as IBM, Sears, GM, and Citibank, has demonstrated that dom-
ination does not guarantee success (Loomis, 1993; Schwalbach,
1991). Indeed, success may carry with it the seeds of failure (Shaw
and Perkins, 1992).

Therefore, the challenge revolves around identifying the
other players' positions and then building coalitions. It often involves restructuring the organization and the market with others in
mind. One visible form of this is the increasing trend of having
customers co-design products. Another is the shaky success of al-
liances—the IBM, AT&T, and Apple chip and the Xerox-Microsoft
alliance, for example.

Partnering for leverage is another generative approach. Partnering allows a firm to expand capability and scope without piling
up assets. Again, it involves recognizing that someone else may be
able to do something better for you than you could do for yourself.
For example, Novell, through third parties, built market coverage
equal to or better than IBM or Microsoft. Mail-order computer giant
Dell, using information technology, built a virtual warehouse. Har-
ley, with its long connection to dealers, eventually won back the
motorcycle buyers—not through control but through relationships.

Generative organizations recognize the value of relationships
and construct and nurture them carefully. Unbalanced deals, those
that disproportionately favor one player, are typically unstable. The
principle of coopetition includes a fundamental appreciation of the
value others bring, our dependence on them, and an interest in their
well-being.

Loving the competition also means accepting internal competition and appreciating that it can be fruitful. While teamwork is still valued, it is placed in a context that recognizes competition as an inescapable and important fact of organizational life. Coopetition also implies the ability to recognize and celebrate someone else's success. It places a premium on people who can define and live with cooperation—combining competition and cooperation in ways that build leverage for the firm.

Diversity

A fourth principle of generative strategy is to build diversity into the system and to value the multiple perspectives it generates. Diversity comes in many forms. Demographic diversity is the one most frequently targeted, as witnessed by the growing number of diversity programs in corporate America.

The key to this strategy is simple: valuing diverse backgrounds, skills, and points of view. Although the thought is simple, it is quite difficult to execute. Humans prefer those who are similar to themselves. Differences can crop up anywhere; demographic differences are obvious, but the unseen differences typically create much more trouble. Consider, for instance, occupational differences.

A finance manager and a marketing manager need to resolve an issue of product positioning. The marketing manager emphasizes the importance of understanding the customer and suggests that the organization needs salespeople dedicated to specific product lines. The finance manager, concerned about the effect on costs, responds, "Let's not forget about the shareholder." The marketing manager believes the best way to serve the shareholders' needs is indirectly—guaranteeing market coverage would guarantee sales and margin. The finance manager wants to see direct action, such as cost control and organizational consolidation. But even more difficult is that their world views differ. The finance manager trades in data and "what is." The marketing manager trades in "what could be." Thus the arguments that persuade the marketing manager carry little weight according to the finance manager's logic.

Diversity conflicts can also be seen between strategic or technical visionaries and operating managers. The visionaries chide managers for being too narrowly focused and being behind the curve on the major market discontinuities. The operating managers chastise the visionaries for being idealistic and out of touch with current customer needs. Again, the different roles focus attention on different information sets, but both conclusions are right.

Diversity is valued because it delivers many benefits. The first is that diversity, de facto, provides many different frames for a problem or decision. People with different backgrounds, experiences, languages, and cultures will necessarily see a problem differently. The value is in leveraging those different perspectives.

A second advantage of diversity is higher sustainability (Huberman and Glance, 1992). Diverse capabilities (not diversification) allow an interweaving of competencies. Different capabilities can support each other in a symbiotic way. For example, the success of a new business depends on the structured rigor of a financial business case and also the creative, unconstrained thinking of marketing or technical innovators. At the corporate level, a portfolio of diverse businesses enables an organization to buffer one line's seasonality against another's consistency, or to share core competencies across businesses.

One of the clearest examples of this benefit is in the area of size diversity. Firms often create business units or geographic units that are within some range of normal mass—not too big or too little. However, sometimes new products have no home because they don't fit in any of the existing units. There are many cases of good ideas developed by large companies, only to be commercialized by upstarts (Smith and Alexander, 1988). Promoting diversity allows small paradigms to exist within larger paradigms.

At Ragú, the search for new products forced then CEO Charles Strauss to create a new paradigm. He said, "We had to create a new business unit. We said, 'Think about chicken, and don't think about anything red.'" This propelled the launch of Chicken Tonite, a successful line for Ragú. While red sauce and white sauce may not constitute a paradigm in the grand sense of the word, in day-to-day business red versus white take on the same kind of power. They affect the thinking and the solutions considered. Promoting diversity allows upstarts and deviants to succeed.

Finally, the explicit value placed on diversity enables all people to contribute. It recognizes them as whole human beings, with importance and identity, and creates a positive cycle of confidence, action, and learning. It also provides a platform for connection and communication as a means of uncovering distinctions and differences.

The Importance of Netware

Fluid organizations constantly combine and recombine skills, attentions, processes, and so on. Many organizations, to keep up, try to create the smallest units or building blocks possible. Then, to build a specific product for a specific market, they simply combine the two relevant units—which uncombine when the task is done.

One result is that social relationships are constantly formed and broken. Employees need to be able to work with strangers at a moment's notice and say goodbye to colleagues just as rapidly. Integrating new relationships and new information is difficult and stressful; so is ending relationships. The continual forming and reforming, the constant challenge of getting to know new people and working out new working relationships, can lead to overload.

Netware is the collective term for the tools and vehicles that allow people to achieve genuine communication rapidly. The tools of netware are many: common principles of expected behavior, common problem-solving formats, electronic and video mediums, and so on. Netware provides a communication highway between all organization members, so people can come together and set about working with minimum "getting-to-know-you" time.

This is one aspect of the learning organization: Diverse, unacquainted individuals must be able to come together and reach a common understanding about complex issues. These issues cannot be resolved with the tools of quality, engineering, or financial analysis. Facts and numbers will not lead to agreement or alignment because facts themselves are often gross abstractions. Judgment, reasonable discourse, and mutual acceptance are required. And they represent the crux of netware.

Judgment is required because after all the data and facts are on the table, people must somehow reflect on their value. They may conclude that new ideas and information—uncollectable because they are nonexistent—are more important than historical, collectable data. Many times, particularly in regard to the future, facts and figures are not conclusive or directive, and the decision must come down to gut feelings.

Reasoned discourse is also critical. Dialogue is the primary method for doing the work of identifying issues, resolving problems, and making decisions. By using more effective dialogue, the executive, team, group, or organization operates at a higher level of performance. The tools for effective discourse are no secret, but they are rarely practiced. In organizations that do not have common approaches to discourse, conversations are a free-for-all in which any topic is fair game. In organizations where group-discussion guidelines are widely understood and valued, teams can cover difficult and complex topics more quickly and far more effectively.

The last component of netware is mutual acceptance. We prefer the word *acceptance* to *trust* because the expression "trust me" is much overused and often describes a melange of phenomena (Gabarro, 1987). One may distrust intentions (that is, the other person has selfish or malevolent intentions), competence (the other has good intentions but lacks the ability to act on them), personality (the other has the right intentions and the right capability but may be inconsistent in applying them) or other characteristics.

Lack of mutual acceptance is often the culprit when behavior and strategic choices are not aligned. For example, the organization is performing poorly, multiple explanations exist, and behavior is scattered in many directions. People are trying to improve product quality, redefine the product line, cut staff, and increase R&D—all at the same time.

When this lack of alignment is discovered, it is usually attributed to malice, not different information or logic. It has been called the sinister attribution error (Simpson, 1993). People dismiss a different point of view because they think its advocates are playing politics, biased, self-interested, or have some other sinister motivation. The attribution is in error because it doesn't take into account alternative, sensible explanations for the same behavior. Because of this attribution error, people make little effort to learn about the competing logics in their organizations. This relieves them of having to work to understand the different points of view.

However, where there is mutual acceptance, people must

work to understand what other people are saying. They value the diversity of their views and their different perspectives and build on them to reach a deeper understanding of the problem.

Building the Capability for Generative Strategy

There seem to be certain critical steps to building a generative organization and generative strategic capability.

1. *Build a strategic language system.* Oddly enough, building a language system is a major contributor to enabling strategic action. Once they agree on terms, people are able to discuss the underlying market dynamics and the options before them. It allows them to argue about choices, not about terms. It minimizes the possibility of talking past one another.

The language system also needs to be supported in a number of ways. Short and simple documents that build on the language system should be created. These documents reinforce the use of the terms and enable paper-based communication between players.

2. *Build listening devices.* Because operating managers find their attention driven to urgent quarterly matters, they often lack the time, data, and even perspective to get a different view on the problems at hand. New, innovative perspectives most often come from the periphery (Brown, 1991). Younger employees, outsiders, technologists, and field personnel often have insights that are overlooked at the core of the firm. Some organizations have institutionalized processes to forward these perspectives to the seniormost level. Outside consultants can also be helpful in this regard. They can provide an external view that includes comparisons with other firms, and they can often identify and untangle the internal competing perspectives.

3. *Build fluid processes.* To overcome the issue of level of organization (from CEO to product manager), there must be a hierarchy or network of strategies, each clearly linking to the strategies above and below it. Policy deployment (also known as hoshin planning) recognizes this, linking together objectives such that the hows of the corporation are the whats of the business group; the hows of the business group are the whats of the business unit, and so on.

Perhaps most important in building strategic capability is simply getting people in a room together and sharing ideas in a productive way. Most firms have moved away from traditional presentations because they often set up very dysfunctional dynamics—the presenter becomes more and more defensive and the reviewers become more and more challenging—and because they place too much emphasis on data. The goal is to build a process that enables key decision makers and stakeholders to engage in dialogue about choices and assumptions. For every problem, there are massive data available, and all participants have crafted their own interpretations and conclusions from their own unique set of data. The important objective is getting people together to share their data and their conclusions in constructive synergy.

Many techniques already exist to do this. Strategic choice (Bliss, 1992) provides a process in which key decision makers co-create the strategic agenda for the firm. Strategic profiling (Biggadike, 1994) and future mapping (Mason, 1994; Stewart, 1994) build creative processes of strategy definition and choice. Expert systems such as Corporate Memory (Corporate Memory, 1993) allow stakeholders to address strategic issues using a shared electronic problem-solving tool.

All these techniques use data to aid, but not dominate, problem solving. All depend on a few key features: simplicity, human interaction, future orientation, customer amenities, and portable tools and technologies.

4. *Build a strong culture.* One thing that helps people cope with the challenges of constant change is solidity of direction and day-to-day behavior. Having a clear set of practices for team startup, including how to identify objectives and outputs, how to set direction, and so on, can minimize potentially massive transition costs. Xerox's quality process provided just such a set of practices. Even today, when a quality improvement team or a new division is formed, there is shared understanding about how to approach the problem. By being able to start working on the problem immediately, the teams save a lot of startup costs.

5. *Build communities of practice.* A community of practice is a group of individuals with a common interest that shares a common language system and interacts to produce something. Us-

ually, the members do not report to the same formal work group or have the same sets of skills. Often the community is stealthy, unseen, and unsanctioned by management. Community members seek each other out because they share an interest in accomplishing specific work objectives.

Usually organizations are indifferent to or even hostile toward these informal groups. However, communities of practice are usually wellsprings of organizational competence and tend to be directed at market-relevant goals. The techniques for supporting and leveraging these communities are just developing, but they provide a powerful source for generating new strategies.

6. *Build time for reflection.* The literature is filled with the biases built into human decision making. Executive decisions are no exception (Bazerman and Neal, 1992; Whyte, 1991). This calls for executives and executive teams to build self-reflection into their processes. They must use checkpoints to ascertain whether they are progressing in the right direction, perhaps even meet together when there is no specific agenda to discuss.

Summary

Generative strategy addresses two elements of discontinuous change directly: the challenge of recognition and the challenge of strategic choice. Because of their fluidity and diverse frames of reference, organizations using generative strategy often see opportunities before others do. Because of their netware skills, they are better at outlining choices, discussing them, making a reasoned choice, and taking action.

9

Organizational Architecture: Designing for High Performance

David A. Nadler

Paul Allaire, the Chairman and CEO of the Xerox Corporation was pondering what to do next. It was the middle of 1990, and Allaire, President and Chief Operating Officer since 1986, had just been named CEO upon the retirement of David Kearns. For the past year, Allaire had been deeply involved in an effort to develop a new ten year strategic vision, known as "Xerox 2000." He was feeling very satisfied, and in fact excited about this work. At the same time, he was very concerned about the ability of the Xerox organization of more than 100,000 people to make it happen. The company had made tremendous strides during the 1980s, coming back from the brink of extinction at the hands of the Japanese. This had been accomplished by a broad based cultural change process centered on quality improvement, known in Xerox as "Leadership Through Quality." Quality had been a tremendous success, as symbolized by Xerox' winning of the Malcolm Baldrige National Quality Award in 1989. However, it had failed to change some of the basic ways the company related to the marketplace, developed product, and managed innovation. Since 1988, Allaire had been talking about his "change agenda," which attempted to focus people on the customer and the marketplace and enhance innovation, but the results so far had been disappointing to him. He felt that not enough progress was being made and that the organization seemed very resistant to change. So, in 1990, Allaire came to the conclusion that the basic organizational architecture of the corporation had to change so that Xerox people would have a clear line of sight from customers to offerings and greater control over their own destiny. He didn't mean merely another reorganization. In the previous decade, the company had been reorganized four times, but Allaire realized that while the boxes had been moved, these reorganizations had not fundamentally changed the way the company was run. They were changes in structure, not changes in governance. He therefore began an effort to re-architect the company, an effort that would not reach maturity until early 1994. His goal was to fundamentally change the way the business was run [Howard, 1992, p. 107].

Allaire's decision to rearchitect Xerox was an important turning point in the life of that corporation. But it was not unique: many CEOs have come to the same conclusion. Redesign of the fundamental structures and processes of the organization can be a powerful lever to bring about discontinuous change. As a result, changes in organizational structures and processes show up as central elements in many CEOs' change agendas.

Why are structure and process change so prevalent in times of disequilibrium? Part of the answer stems from the inherent limitations on CEO action. Contrary to the illusions held by many, the CEOs of large and complex enterprises have relatively few levers to use in the short term to bring about dramatic change. They can make major strategic moves, such as entering new markets, acquiring or divesting operations, or changing investment patterns, but there is a limit to how many actions can be taken, and many of these take a good deal of time to execute. CEOs can change people, through hiring, firing, and placement, but again there are limitations. They can bring people in from the outside, but this takes time and the odds of success are at best mixed. This leaves the potential for moves of staff inside the organization, but here the CEOs' reach is often limited to the few reporting levels with which they have direct contact. CEOs can change the reward system, but this again takes time to have impact, usually several years. So, one of the few areas where CEOs can take immediate, visible, and dramatic action is basic structures and processes—or, as we call it, the organizational architecture.

But deciding to change the architecture is not merely the result of a process of elimination. It turns out that this is a powerful tool for affecting the behavior of large numbers of people in very dramatic ways. Organizational architecture has high visibility; people can immediately see changes that are very tangible. It can have immediate impact. As people are given new roles, new tasks, and new relationships to manage, they instantly feel the effects of the change. Architectural change can be constructively disruptive. By reconfiguring roles, relationships, and work, it can serve to aid in frame breaking and frame bending by destroying some of the old patterns of interaction and performance.

Architecture is a tool that can be used and also misused. In some cases, changes of organizational structure are used as a substitute for real strategic changes. In other cases, the changes are described as discontinuous, but are (as in the case of the four previous Xerox reorganizations) incremental changes surrounded by discontinuous verbiage. In yet other situations, changes of structure and process do not succeed because of inattention to other elements—people and the informal organization. A way to increase the probability that structure and process interventions will lead to the desired discontinuous change is to broaden our thinking and consider *organizational architecture* as a different way of approaching organization design.

The Concept of Organizational Architecture

Architecture is defined as the art and science of designing and erecting buildings. But architecture is more than an activity, it is a way of doing work. It is a framework that specifies approaches to designing, structures, and relationships.

Organizational architecture is a logical extension of this thinking. When we talk about organizational architecture, we define it as a framework or a system for design and construction of human organizations and also a way of thinking about that design process. It involves shaping organizational space to meet human needs.

A Metaphor for Design

One perspective on organizational architecture is that it is a metaphor for design that helps us think differently about what organizations may look like in the coming years.

In physical architecture four factors are important in shaping the development of an architecture. The first is *purpose*, the fundamental function that the particular building is intended to perform. A building's purposes define the design problem an architect must solve; they are the driving force of the entire design process. As new purposes develop, new designs are developed. For example, in the late 1880s large retailers such as Marshall Fields emerged. Their need to display large amounts of merchandise in open spaces necessitated the development of new buildings, known as the commercial loft.

A second factor is the available *structural material*. Any architect's vision for solving the core design problem is profoundly shaped by the physical materials and techniques available for realizing that vision. New structural materials enable new and different designs. For example, the development of structural steel enabled the design of buildings with steel frames and curtain walls hung from the frames, as opposed to the traditional load-bearing wall approach to construction.

A third factor is the more elusive quality of *architectural style*. Style means much more than aesthetics, although that is certainly part of it. When the drive for new design solutions raised by new purposes is combined with innovations in structural materials, the product is often a new architectural style. It is the holistic solution an architect develops to integrate a building's purpose and its materials.

The final element is collateral technology—technologies that, while not absolutely necessary for construction of the building, are necessary for it to function effectively. For example, large skyscrapers can be built without high-speed elevators or central air conditioning, but it is difficult to imagine people living and working in them without such technologies.

When purpose, materials, style, and collateral technology all change, then radically new kinds of buildings get designed and constructed. A parallel pattern seems to apply to organizations. A study of large business organizations in the late 1800s illustrates this pattern (Yates, 1993). New industries presented their owners with new business purposes, and new materials—the typewriter, carbon paper, the duplicating machine, and the vertical file—were developed for realizing these new purposes. Using these materials, managers could issue orders via memos, collect relevant data from the field on standardized reports, and organize information in filing systems so that topics could be easily accessed by managers on demand.

The combination of new purposes and new structural materials led to a new organizational style—what is commonly thought of as the machine bureaucracy, with its narrowly defined jobs, small spans of control, functional divisions, and steep hierarchy. This new style of organizational architecture reached its fullest expression with the development of the modern corporation's equivalent of collateral technologies—the disciplines, techniques and methodologies of scientific management.

Today, the factors that influence organizational architecture are again in change, to a degree unmatched since the emergence of the large corporation almost one hundred years ago. Continuous technological innovation, fast-changing markets, and the necessity of operating on a global scale are redefining the fundamentals of corporate purpose. The imperatives of quality, speed, and customer responsiveness are replacing the traditional emphasis on bureaucratic control. As a consequence, organizations must be designed for radically enhanced productivity, to produce increased innovation and speed, and to be capable of managing change.

Companies also have new structural material at hand to shape their organization to achieve these new purposes. Two are of particular note—one is new and another has long been available but until recently was largely unused. The new material is information technology, based on computer and advanced telecommunications. These technologies are the structural steel of the current revolution in organizational architecture, making possible profound changes in how companies organize and manage work. Computer networks, electronic mail, digital scanning and printing, desktop video conferencing, and collaborative software allow organizations to function independent of time and place to disseminate information more broadly and more quickly and to facilitate collaboration and teamwork. Knowledge-based systems codify technical knowledge, make explicit the expertise of the organization's members, and leverage organizational learning. In general, this technology enables new forms of design by performing three functions previously performed by the hierarchy: communications, linkage, and knowledge enhancement (see Gerstein, 1992).

The second structural material is the team. For decades, we have known of the power and capability of teams as a key building block of organizations (see Likert, 1961), but many enterprises continued to view the individual and the individual job as the core building unit, following the concepts of scientific management. It is only as a result of recent work on teams and empowerment (Lawler, 1992; Katzenbach and Smith, 1993) that senior managers have become aware of the power of teams and the value of using them as a basic design element in organizations.

Today, just as a century ago, new purposes and new structural materials are spawning radically new organization styles. The traditional functional hierarchy is giving way to more decentralized enterprises where self-managed teams have end-to-end responsibility for satisfying customer requirements. But this new organizational architecture will be incomplete if companies do not also develop new collateral technologies. In particular, new architectures will require new approaches and models for leadership, new methods for selecting and developing people, new techniques for performance management and rewards, and finally, organizational learning as a key collateral technology to enable these new enterprises to function and grow.

A Metaphor for the Design Process

Another perspective on organizational architecture is focused on the *process* of design, as opposed to the *content* of design decisions. Here, architecture again provides a metaphor, this time for the design process.

In physical architecture, the architect works to understand the needs of the client, the purposes of the building, and then draws on available materials to develop the "theory of the case" for the design, usually represented through architectural renderings. Once the basic concept of the building is agreed upon, then the engineering work of detailed design begins.

An architectural approach to organization design takes a similar approach. The first step is diagnosis, to determine the problems which the design is intended to solve. The second step is the development of a clear design intent, a statement of what the new organizational architecture is intended to accomplish. Next, several alternatives are developed, staying at the level of detail of an architectural rendering. The alternatives are assessed against the criteria implied by the design intent, and then the key client (usually the CEO and the senior team) makes a choice. The process now moves to the next step: detailed organization design. This includes unit design, design of processes, selection and placement of people, development of operating mechanisms, and so on, and it frequently overlaps implementation of the new architecture. In practice, the design process is rarely as linear or as neat as implied here. Design is an inherently messy, interactive, and iterative process, involving a lot of back and forth between designer and client.

There are various ways of structuring the design roles. One

approach that has worked successfully, particularly at the topmost
levels of the enterprise, is outlined in Figure 9.1. The CEO is both
the primary client and the organizational architect. The CEO and
the senior team charter an architecture team to do the diagnosis,
clarify the design intent, and develop alternatives. The CEO and
senior team choose an alternative and then charter a second team
to do the detailed design work. The senior team reviews, and approves the design, then charters an implementation team.

Limitations of the Metaphor

The architectural metaphor can help us think differently about organizations and understand the design process. At the same time, it
is important to use the metaphor with caution. Human organizations are dynamic living systems; the inherent variation in human
and social behavior brings great uncertainty. Taken to an extreme,
the architectural metaphor may lead us to think in too static terms
about the design of.organizations.

A second limitation concerns change. In most cases, the architect is designing a new structure. Organizations grow incremen-
tally over time; rarely does the organizational architect sit down to
design a brand-new structure, starting with a clean sheet and no
constraints. In fact most large-scale organizational architecture is

Figure 9.1. A Design Process for an Organizational Architecture.

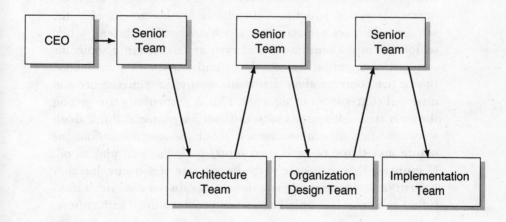

redesign rather than design. Imagine that an old building with load-bearing walls is being redesigned. The task is to build the new load-bearing frame inside the current building, then demolish the old building and create the new structure, while enabling people to continue doing their work. That, unfortunately, is the challenge inherent in re-architecting organizations as an element of discontinuous change.

Organizational Architecture as Discontinuous Change

Changes in fundamental organizational architecture are almost always discontinuous changes. Therefore, the concepts of managing discontinuous change are directly applicable to architectural change. In addition, architectural change poses some very specific questions and challenges.

- *Changing structure versus changing governance.* One of the key challenges of architectural change is to truly affect governance—how the enterprise is actually run, day to day, and in particular how key decisions about strategies and resources are made. Many attempts at change fail because they affect structure but fail to change the basic mode of governance.
- *Hardware drives out software.* We think of the explicit and formally designed elements of an organization, such as structure, processes, and systems, as the *hardware* of organization. The emergent and less tangible elements, such as culture, behavior, norms, leadership patterns, and so forth, can be thought of as the *software*. Both are necessary, but alone neither is sufficient. While senior executives understand and even are enthusiastic about the concepts of organizational hardware and organizational software, in practice concerns about hardware seem to take precedence and drive out concerns about software. This is particularly true during the early stages. It appears to be difficult for people to think about software when they are concerned about the structure, about the nature and shape of their own units, staff, budgets, and so on. Cognitively they are aware of the importance of software, but they have trouble focusing on it emotionally because of these other overriding concerns. It is only later, when problems arise with culture,

behavior, and related issues, that people again return to software. Sometimes it is too late.

- *Understanding the implicit structure.* The informal organization is a very important and critical part of the architecture of an organization, and that fact is often forgotten during change. An interesting example occurred with General Motors, which was restructured into two major groups in the 1980s (Keller, 1989). Many of the organization's processes were accomplished through the informal organization, and when the reorganization was done, those informal processes were unintentionally destroyed, crippling the company's ability to get work done.

- *Unlearning.* Organizations are the embodiment of shared learning about how to get things done. A major and discontinuous change of architecture is a commitment to getting things done differently. While part of the challenge for individuals is to learn new ways of working, an even greater challenge is to collectively unlearn the patterns of action that have become embedded and have been reinforced by the previous organizational architecture. These habits die hard and can serve to undercut the effectiveness of the new architecture.

- *Staffing new architectures.* Ultimately, a new architecture evolves into a design, and that design must be populated with people in key roles. Staff therefore becomes a major issue, particularly in large-scale architectural change where old jobs disappear, many new jobs are created, and large numbers of staffing decisions must be made in a short period. The core dilemma is that architectural change frequently creates jobs for which few people were prepared in the old organization. Architectural change means fundamentally different ways of doing things, and therefore basically different types of jobs and managerial roles.

An example can be seen in the early 1990s when many companies, such as AT&T, IBM, and Xerox moved away from large functional structures to smaller, stand-alone business units, to be headed by business unit presidents or general managers. The problem was that the presidents were drawn from a pool of people with functional backgrounds, because that was all the experience one could get in the old organization. The change of architecture called for new skills and experiences that inherently were not there.

- *Depreciating intellectual capital.* The increasing rate of change inherently increases the rate of depreciation of intellectual capital. As organizational architectures change, some competencies become more valuable and others become less valuable. In general, the larger the change, the greater the writeoff of intellectual capital, particularly the knowledge that is structure-specific. New learning will need to occur to replace the lost capital.

Implementing Architectural Change

Companies that have experienced architectural changes have provided us key lessons about dealing with the predictable problems and challenges.

- *The design process.* An important tool in effectively managing architectural change is the design process itself. A basic principle is participation. When as many people as possible are involved, relevant knowledge is brought to bear, a constituency for change is built, and the implementation process inherently starts as the design work is being done.

Different tasks require different kinds of involvement. For example, architecture teams frequently are drawn from three to four levels below the CEO. These individuals have less of a personal agenda about architectural decisions and bring much more knowledge about how the work is actually done. Later on, it is critical to involve the key leaders of the new organization so that those who design the new structures, processes, and behaviors will be the very same people who are responsible for enacting them.

- *The design intent.* A major help in learning, unlearning, and managing implementation is a very clear and concrete statement of design intent. A well-articulated design intent can be a device to focus energy and resolve conflicts during the change. When differences arise, it is possible for all parties to go back to the design intent and find "first principles" to help determine the appropriate course of action.

- *Selection.* Given the centrality and scope of the staffing question, selection must be a very key event in the implementation process and should involve the CEO and senior team. It appears to be helpful to make use of some type of structured selection logic (see Nadler and Gerstein, 1992c). Done well, selection can be a powerful tool in moving along the organizational change.

• *The design of processes.* Those who focus on hardware to the exclusion of software frequently make another mistake that adds to disruption: They tend to focus on structure to the detriment of processes. As it turns out, the key processes used for running the organization (planning, budgeting, production planning, pricing) are ultimately more significant than the structures alone. At the point where organization design begins, great attention must be paid to the design and implementation of the key processes. This should be done early and with significant resources devoted to it.

• *Forcing focus on software.* Since the natural tendency is for hardware to drive out software, it is critical to force the focus on software—on organizational culture, on informal organization, and on patterns of behavior. Expect resistance at first. Build in major amounts of time to teach people new behaviors, to promote shared learning, to build new organizational capabilities, and to build the new required culture.

• *Mechanisms for continuous learning.* Even the most effective architectural interventions don't get everything right the first time. This reflects both the primitive state of the science and art of design and the fact that organizations exist in dynamic environments that quickly make many design features obsolete. It therefore becomes critical to build in mechanisms to enable continuous learning and improvement (Shaw and Perkins, 1992). Typically, this involves periodic assessments, using mechanisms such as surveys, interviews, observations, reviews, and events for reflection and learning.

Summary

The final years of the twentieth century will witness a major revolution in the design of organizations throughout different sectors of the economy. As profoundly new challenges are being presented to organizations, leaders are drawing on new technologies and new structural materials to develop new architectures.

The concept of organizational architecture is meant to capture the importance of system-level design, using new concepts, new approaches, and new processes. But architecture doesn't happen automatically. For the enterprise it happens only when the person at the top, the CEO, takes responsibility for making it happen. In effect, this means that the CEO takes responsibility for ensuring the integrity of the organization's design.

Does this mean that the CEO must become an organizational architect? Yes. The chief role of the CEO in the corporation of the future will be to imbue a company's design with clarity of purpose, to ensure that the design can fulfill the strategic requirements of the business, and to utilize the most appropriate organizational building materials. But the CEO's role goes beyond responsibility for design, to implementation. In this respect, the CEO is more akin to the "master builder" of the Middle Ages—part designer, part construction manager, part craftsman, part field-test problem solver. In the coming decades, successful organizations will be built by executives willing to get their hands dirty in the messy process of organizational change.

10

Transformative Culture: Shaping the Informal Organization

A. Elise Walton

Discontinuous change often begins with a focus on hardware—strategy, structure, work processes, roles, and accountabilities. Yet these hardware changes create only partial change. Full and complete change means changing people's *behavior,* and that invariably means changing the software.

Organizational software—the values, culture, climate, informal operating style, rituals, communications patterns, and so on—has a big impact on behavior. Equally important, the software decodes the hardware—it infuses concrete signals and actions with meaning. In the midst of most major changes, the leaders of the enterprise experience an "ah-ha"—the flash of insight that software is on the critical path to successful organizational change.

Yet changing the software often presents the most vexing and challenging aspect of leading discontinuous change. Software, particularly culture, is by its nature difficult to change. The "hard stuff"—strategy, structure, and processes—is actually a lot easier to change than the "soft stuff"—culture, practices, and norms. So the transformation of organizational software is both important and difficult.

Definitions and a Perspective

Among the many definitions of culture in general and organizational culture specifically, we've found the following useful: "Organizational culture is a set of commonly shared values and beliefs, which influences the behavior of people, and is reflected in work practices—how we do things here."

Values are fundamental axioms or feelings about the goodness or badness of some quality, such as innovation, individualism, and so on. Values are accepted in their own right and need no proof. Beliefs are perceptions about the connections between events and outcomes, such as "people who work hard will be rewarded" or "individualism leads to the greatest good for society." It is those values and beliefs that are *commonly and widely shared* by a group of people that make up culture. The evidence of the influence of culture can be seen in work practices—through language, norms, rituals, myths, informal processes, and other aspects of the informal organization.

Software typically has multiple levels.

1. *Patterns of behavior.* Behavior is the visible indicator of a culture—its reflections and representations through observable actions, events, or structures. It is concrete in the sense of who said what, nonverbal action, published writings, and so on. It is the "fact" of culture—the things people can see and usually agree on.

Behaviors develop to serve underlying purposes. For example, many firms have a list posted on the walls in their meeting rooms, to remind people of the type of behavior that is expected in meetings. In themselves, the posters have little impact. However, in referring back to them, people can politely remind each other of agreed-upon etiquettes—and usually improve the effectiveness of their meetings.

2. *Beliefs.* These are the ideas, the "if-then" reasons, that

people use to craft and interpret behavior. This is a discussible and debatable area, relatively amenable to observation.

Attribution errors are common (Heider, 1958). Someone has an intention and designs behavioral strategies to realize that intention; observers see the behavior and infer the person's intention. A common example is the dilemma faced by managers learning to work under new empowerment efforts. The manager wants to give people latitude in how they do their jobs and therefore leaves them to work alone much of the time. The employees only see that they are being left alone, and interpret the manager's distance as a lack of concern.

3. *Values.* Underlying attributions are premises, values, or what we sometimes call world view. These are the underlying fundamental assumptions and concepts about human nature and the way the world works. They are intensely held and deeply embedded. They cannot be proved or disproved, and they are less disputable— for example, all people are created equal, or all people have a right to life, liberty, and the pursuit of happiness. Often, world views are inherited and built early in life (or in an organization's life).

It is at this level that crosscultural "errors" occur. The conflicts and misunderstandings that occur are driven by differences in fundamental beliefs. Here, too, are assumptions about feelings and how they may be expressed. For example, southern Europeans may argue with loud, emotional gesticulation, a style likely to make a more formal northern European uncomfortable. An Asian may believe respect for superiors is most important and maintain a substantial degree of formality with the boss. An American may believe friendliness is important and will demonstrate less formality with superiors, asking about family or making jokes. Without assessment, the American might find the Asian stiff, the Asian might find the American rude.

Motives and needs may also be part of values. While certain human needs are universal (biological needs for food, water, and air), the expression and scope of these needs vary widely and are often shaped by culture. The need for food, physical space, and individual attention can diverge greatly depending on culture.

Two observations are in order. First, culture is reflexive. Beliefs shape behaviors, but behaviors also shape beliefs. Values affect beliefs and behaviors, but in turn beliefs and behaviors affect values. Second, often one set of beliefs and values is espoused while another set may be inferred from behavior. This lack of alignment is one of the greatest causes of organizational dysfunction.

One company publicly espoused a belief and a value about merit; the spoken belief was "We listen to ideas based on merit," and the spoken value was "A meritocracy is the only possible structure for an ethical organization." However, the behavior that most employees witnessed was that senior managers' ideas were listened to more thoughtfully and acted on more frequently than junior managers' ideas. The culture in action contradicted the espoused culture. The belief in action was "Senior managers' ideas count more than junior managers' ideas," and the value in action was "Might is right."

One of the critical issues in redesigning cultures and individual behavior is that often it is not a matter of changing one culture but changing many. For one thing, individual behavior is a complex medley of different cultural roles, situational influences, and individual dispositions. One person may be gregarious with customers, autocratic with subordinates, and shy in social settings. For another, most large organizations are mixtures of multiple cultures. This means that few interventions will work globally across the organization.

Quality, for instance, has been embraced by manufacturing and operations units as a way of improving performance and work behavior. However, in the same organization, researchers may reject quality. Occupational culture explains why. Researchers have been taught to value skepticism and questioning; also, trained in advanced analytical methodologies, they consider Paretos, flow charts, and other quality tools simplistic. The research community is typically filled with people who greatly value autonomy and independence and who rebel against the "newspeak" of quality.

Three types of forces shape the values and beliefs of an organization: *external, historical,* and *internal.*

• *External forces* are those outside the organization that contribute to shaping values and beliefs. These may be regional, occupational, organizational, or local cultures as well as environmental factors such as regulation, technological changes, and competition.

- *Historical forces* have a very strong influence on the values and beliefs that develop over time. How the organization was founded plays a particularly important role (Schein, 1985). How the organization deals with crises during its lifetime also creates cultural lore and beliefs. A final historical force is development of organizational referents or role models. For example, in many high-technology and information-technology companies, the organizational referent is Motorola. People talk about how things are done there, and it is held up as the model for action. For many diversified companies, General Electric is the referent; in wholesale banking, it's Morgan Bank, and so on. The referent is the expression of the aspirations of the organization—what it would like to be, wishes it could be, hopes to be. The referent in particular shapes beliefs. The implication is that "if we act like them, then we will be successful like them." Behavior is, in turn, shaped by this, sometimes in a thoughtful attempt to be like the referent and at other times in surface-level mimicry.

- *Internal forces* shape values and beliefs. These are the critical factors in the organizational context—leadership behavior, structure, strategy, rewards, management appraisal and feedback, information, communications, and so forth.

In general, it is easiest for managers to affect the internal forces as a leverage point for culture change, and it is these changes that we focus on below.

Changing Organizational Culture: Basic Principles

Culture, by definition, is difficult to change. It is built up over many years and based on many interpretations and stories. The institutional memories and routines that codify culture are not easily erased. In fact, culture's resistance to change is both its strength and its weakness. Culture change at an enterprise level is possible, but requires a long time.

In changing organizational culture, there are three critical areas that need to be addressed and resolved:

1. Content of the change—the vision of the new culture
2. Leverage points for change—what and how to change
3. Tactical choices—when and where to change

Cultural Vision—The Content of Culture Change

The first starting point for culture change is developing a vision of the new culture. In discontinuous change, the cultural vision must build on the new corporate identity and values. Typically, this is an in-depth effort conducted by the CEO and the senior team. A great deal of time goes into debating choices and agreeing on language. This is an essential effort; care must be taken to guard against spurious agreement. Each member of the senior team must understand the meaning of the new cultural values. In addition, those values must be tested against the new view of the business. They must be consistent with the organizational context and the business vision. Typically, the result of this effort is an articulation of the new cultural values.

By late 1991, Bob Allen at AT&T had assembled a number of complicated related businesses. Clearly, there was great potential for market conflict among them—one business unit sold to another's competitor, another partnered with the customers of a different business unit, and so on. Allen recognized that no formal system would allow the organization to solve all problems routinely, and that internal coordination would have to rely heavily on the behavior of individuals toward each other. If the whole organization were to act in the overall best interests of AT&T, then a certain culture would be necessary. This culminated in what AT&T calls Our Common Bond (see Exhibit 10.1). This statement of cultural values clearly focuses on areas that are required for cultural synergy and customer focus.

In the past few years, some common themes in culture change have emerged. These themes tend to line up with current thinking around best management practice; for example, simplicity, empowerment, customer focus, and line-driven. The themes of culture change are increasingly driven off a preliminary cultural diagnosis or culture audit. The values of the new culture are often intended to eliminate the evils of the existing culture.

Exhibit 10.1. AT&T's Value Statement.

Our Common Bond

We commit to these values to guide our decisions and behavior.

Respect for Individuals

We treat each other with respect and dignity, valuing individual and cultural differences. We communicate frequently and with candor, listening to each other regardless of level or position. Recognizing that exceptional quality begins with people, we give individuals the authority to use their capabilities to the fullest to satisfy their customers. Our environment supports personal growth and continuous learning for all AT&T people.

Dedication to Helping Customers

We truly care for each customer. We build enduring relationships by understanding and anticipating our customers' needs and by serving them better each time than the time before. AT&T customers can count on us to consistently deliver superior products and services that help them achieve their personal or business goals.

Highest Standards of Integrity

We are honest and ethical in all our business dealings, starting with how we treat each other. We keep our promises and admit our mistakes. Our personal conduct ensures that AT&T's name is always worthy of trust.

Innovation

We believe innovation is the engine that will keep us vital and growing. Our culture embraces creativity, seeks different perspectives and risks pursuing new opportunities. We create and rapidly convert technology into products and services, constantly searching for new ways to make technology more useful to customers.

Teamwork

We encourage and reward both individual and team achievements. We truly join with colleagues across organizational boundaries to advance the interests of customers and shareowners. Our team spirit extends to being responsible and caring partners in the communities where we live and work.

By living these values, AT&T aspires to set a standard of excellence worldwide that will reward our shareowners, our customers and all AT&T people.

Most executive teams find themselves able to reach the definition stage. The danger here is that the senior team considers its work done once the culture statement is put on wall posters and laminated cards. When the senior team's involvement ends there, the new values become just another organizational flop; the most attention they get is ridicule or derision. People look for new signals and behaviors that support the new words, but see none. In that case, articulating and communicating of new cultural values is dysfunctional; it has the opposite effect of what was intended.

The vision of the new culture must be followed with leadership attention and support. These occur both in the organizational context—building systems that are supportive of and congruent with the new cultural values—and also in specific interventions—events and actions that directly target behavior.

Leadership is essential for successful culture change. Cultural leadership is typically drawn from the CEO, the senior team, the "colonels," and key catalysts. The CEO must be intimately involved; he or she must be seen as truly committed to the change and deeply involved in it. But to truly "take," the change must move beyond the CEO. The senior management team must also be able to describe and live the new culture. Finally, culture change is most successful when there are also key champions at all levels of the organization. Supporting voices must be heard from all quarters, or else the change is viewed as a passing executive fancy.

Interventions—What and How

As part of the development of the cultural vision, leaders must ensure that the values fit the organizational context and that the organizational context fits the values. Full-blown culture change requires change in all the key elements of the organizational context, including structure, business processes, measurement, appraisal, and rewards.

The organizational context provides the greatest leverage for shaping values and beliefs. Changes in leadership, strategy, structure, and human resource management are alternatives to focusing directly on the culture. Actions—changes in the organizational context—are interpreted as signals, and these signals speak louder than words. When the hard does not match up with the soft, the soft loses. Most employees will infer the actual, or real, culture from the hard elements of organizational context. For example, for an organization promoting customer focus, those closest to the customer must have an important role in decision making. Organizations that espouse line-driven entrepreneurship should have small corporate staff and low overhead.

Sometime early on in the culture change effort, values must be articulated in terms of expected behavior. Often, values are so abstract that any behavior can be justified. Statements that pose one value as superior to another are particularly helpful because they give employees a sense of priority. In fact, this is one way in which values are demonstrated—by taking precedence over other motivations. One of the important things to change is what the organization pays attention to. Information and communication are strong indicators of culture and powerful shapers of behavior.

In a recent culture change, rewards were restructured so that a significant portion of each president's bonus depended on overall company performance. This scheme was designed to induce the presidents to make tradeoffs and sacrifices in the best interest of the company: the money should flow to wherever it earns the most return. The reward system was changed in support of a planned culture change to a more team-based culture. After eight months, the behavior change had not occurred. Presidents still protected their own budgets, and only a few had made genuine divisional sacrifices for the greater good.

One president concluded that this phenomenon indicated the triumph of ego over self-interest. Ego may indeed have been involved, but the culture providing information, communication, and decision guidelines also shaped the presidents' behavior. The old culture—the informal system—still ran the organization using the old financial and business reporting systems. Presidents may have wanted to "do the best thing for the company," but without information systems to support the new teams, it was difficult for them to make informed tradeoffs. The old culture—the formal and informal operating practices—was still driving decisions.

In contrast, at another company change to a trust-based culture was made easily because the company had standardized a common financial language, which provided necessary and usable information. Understanding alternative resource applications required little "translation" and division presidents were well equipped to understand the tradeoffs they were making.

One powerful intervention is an upward feedback process. Cultural values are used to generate specific behavioral statements to show the cultural value. In AT&T's Our Common Bond (see Exhibit 10.1), each value has several behavioral descriptions. For example, the value "highest standards of integrity" is amplified by these behavioral statements:

1. Upholds ethical standards even if profit is at stake
2. Acts in ways that are consistent with what he/she says
3. Backs up those who behave with integrity in difficult situations
4. Does not "shoot the messenger"
5. Keeps promises and commitments
6. Admits when he/she makes mistakes

These behavioral statements were included in a survey sent to the staffs of the senior executives. The process began with the management executive committee and cascaded down from there. Each executive conducted a feedback session, with the support of an outside coach, in which the results of the survey for his or her staff were discussed. These sessions approached culture change from two positions: first, it gave the team a chance to discuss its own climate and culture, and how well it was achieving Our Common Bond; second, it focused attention on the manager's style and how well that reflected Common Bond values.

These sessions were extremely helpful in beginning the process of culture change. They forced the executives and their teams to invest a substantial period of time discussing, debating, and building a shared understanding around cultural values. Needless to say, this helped improve relationships in the team and build more constructive behavior. Most managers learned how their own behavior was being perceived by their staff.

For example, one of the indicators of integrity was "keeps promises and commitments." Ratings on this item varied widely within teams. In discussing the differences, teams often had to unearth underlying premises about what constitutes a promise or commitment. A manager might say in passing, "We should cover that topic at your next review" or "We should think about increasing the staffing in your department." A staff member would take this as an implicit commitment but the manager might forget or consider it not worth following through. The discussion helped create better aligned expectations and behaviors. Managers became aware that casual or gratuitous remarks might be taken seriously; staff became aware that not every proposal need constitute a commitment.

An equally important element of the Common Bond feedback sessions was the ability to build organizational synergy around the values. Too often, feedback done in isolation affects only the one group and does not migrate into cross-group improvements. One team "gets religion" but their peers and other managers don't understand the new values they're talking about and know even less about how to be supportive of the behavioral changes.

At AT&T the feedback sessions were done concurrently. There were senior management forums in which Bob Allen and others discussed the results for the officer group overall. Suddenly, executives, teams, and organizations with long-standing conflicts had a new standard of behavior to achieve and a shared language system with which to talk about it. All executives, having received direction from the CEO and personal feedback from their staffs, felt a high motivation to change. Moreover, the others around them expected to see change, thus creating a positive, self-fulfilling feedback loop.

The feedback sessions and forums were followed with a series of executive office visits. Each member of the management executive committee was assigned to interview an executive lower in the organization—in the *other* person's office. Bob Allen and his team had one-on-one conversations with many different people about how they saw the cultural values working, particularly the Common Bond. This also created a positive effect. It demonstrated a high level of leadership commitment, and, equally important, it built in a feedback loop. Allen was able to ascertain how well the culture change was working from a bottom-up perspective.

During the time from the articulation of the values through the feedback, a team of senior executives and high potentials worked on the values deployment approach. This team met monthly or more frequently and made many of the key decisions about rolling out the values. The team itself became very close, forming a support network for the change. Finally, the team members became informed, experienced spokespersons for the new value system.

Rewards and punishments are an important area for intervention. This is what employees most frequently mention as the real indicator of commitment to cultural values. Often rewards are aligned to new cultural values, but formal reward systems (such as compensation) *lag* the desired behavior change. That is, the rewards take effect after the aspirations have been achieved, thus limiting their impact. Occasionally reward systems are so complex or abstract that they have little effect on day-to-day behavior. Rewards for values whose behavioral correlates are poorly understood or practiced may be the most dangerous. This is equivalent to offering a pigeon $10 for every mile driven—the reward is irrelevant because the behavior to be rewarded doesn't exist. Such rewards create superstitious learning and erroneous cause-effect theories.

Another key reward intervention is in the area of employee flows: selection, promotion, and termination. Successful culture change efforts eventually assess behavior as part of the formal human resource review and planning process. Simply paying attention to behavior through the annual processes helps. However, when career success and status depend directly on behavior, the cultural values take on real power.

The area of employee flows offers a more immediate proof of the system. People typically look at tests of the system: Are the "good guys" getting promoted? Are the violators being penalized? Who gets promoted and who gets sidelined are signals that are carefully watched. Promoting a person whose behavior reflects the new values provides a concrete example of the expected new behaviors. When a person is promoted or moved aside for cultural reasons—either cultural alignment or cultural conflict—the decision must be publicly acknowledged and discussed.

Dealing with executives who do not support the new cultural values is a key intervention. Certain executives become well known for failing to live up to the new values. Often their failures are in the area of interpersonal skills and behaviors—teamwork, empowerment, open and honest communication, and so on). When they are permitted to continue violating the new norms without sanctions, they undermine the credibility of the new cultural values.

This creates a particularly tough dilemma when someone is delivering excellent operating results but behaves in ways that seriously conflict with the new values. Senior management may be reluctant to put the business at risk and so will overlook the person's behavioral shortcomings. But if this person remains in power, observers will conclude that the *real* cultural premise is operating performance and the other stuff is just talk.

These behavioral issues must be addressed proactively. Typically, the problem executive is first given a coach who works one on one with that person on behavioral issues. The coach typically interviews the executive's colleagues, staff, superiors, and sometimes even family. This is combined with in-depth psychological testing and analysis. The executive is given enough time to work through the information, to plan action around personal choices and behavioral options, and to begin to implement a new managerial style. However, if this support is refused or if progress is not made, then the executive must be moved out of the position.

As an intervention, it is important to highlight and communicate the reasons for the executive change. The rumor mill is quick to generate alternative interpretations for the executive's move, such as politics or performance. The lesson must be repeatedly communicated: executives do not live by results alone—they must also live by the cultural values. Few other messages reinforce the new culture so powerfully.

Other interventions can also be made to support the new culture—educational events, stories and "moments of truth" case studies, new rituals, and so on. Many of them serve to reinforce the new culture—particularly on a behavioral level. The fundamentally important element is to keep dialogue open and alive and to shape the social construction of knowledge that occurs about the new culture. The executives, in partnership with the organization, must ensure that everyone is reaching the same conclusions and interpretations.

In addition to changing the organizational context, many organizations are working to intervene directly in the culture. This is typically done by measuring the features of the culture, discussing them, defining a new cultural vision, and identifying any gaps between current and desired cultures (see Kilmann, Saxton, Serpa, and Associates, 1985; Cameron and Quinn, forthcoming).

Tactical Choices—Where and When

In addition to ensuring a supportive organizational context and designing a series of interventions to support change, the culture change program typically has to fit into a broader series of organizational changes and compete with them for attention. This raises tactical questions: when, where, and how to intervene for the greatest leverage. Tactical choices depend upon the unique organizational situation.

First, there is the issue of when to intervene in culture. There are two basic approaches to software changes. We use the concept of software as a platform—that is, the culture and the values are the very foundation upon which the overall change agenda rests (Brown and Walton, 1993). This means that the CEO, the executives, and the entire transition team must be thinking about the software *at all times* during the change process. The change process must ensure that the organizational context enables the cultural values and that they are worked into various speeches and announcements, albeit in the background.

Second, direct interventions into culture are better sequenced in an integrated change effort and done separately from the hardware interventions. Because hard drives out soft, when a great deal of attention is paid to structural changes, executive changes, new systems, and new work processes, the attention to culture change (if presented simultaneously) will be diminished.

One effective sequence is for the direct interventions into culture (upward feedback processes, forums, and so on) to occur somewhat after the initial announcements of structural and work process and changes. In this case, culture is presented full center with complete attention directed to the culture change. Culture change must now take the foreground if it is to be effective. Alternately, the culture changes can come first, with training sessions, events, and projects that focus on the new values. Many quality programs begin with an educational campaign and a quality project. This builds a supply of skills and an orientation that will solidify during future hardware changes.

There is also the issue of where in the organization to intervene: from the top, from the bottom, or from the periphery. Culture change requires a multi-perspective approach that we call top down, bottom up, and lateral (or periphery in). Top-down changes have the advantage of focusing energy and using leadership's authority and charisma to "pull" change. The top of the house makes a decision and then communicates it. Typical top-down changes are those involving structure, reward systems, reporting relationships, and the movement of key people. Frequently, in culture change, this includes realigning reward systems to reflect new cultural values, hiring or promoting people with the right skills and behaviors, and mandating other behaviors.

Top-down change has special advantages. One is speed. Unilateral decisions made by a single person or team can be made faster. Second, top-down change is universal: it typically addresses the whole organization at once. As in the AT&T case, the synergy can work *across* groups as well as within them. Finally, top-down change is advantageous because it creates a "demand pull." That is, people see that there is a market for culturally aligned behavior, and that success in this market corresponds with personal success—promotions and recognition. There is a pull for new behaviors—and people produce to meet the demand.

The culture change must also focus on bottom-up interventions. These interventions seek information and opinions from lower levels in the organization. They include training and forums, which increase people's capability to behave in ways consistent with the new culture. They identify the motivations for culture change at all levels of the organization. In that regard, bottom-up change is similar to supply-push change. It makes more of the right behavior available (in individual repertoires). It uses the energy of the whole organization and checks that the executive team is in touch with what is really happening.

Finally, the change process should include lateral changes, using what has been called an agricultural model (Beer, Eisenstat, and Spector, 1990). Change occurring in one location should be migrated to other locations. This can be done through intergroup exchanges, the movement of key managers, and field visits. In addition, building the capability for lateral change may mean building up some peripheral competencies—for instance, building pilot sites for change and communities of practice around the new culture. These areas, protected from some of the mainstream pressures, have the chance to make the change operative early on and so provide learning and insight for the rest of the organization.

Lateral change seems to be an increasingly popular approach to culture change, particularly given the network configuration of many organizations. It builds on peer relationships to transmit messages, which often have higher credibility than messages coming from senior management.

Table 10.1 summarizes the strengths and weaknesses of these three types of changes.

The change program must also consider *how* to intervene, especially given existing organizational and local contexts. Interventions that succeed in one location may work less well in another. One of the critical areas for consideration, then, is the local context of the intervention and how to intervene in the local culture.

Take the case of two interventions: quality circles and team building. Each promotes a certain set of values and behaviors, but with a somewhat different focus. Quality circles are a better fit with Japanese culture than with U.S. culture, which suggests a common-sense explanation for why quality has been more successful in Japan than the United States. Likewise, team building is a better fit with U.S. culture than with Japanese culture, and this may explain its greater use here.

Our experience suggests that interventions which are far afield from the local culture are not likely to create change. If the interventions are too divergent, they will be dismissed. In fact, this is why much of the work from the 1960s and 1970s on T-groups and team building has disappeared. Its premises and methods are too different from management practices and accepted operating styles in current organizations.

Finally, the cultural interventions must shape the nature of participation. Tactically, the agenda will decide who participates and when. Implicitly, the program decides how much debate is welcome and when debate will be cut off. Debate is essential to culture, as is the shared understanding and commitment of all members of the organization. However, it is unlikely that all members will buy in equally or equally rapidly. Endless debate can be

Table 10.1. Strengths and Weaknesses of Three Different Intervention Points.

	Examples	Strengths	Weaknesses
Top down	• Definition of new cultural values • Self-assessment • Reward system alignment • Executive changes	• Speed and immediacy • Unilateralism • Universality • Demand pull	• Enacted behavior possibly different from intent • Resistance • Ignores the local context in which change fits
Bottom up	• Education, training • Forums, town meetings • Upward feedback • Empowerment • Staff support (coaching, etc.)	• Puts behavior decision closer to action and information • Supply push (builds a supply of behavior) • Checks for consistency, enactment	• Middle management is squeezed • Lower levels less ready for or capable of action
Lateral	• Beta sites, skunkworks, communities of practice • Field visits, customer visits • Migration strategies (leaders, groups) • Intergroup exchange • Serendipity, chance	• Utilizes emergent learning • Less threatening • Is local • Has "real world" credibility	• Possible lack of support from other areas: "It won't work here." "Those guys don't know what they're talking about."

unproductive and even detrimental to the new cultural values, particularly when the new values focus on action. Therefore, mechanisms for reaching critical mass, and for moving the process forward once it has been achieved, are essential. Debate about which values turns into debate about how to enact and realize the chosen values. Dialogue continues, but certain elements of the debate are concluded.

Conclusion

In summary, we believe that culture change is possible. It is a long process and takes several years to complete. It requires a great deal of effort and commitment from senior management and eventually the whole organization. But it *is* possible. A range of interventions and tools exists to manage culture. These can occur in the background—as ways of facilitating elements of the organizational context. Interventions can also be directly aimed at culture and behavior, such as feedback, selection, and communication processes. While a great deal has been learned about organizational culture, new learnings emerge daily and we continue to add to our knowledge and experience.

At the end of the effort, though, the real test is behavior and its common interpretations. Changes and interventions in support of the culture are a process to reach an end state. The test of success is behavior change, not plaques created, projects launched, training conducted, or any other efforts expended. It is essential to evaluate whether the end state has been achieved and to continue pressing for change until it has.

11

Business Processes: Embracing the Logic and Limits of Reengineering

Robert B. Shaw
Mark C. Maletz

Many of our largest companies are engaged in initiatives to fundamentally change the way work is performed. This revolution in the workplace began as a relatively isolated phenomena in a few manufacturing environments but has spread across all sectors of the economy. It involves new ways of thinking about the design and management of organizations. The intent is to create business processes that are capable of delivering dramatically higher levels of performance over a sustained period of time. This process is called reengineering, and it is one important type of discontinuous change.

Reengineering, like any single approach to change, has inherent strengths and limitations. Its strengths include a focus on business processes (versus functional roles) and the power of information technology when appropriately used. Its limitations, which derive primarily from an "engineering" view of organizations, can be mitigated by a broader and more fully integrated model of organizational change and skillful use of change-management techniques. From our vantage point, we see reengineering as a necessary but insufficient approach to organizational transformation—necessary in that organizations must become radically more productive; insufficient in that it can address only a subset of the problems facing organizations today.

The Reengineering Imperative

Peter Drucker (1992) has suggested that the productivity explosion in developed countries over the past century was the most important social event of our time, and one with no precedent in history. The overall standard of living and quality of life in developed countries far surpasses what was possible even fifty years ago. This increase, based largely on productivity improvements in manufacturing and transportation, is now under attack as more and more people work in service and knowledge jobs—a sector that has shown only limited improvements in productivity. Reengineering has become increasingly visible because it offers a powerful new approach to improving productivity, particularly in the area of service and knowledge work.

Most of the conventional wisdom about how to improve productivity dates back to two approaches developed close to a century ago. At the turn of the century, an American named F. W. Taylor developed a "scientific" model of organization. Taylor used the metaphor of the machine to explain organizational behavior. He believed in careful and comprehensive analysis of work, and the removal of any possible cause of variation in approach. At approximately the same time, the German sociologist Max Weber articulated a management model he called bureaucracy, built on a coherent and well-thought-out theory of organizing. He believed organizations should be built around a clear system of hierarchical relationships and governed by a clear and consistent set of written rules and procedures. The "machine bureaucracy" that emerged from the fusion of Taylor's and Weber's ideas achieved previously unattainable levels of performance, and became the template for industrial organization that persists to this day.

However, the machine bureaucracy model, while tremendously successful, ultimately suffered from three significant problems that became apparent by the middle of the twentieth century. First, the model was built for the management of relatively stable and predictable situations. It broke down under conditions of uncertainty and instability because of the inability to reconfigure and the lack of emphasis on discretion by individuals. Second, the model assumed a relatively uneducated work force and focused primarily on manufacturing work. As workers and the work changed, the organizations built on this model had a more difficult time motivating and satisfying their employees. Third, over time, organizations based on this model experienced their own entropy; they tended to become more complex, less responsive, more inwardly oriented, and more unwieldy. Attention to the internal rules became more important than adapting to changing marketplace conditions.

The limitations of the machine-bureaucracy approach became more evident as pressures in the business environment increased during the 1980s, and reengineering emerged as an alternative.

The Logic of Reengineering

Reengineering is an approach to the design of work in organizations. In its simplest form, it is a way of building organizations that bring together people and technology in a manner that results in high performance. More specifically, it has been defined as "the fundamental rethinking and radical redesign of business processes to achieve dramatic improvements in . . . cost, quality, service and speed" (Hammer and Champy, 1993, p. 32). One key element in most reengineering approaches is the attention to business processes, the activities within an organization that add value from the perspective of the customer. People or groups who assume responsibility for a core process (such as order fulfillment) are called process owners. The focus in reengineering is on the entire process, culminating in output that is of value to customers, versus a view of work as a series of distinct tasks performed to internal standards and metrics.

Reengineering has introduced—or more accurately reintroduced—a number of important ideas in the management of work.

Many of the core ideas are evident in other approaches to change. The strength of reengineering resides in how these fundamental themes have been packaged in a manner that provides clear and forceful guidance. We think of these as the "big ideas" that give reengineering its power.

Reengineering has made it acceptable to talk again about productivity. For years, it was taboo to talk about productivity in polite company because the topic had connotations of industrial engineering (and the dreaded time-and-motion "efficiency studies") or simplistic approaches to cost reduction (such as an across-the-board cut in work force). In the past many people considered productivity as within the domain of a small group of staff specialists or a "brute force" approach associated with a crisis of some type. Reengineering provides a perspective on productivity that enables people to see it as a competitive necessity.

A second "big idea" of reengineering is the focus on value-added core processes. Many change agents have looked at organizational effectiveness from the perspective of individual traits ("we need the right leadership"); organizational structures ("we need the right organizational structure"); informal processes ("we need the right organizational culture"); or job-specific tasks ("we need to define work tasks as clearly as possible"). Reengineering champions, like those in sociotechnical redesign forty years earlier, stress the need to start with customers and work "outside in" to determine what work adds value.

In particular, reengineering pays attention to "core" business processes that add value, most of which cut across functional boundaries. This way of looking at organizations can produce significant gains as companies move beyond the limitations found in traditional lines of authority. Reengineering proposes that business processes become the basic building blocks of organizations, resulting in what some call the horizontal organization that operates as a set of processes, with process owners instead of functional heads.

Another contribution of reengineering was pointing out the dangers of incremental change, and particularly total quality management, at precisely the time when most executives and consultants were enthusiastically embracing it. Reengineering proponents suggested that there comes a time in the life of each organization when incremental change leads to only deeper problems. Reengineering stresses the need for bold change, beginning with an approach to design that essentially does away with current processes. The argument is that big leaps are essential in many cases, and incremental change will only create the illusion that the organization is closing a competitive gap.

Reengineering is, at its core, discontinuous change—reinventing how work is done, abandoning past work practices, "starting over" with a blank page. The goal is to determine what adds true value from the customers' perspective and then to create radically more effective processes to perform that work. Incremental techniques, in contrast, strive to improve upon current practices. In many cases, traditional quality programs are forms of incremental change, approaches designed to achieve ongoing improvements in the current processes.

Finally, reengineering demonstrates that dramatic improvements are possible when information technology is used appropriately—that is, when used in synch with the redesign of core processes. Rather than applying technology to improve current processes—what some call automation—reengineering either eliminates or dramatically redesigns the work processes, using technology as a tool toward that end. The power of reengineering comes with combining information technology with blank-page redesign. The capacity of information technology has increased exponentially over the past decade; reengineering provides a model on how to leverage it to greatest advantage.

The Limits of Reengineering

There is no denying that many reengineering efforts either failed to meet expectations or were totally abandoned. Reengineering advocates argue that the task is a difficult one requiring courage and dedication, and the failures that have occurred can be explained, at least in part, to the absence of these necessary qualities. Failures in implementation don't necessarily undermine the approach to change, and poor implementation planning and execution is the source of many reengineering failures. However, there are inherent limitations in the theory that drives reengineering—limitations that in many respects are closely tied to its strengths. These limitations do not make reengineering any less powerful as a way of changing organizations, but they must be understood.

First, reengineering is an approach to organizational renewal that begins with customer needs and then moves to the work itself. As a result, it is necessarily incomplete. Most approaches to reengineering result in a reductionist perspective focused on operational effectiveness and efficiency—an approach that largely fails to take into account the big picture—particularly in regards to business strategy and the complex interdependencies among different aspects of organizational life. Reengineering largely ignores strategic demands and choices because the focus is on improving operational processes as they impact an organization's current set of customers. In this respect, reengineering replicates at a higher strategic level the same shortcomings its advocates find in incremental approaches to organizational change (namely, taking as a given that which may or perhaps even must change). Practitioners of any given approach to organizational change should surface primary issues before the secondary issues—in the case of reengineering, surfacing strategic issues and choices prior to operational redesign work. While an outside-in approach to design may help evaluate the value of each business process, we do not believe customers cannot provide strategic direction. The reengineering toolkit does not provide any tools to evaluate the linkage between strategic intent and business process redesign.

A number of reengineering efforts derail because the strategic context in which the redesign was positioned changed significantly—rendering the new operational design worthless. Design always occurs in relation to a fluid environment, with shifting strategic directions and larger organizational forces, where reengineering has little effect. More dramatically, some business processes exist because they compensate for larger strategic mistakes. One company, for instance, reengineered its order-processing capability for centralized operations; however, midway through the design effort, the firm moved to a decentralized organizational structure that significantly changed the demands on the order-processing system. The result was an expensive centralized "super-highway" when the firm no longer needed it. This is not to suggest that reengineering is flawed because its scope is limited in regards to strategy. It is to suggest that reengineering is necessary in many situations but it is never sufficient in and of itself.

The reductionist tendency also applies to organizational behavior. Reengineering focuses primarily on the technical side of work. Practitioners would be wise to remind themselves to recall the key word in reengineering is *engineering;* this engineering mentality offers tremendous benefits but also has a down side. For one thing, reengineering typically does not take into account the social side of work. A large majority of the reengineering efforts begin with the redesign of core business processes and focus on the social side of the workplace only to the extent needed to ensure that the technical design is capable of being implemented by humans. Reengineering is not particularly concerned with creating jobs that are motivating and interesting or an environment that fosters learning and innovations. Designing work processes with minimum specification so that they can evolve to fit local needs is seldom considered; making room for appropriate social systems is even less so. Champions of reengineering have suggested that these types of shortcomings are "user errors." However, these limitations, while they can be exacerbated by those lacking change management skills, are inherent in reengineering's "engineering" focus.

Reengineering designs are often positioned as the answer to a host of organizational problems; one firm called its new design the "perfect solution." But reengineering often results in "hardwired" solutions that are far too rigid for today's business environment. Reengineering efforts typically build work-process blueprints that lack the adaptiveness needed in more decentralized systems. Thus, reengineering, in some respects, contradicts the movement in organizations to emergent designs that provide greater rather than less flexibility (which mirrors a similar movement in our political world). There are few permanent engineering solutions to core organizational problems, yet reengineering assumes that such solutions are not only possible but desirable. Organizational life is messy and will become more so in the future. Those facing uncertainty often seek that which appears to be more permanent as much to comfort themselves as to help their organizations. As we move to redesign our organizations, we may need architects more than engineers.

A second potential weakness in reengineering involves the challenge of managing change itself. Many reengineering teams don't know how to move from the design to the complicated process of implementing that design, and so they hit the wall in terms of resistance. One Fortune 100 company spent $25 million on a reengineering design proposal that was never implemented; all the work went into producing an elegant design and very little effort was invested in managing the change process from start to finish. Change management is not something you do when done with the design. It begins with the initiation of the project and must be part of the design process. This is necessary because in most discontinuous design efforts there is the reality of "local losers" (versus doing what is beneficial for the overall good for the corporation); the traditional power base is reduced as the changes are made; new processes put short-term financial strains on the organization; the reengineering business case is often difficult to justify the investment; and the assumptions behind those cases are often questionable.

While proponents of reengineering recognize this potential point of vulnerability, few have any systematic model for thinking about or managing large-scale change. Failure to build support in the organization for implementation of the changes results in longer time frames and higher costs because resistance is not adequately addressed. This situation is made worse by the fact that most reengineering efforts are usually top-down initiatives, often led by information technologists who created design teams that are sequestered from the rest of the organization.

Reengineering also lacks sufficient theory and practice about organizational renewal. Even positive applications have unintended consequences that can create as many problems as they solve—redeployment and reduction of staff; destruction or significant alteration of the existing organizational culture and informal processes; new demands on individuals and groups. Reengineering has few approaches to deal with the down side of successful implementation.

In sum, reengineering is but one part of a larger strategy that needs to be in place. It can take you only so far before other, complementary approaches to organizational change are needed.

Significant Challenges

Those leading reengineering changes need to embrace a broader model of organizational behavior and work through the necessary linkages described in earlier chapters. They also need to actively support the change process, to see it as part of the design process, and realize the effort and skill it demands.

In reengineering efforts the CEO and the senior team must be active partners in the change process. They work closely with the design team to co-design the future state and co-manage the change. This requires a clear sense of shared responsibility and a commitment to empower the design team. It also requires that they actively participate as change agents and communicators of change to the organization.

Senior managers who collectively have the authority to drive process transformation are typically organized into a steering committee, chaired by a process owner who acts as the sponsor for the reengineering effort. Those leading specific reengineering efforts—especially the steering committee—face five key challenges:

1. Establishing strategic direction and a framework for design
2. Maintaining a clear and consistent customer focus
3. Monitoring the business and organizational environment
4. Coordinating an effective communication strategy
5. Ensuring participation in design

Steering committees that successfully meet these five challenges have the best chances of successfully achieving the desired improvements.

Establishing Strategic Direction and a Framework for Design

Reengineering efforts are most effective when they are shaped by a clear strategic direction and a framework for the desired change. The strategic direction need not be reflected in a formal and detailed statement of strategy, but it should paint a clear picture of the organizational future within which the new process is to operate. This strategic direction should address the three dimensions of a total work system—procedural, structural, and social. For example, the procedural dimension of a strategy for new product development might focus on the need for co-evolution of new product designs through multiple, short-cycle iterations involving customers and product designers. The structural dimension of this same process might emphasize the use of cross-functional teams and shared accountability, and the social dimension might focus on the interpersonal dynamics required to achieve effective partnering between customers and designers.

Conventional approaches to strategic direction are inadequate for reengineering efforts. The resultant strategic plans seldom describe the future with enough texture to be usable in shaping a new process design. Moreover, conventional strategic plans seldom address the three dimensions of work. An additional complication is that in many organizations, strategic plans are the domain of a central planning group, and thus steering committee members have little practice in strategic thinking.

One steering committee, realizing it needed to develop a strategic direction, allocated three hours for the task. At the end of three hours, they had generated very brief and essentially meaningless vision and mission statements. In the end, the committee spent more than twenty hours over a three-week period to complete and gain consensus on a strategic direction for the reengineering effort.

Often the principal challenge in completing a strategic direction involves finding ways to communicate the new direction through meaningful images. For example, one team developed a strategic direction that emphasized teamwork and resource allocation for a large community of system developers. The formally documented strategic direction, however, was difficult to comprehend, until one of the steering committee members suggested that what they needed was "just-add-water programmers." Comparing programmers to dehydrated food, stored on the shelf until needed, is somewhat strange, but the image communicated a clear focus on a key issue—the organization employed so many programmers that management invested more time in keeping them busy than in selecting the right things for them to work on.

Once a strategic direction has been developed, the steering committee must establish a framework for the new design. This includes the articulation of customers, values, objectives, and boundaries. The customers will be easily definable if the strategic direction is sufficiently clear. The values should characterize the new culture that should evolve as the new design is implemented. The objectives should include measurements and targets that can be used to determine if the objectives are met. In addition, the framework should specify the boundaries or constraints within which the design team must operate. Although reengineering often results in a new and fundamentally different process design, there is really no such thing as a true blank sheet. Every design team operates within some constraints, and it is extremely important to identify them as soon as possible. For example, budget constraints typically limit the implementation plans. Human resource policies limit the options for reward and recognition systems.

Maintaining a Clear and Consistent Customer Focus

A simple but useful definition of a business process is: "a repeated and repeatable set of activities that collectively create and deliver value for a customer." This definition highlights the importance of developing a deep understanding of the customer and of value from the customer's perspective. This focus on the customer must begin with the steering committee at the very beginning of the reengineering effort. Customers should be identified as part of the project framework, and steering committee members must begin to develop an understanding of the customer's sense of value. This often requires more customer contact time than steering committee members are accustomed to.

Customer contact may be difficult at first, especially for steering committees that have not previously established good working relationships with customers. In fact, reengineering efforts are often initiated in response to dissatisfied customers. In that case, customer contact may be extremely uncomfortable at first. One company routinely promised customers product delivery in one week, but usually took three weeks. The managers in charge of the process had isolated themselves from the customers, and they refused to acknowledge the many late deliveries. When steering committee members first approached the customers to discuss the delays they were met by hostility. A positive working relationship ultimately developed, but only after many weeks of uncomfortable interactions.

Steering committees must also actively work to help develop a sense of partnership between customers and the design team. Design team members are often hands-on participants in the day-to-day performance of the process. They have established working relationships with their counterparts in the customer organization but usually have not had contact with the customer's executives. The steering committee can help the design team interpret the executive-level customer's needs while the design team in turn helps the steering committee understand the customer's employees. In this way, steering committee and design team jointly create a new *lens* for understanding the customer from multiple perspectives.

An important distinction that underlies customer value is *live time versus dead time*. A key objective of reengineering is reducing time that does not add value—dead time—while simultaneously increasing value-adding time—live time. This is a challenge because intuitions about live time and dead time are often not particularly good.

Consider the practice of a large technical service force at a major manufacturer. The tech reps installed and repaired equipment. They also had more customer contact than any other class of employees at the company, but their insights about customer needs and behavior were seldom solicited. There was a communication gap between senior managers and the tech reps, and it led to erroneous assumptions. Senior service managers assumed that the several weeks of training that the tech reps received each year was live time, that it contributed to their ability to add value for the customer. They also assumed that the hundreds of people producing and updating product repair manuals were contributing value and therefore engaged in live-time activities. Unfortunately, the tech reps used an oral culture; they learned by telling war stories that became part of their collective diagnostic knowledge. Hours spent in formal classroom training proved to be dead time. Furthermore, tech reps seldom consulted the written documentation, which rendered its production dead time as well. Time spent telling war stories with other tech reps was the real live time, but to the managers this appeared to be nothing more than shooting the breeze.

The distinction did not become clear until a reengineering steering committee engaged an anthropologist to observe the tech rep community. The decision was initially met with humor: Since anthropologists were viewed as "those people who study primitive tribes" and since tech reps were viewed as somewhat primitive, it seemed only fitting. But this anthropologist, a specialist in workplace behavior, was able to clarify the actual practice of the tech reps and the way they added value to the customer. This drove a new design that enabled the tech reps to engage in storytelling more effectively: using radio technology, they could talk with one another while repairing equipment and thus tap into the collective diagnostic knowledge of their community. The radio technology also enabled the tech reps to check in with customers the next day to ensure that the repair had been successful. This proved to be of significant value to the customer, and was reflected in increased customer satisfaction ratings.

Monitoring the Business and Organizational Environment

The business environment comprises the customers and other external agents and elements that are not part of a business process but that do interact with or affect the process. Examples of external agents are regulators and shareholders. External elements include the economy, the political environment, and market geography and demographics. The organizational environment reflects all aspects of the work system associated with a business process, including the culture, morale, and sense of urgency concerning the need for change. Steering committees must develop an ability to sense the business and organizational environments and the changes that they will inevitably go through during the course of reengineering.

Just as there is no such thing as a blank-sheet design opportunity, there is no such thing as a static business process that can simply be reengineered and transformed from its current state to a new and improved state. Business processes are in a constant state of change; they do not remain fixed while a design team contemplates design alternatives. Morale, interpersonal relationships, and informal work practices always change during the life of a reengineering effort. Often, the organizational structure also changes, at least the players. Even the business environment and customer requirements typically change during the reengineering process. The steering committee must watch for these changes and bring them to design team discussions. Design teams must also engage in similar observation and assessment activities throughout the effort. The steering committee and the design team must then work together to make sense of the observed environmental changes

The steering committee members also play a central role in the organizational changes that occur during reengineering. At a minimum, they authorize changes associated with organizational structure; often they actively participate in restructuring that is directly tied to the reengineering work. They can also help to reshape the social dimension of work through their leadership role. This includes creating a willingness to participate in the change effort and a sense of excitement about the change.

Frequently, steering committees must also confront the reality of reductions in staff levels that occur concurrently with a reengineering plan. When this happens, it makes change management significantly more complex. When reengineering and downsizing occur in parallel, a natural assumption is that they are linked efforts. Employees may assume that the design team is responsible for the downsizing, which will hamper open communication between them. Even if downsizing does not occur in parallel with a reengineering effort, it often does occur as the new process is being implemented. This is because new processes are substantially more effective than the processes that they replace. Steering committees should address this possibility early in the effort and determine their response. If downsizing is a high likelihood, then that fact should be part of the reengineering communication strategy.

To help monitor and assess the change that occurs during a reengineering effort, steering committees and design teams often use semiformal stakeholder-management techniques. Stakeholder management consists of identifying key stakeholders (external and internal) and then assessing their knowledge of the effort, their level of influence over the outcome, and their level of commitment to the success of the effort. Level of commitment is described on a scale from "blocker" (one who proactively tries to prevent the effort from succeeding) to "sponsor" (one who proactively works to ensure that the effort succeeds). Stakeholders can be repositioned through effective stakeholder management: providing additional information, building relationships, addressing stakeholder concerns, or perhaps even reducing the authority of a blocker. In one reengineering effort a blocker was removed from his position by the head of a steering committee when it became clear that he could not be convinced to let the effort proceed (supporting it was never even a possibility).

Stakeholder management, despite its semiformalized nature, is never straightforward. It is often difficult to accurately assess the positioning of a stakeholder. And there are complications: a stakeholder who appears to be supportive publicly but who blocks the effort behind the scenes; the truly supportive individual whose subordinates block the effort; and the supporter who lacks sufficient knowledge of the effort and therefore communicates inaccurate information to the organization. For obvious reasons, care must be taken to keep the results of stakeholder assessments confidential.

Another aspect of organizational change concerns the question of *quick hits* that may be implemented while the design team works on the new design. In the course of their work, design teams often come up with specific improvement suggestions that the steering committee can implement quickly and with relatively little effort. Usually they relate to formal procedures, authorizations, and information flow and associated technology. Steering committees should establish an informal policy about quick hits so that the design team and the rest of the organization know how to handle these change ideas.

The organizational environment also affects the steering committee and design team on a more personal level. For both groups, the key theme is balance and duality. Steering committee members collectively serve as process owners for the business process that is to be reengineered. They also retain their departmental and functional responsibilities as individuals. They must therefore balance their obligations as a team of process owners with their individual interests and responsibilities. Excessive emphasis on either side can lead to problems. Ignoring functional responsibilities can lead to failure in the current process before the new process is ready; excessive emphasis on individual interests, especially turf considerations, can significantly complicate the task of reaching consensus on a new design and then implementing it.

Design teams face an analogous challenge. They must work effectively as a crossfunctional team while simultaneously remaining engaged with their home organizations. They must be members of both communities, and balance the sometimes conflicting loyalties. For example, a design team member may know that a design alternative would result in the elimination of her home department. Personal friendships and loyalties would drive disclosure of this possibility while loyalty to the design team (and knowledge that it was only one of many alternatives) would prevent disclosure. The challenge is amplified by the fact that design team members ultimately return to the work force.

Some design teams have a tendency to become isolated from their home departments. The steering committee can help to prevent this by insisting that design team members routinely spend time with their home organizations; one day a week is the recommendation. The day can be spent in change management and communication and in informal relationship building, or in formal interactions such as attending staff meetings and conducting briefings.

Coordinating an Effective Communication Strategy

Developing and implementing an effective communication strategy is perhaps the greatest challenge that a steering committee and design team face. Reengineering efforts almost never fail as a result of flawed process designs. When they fail, it is because of ineffective change management, failure to properly address cultural and social issues that relate to the new design, and particularly because of insufficient communication. Design teams should spend 20 to 25 percent of their time in communication-related activities. Steering committees should actively participate in communication both as a group and as individuals.

Communication should be broadly defined to be a part of all interactions between those involved in reengineering and those who will be affected by the effort. This includes formal and informal communication. It also includes gathering feedback, participatory design, and *walking the talk* to demonstrate the new values that the new design will embody. As an example, customer focus is an important value in every reengineering effort. To reflect this value, steering committee and design team members should be seen actively working with customers throughout the reengineering project's life cycle.

Many reengineering efforts fail to allocate sufficient time to communication, partly because many people define communication as consisting exclusively of written memos and reports. In fact, written communication is only a relatively small part of a good communication strategy. Briefings, discussion sessions, focus groups, video news releases, and electronic bulletin boards can all be elements of a communication strategy. The steering committee should help to first shape the communication strategy, and then participate in its implementation.

There are two keys to shaping the communication strategy. The first involves articulating the messages that should be communicated. For example, the change drivers, new values, and desired improvement objectives should all be included in the target messages. The second key involves identifying the modes of communication, the channels that will be used to communicate the target messages. It is important to understand that communication is more an art than a science. There are techniques that aid the art, but communication is fundamentally a function of the people involved. Steering committees and design teams can often benefit from specialized training to enable them to become more effective communicators.

One pitfall to avoid is to confuse communicating with selling. There is an element of every communication strategy that involves selling the change effort and the new design, but this should be only a relatively small component of the communication strategy. Greater attention should be focused on soliciting feedback and on enabling coproduction, participation, and dialogue. Communication should also provide clarification and insight into the design process. One company developed a new process design that required an advanced degree in operations research to comprehend. The steering committee then commissioned a simple simulation to illustrate the differences between the old static model and the new dynamic one.

Two specific communication challenges that steering committees often face are the *program du jour* phenomenon and the *relabeling* effect. *Program du jour* refers to the assumption that reengineering is just a fad or simply another program. Skeptical employees may try to outlast reengineering, rather than embracing it. Relabeling is an alternate reaction in which the work force begins to label all recent successes and all ongoing change efforts as reengineering. In one case, a CEO who had just publicly committed to sponsoring reengineering found more than one hundred references to ongoing reengineering efforts in the next month's briefing materials. The steering committee can address the *program du jour* effect by consistent and ongoing communication. It is also helpful to consider the number of programs in effect throughout the organization and try to reduce the set if there seems to be too many.

An important communication challenge for steering committees involves managing linkages between reengineering efforts and other change initiatives. For example, it is not unusual for a reengineering program to focus on a process that is also the subject of a new information technology development effort. To achieve maximum benefit from both, these two efforts must be linked, and this linkage is best accomplished through the active involvement of the steering committee. One steering committee, preparing to launch a reengineering initiative, identified a dozen related efforts. Three were put on hold (since the new design was likely to invalidate their results), and the design team was linked with the other nine.

If the organization has initiated total quality management programs, it is helpful to monitor the efforts of quality improvement teams. Often, they have collected and analyzed information that can be of value to a design team. At a higher level, it is also important to develop a clear message about the relationship between quality and reengineering. Many organizations that have both quality and reengineering experience a perceived competition, as though only one can survive. However, they clearly share common foundations, such as customer focus and end-to-end process orientation, and can be positioned as two tools in a toolkit. Each applies in different situations and both complement each other. At the conclusion of a reengineering effort, the new process should include the capacity for continuous improvement—quality should be designed into the new process.

Relabeling is best addressed by introducing a set of filters that must be applied before anything can be labeled reengineering. One organization recently adopted the following four filters:

1. There must be a clear customer focus and a clear understanding of the way the process creates and delivers value for the customer.
2. The scope of the reengineering effort must encompass all activities required to create and deliver customer value; it must be an end-to-end process.
3. The scope of the effort must also encompass the total work system—procedural, social, and structural dimensions.
4. There must be a real opportunity to fundamentally change the business process; there cannot be too many boundaries.

Ensuring Participation in Design

Reengineering is most successful when it is performed as an act of participatory design that engages the steering committee, the design team, and the employees that will be affected. For steering committees in particular this means investing time in the effort. On average, steering committee members can expect to spend between two and four hours a week working both formally and informally on the project.

To ensure participatory design means overcoming several challenges. First, both steering committee and design team members must learn to see one another differently. The executive/employee barrier must be eliminated; the executives must learn to appreciate the value that the employees bring to the effort, and the employees must learn to trust the steering committee. Most design teams assume that if the effort succeeds, the steering committee will take the credit and if the effort fails, the design team will be left holding the bag. This must be replaced by a sense of joint accountability and responsibility.

A second challenge involves the different experiences and *lenses* that steering committee and design team members bring.

Steering committees see the organization from 100,000 feet; design teams see it at the ground level. Both perspectives are valuable and can be synthesized to develop an integrated multilevel view of the organization. A third challenge involves committing to an in-depth and sustained level of engagement throughout the effort. There are often occasions when steering committee members grow impatient to see results and when design team members grow concerned about the impact of a year-long assignment on their careers. Both groups must develop staying power and should develop the capability to mutually reinforce one another.

Participatory design must also engage the work force. Meeting this challenge requires multiple techniques, including various kinds of working sessions. Electronic means of participation such as electronic kiosks and bulletin boards can also be used. Another technique is the *open chair*. This symbolic concept involves inviting anyone from the organization to join the design team for half a day. During this time, they act in the same capacity as a full-time design team member. This stimulates participation, and also reduces the aura of secrecy that often surrounds a design team. It also helps to prevent the design team from becoming isolated.

Effective participation by a broad-based cross section of the work force is important in all phases of reengineering. During analysis, it can enrich the design team's understanding of the process. During design, it can ensure that the new process design will *fit* with the people in the organization. This participation ensures that local knowledge is properly understood and incorporated in the design activities.

Finally, participatory design taps the creative energy of the organization beyond the steering committee and design team. This is particularly important because neither group is design professionals. They can use creative assistance from the work force throughout the effort. A facilitation team of trained process consultants can provide process assistance to ensure that the steering committee and design team do not become overly focused on the tasks and techniques of reengineering (because of a common latent bias for activity). Employees' participation ensures that the solutions are not too narrowly considered. Participation leads to the richest possible new process design.

Conclusion

The need for a radical reengineering of the way work is performed is clear and will continue as large companies throughout the world strive to increase their productivity. Few corporations will be able to compete in the future without improving productivity through some form of work-process reengineering. Firms that ignore the productivity challenge will fail. However, those sponsoring major reengineering efforts must be sensitive to the limits of reengineering as an approach to organizational change. Reengineering provides *some* answers to important organizational problems *if* implemented in a savvy manner. Ironically, the promise of reengineering will be most fully realized by those who recognize its inherent limits. In particular, reengineering designs need to balance "hard" technical needs with "softer" social needs that affect the full utilization of individual and collective talent. Moreover, the discontinuous nature of reengineering change (what some call "blank-page design") requires an appropriate set of change-management tools that are largely missing from the reengineering toolkit. Insensitivity to the dynamics of change and inadequate change methodolgies have resulted in far more of the failures in the reengineering area than any technological shortcomings.

Executive Development: Finding and Growing Champions of Change

Richard F. Ketterer
Michael M. Chayes

Selecting and developing leadership talent provides a powerful but often underused opportunity for organizations to more effectively manage discontinuous change. To take advantage of this opportunity, senior managers must create a template for new leadership, a profile of the competencies, attitudes, and experiences that must align with and support new initiatives. Senior managers who adopt this strategy will increase the supply of needed leadership talent while enhancing the capacity of their organizations to adapt to discontinuous change.

Ironically, achieving these goals presents significant leadership challenges in itself. Senior managers must recognize the importance of redefining the organization's leadership requirements, then make the necessary investment in time and resources to translate that recognition into effective strategies for selecting and developing new kinds of leaders.

The Need for Change-Oriented Leadership

Under any circumstances, those leading large organization need a repertoire of critical skills. At the heart of leadership is the ability to develop a vision others can resonate to and mobilize around. Effective leadership also means modeling desired behaviors and holding everyone accountable, including oneself (Bennis and Nanus, 1985, Kotter, 1990). However, radical change, because of the particular demands it makes of the organization, places a special premium on leadership skills and competencies.

The difficulty is that the pace of change is outstripping the capacity of organizations to identify and develop leaders who can direct and guide organizational change. There are several reasons for this. First, radical change means taking risks and doing things in new and different ways—behaviors not generally valued in organizations that have too long delayed strategic change. Also, the skills required to successfully run hierarchical, functionally based organizations are fundamentally different from the skills needed to lead high-involvement "horizontal" organizations. As a result, organizations experiencing rapid change often design the "right" organization only to discover that they lack the bench strength to successfully implement required changes.

Another reason for the gap in leadership talent has to do with the nature of the change process itself. Companies embarking on radical change often start by reexamining their strategy and then redesign their organization and business processes to fit their strategic direction. Much of this work is tangible or "hard"—it involves the design of concrete elements such as organizational structure, work processes, and formal policies and procedures. These elements are difficult to design, but, being tangible, they are generally understood and addressed early in the change process. On paper, at least, tangible elements of a new organization can be implemented as soon as basic design decisions have been made.

Less tangible or "soft" elements, however, are also essential to the success of large-scale change. In fact, it is the synergy between the hard and soft that holds the key to the success. Soft components include the selection and development of leaders, the development of core competencies, and the shaping of culture, norms, and values of the new organization. Unlike organizational structures and work processes that can be mapped out quickly and are then ready for implementation, soft components take longer to design and are more complex and problematic to implement. Being less tangible, and frequently less well understood, they are often neglected in the design process.

Unfortunately, this oversight often limits the success of the overall change effort. Consider organizations changing from a functional to business group structure. Although designing new business units and accompanying work processes is complex, a far more difficult challenge is to find managers with the appropriate set of experiences and skills. In our experience, unless the competencies and skills needed to make the new structure work are defined in advance, the change effort is likely to fall far short of its intent.

Factors Inhibiting Development

In most organizations, there exists a set of assumptions, attitudes, and practices that inhibit the development of leaders. These assumptions and practices are embedded in the mindset of most senior managers and reflect broader societal values about how people learn and develop. Unless these factors are surfaced and confronted, the present leadership gap will remain.

Darwinian Mindset. A key factor inhibiting leadership development is the widespread belief that leaders are born, not made. This fosters a *laissez-faire* approach to development in which the "best and the brightest" are expected to emerge through a process of natural selection. In other words, "real" leaders develop on their own, with little help from others. In fact, one measure of potential is a leader's ability to succeed with little assistance from the organization. Rather than nurturing talent, organizations adopting this view perpetuate the myth that individuals with "the right stuff" will miraculously rescue the organization when crises arise.

Lack of Performance Feedback. Many managers avoid giving performance feedback, particularly negative or "constructive" feedback. The paucity of candid feedback—particularly among senior managers, where the problem is endemic—makes a mockery of the stated goal of most organizations to provide valid performance data to all managers and employees. The irony, of course, is that performance feedback is widely acknowledged to be among the most powerful means of accelerating individual learning and development (Kotter, 1990; Bennis, 1989; McCall, Lombardo, and Morrison, 1988).

Leadership as an Art Form. Another inhibiting factor is the widely held view that the process of developing leaders is inherently subjective. The absence of an "objective" approach leads senior managers to apply their existing assumptions about leadership as a de facto model of development. Thus competencies required in traditional functional structures, such as strong technical knowledge, are given precedence over skills needed to operate in changing environments. The effect is to perpetuate traditional skills at the expense of those required to lead radical change. Additionally, because leadership competencies are seldom made explicit, prospective leaders rarely understand the basis upon which they are being evaluated. Lacking information about the organization's success criteria, they are left to infer what these competencies are, a problem that further handicaps the development process.

Leadership Development as Nonstrategic. Very few organizations define leadership development as a critical strategic challenge. This attitude is reflected in the relative lack of time senior executives devote to identifying and assessing leadership talent, a task often delegated to corporate staff or managers lower in the organization. Unfortunately, delegating this work often results in a superficial, if not invalid, evaluation. Moreover, a low level of commitment in the assessment phase makes it less likely executives will invest in the difficult ongoing task of developing a new generation of leadership talent.

Additional Barriers. McCall (1993) identifies a number of other factors that explain the current gap in leadership talent. These include:

• Tolerating mediocrity in the initial selection of talent
• Allowing towering strengths or skills to obscure fatal flaws

- Giving precedence to short-term factors when making development decisions
- Expecting heroic leaders to save the organization at moments of greatest need
- Creating self-fulfilling situations in which accumulating selection and development errors reinforce one another

All these factors pose a difficult, often invisible, barrier to the development of leadership talent and bench strength. Recognizing and confronting these barriers are the first steps in overcoming them.

Characteristics of Change-Oriented Leaders

It is widely recognized that the key challenge of leadership is to develop a credible and compelling vision, mobilize key constituents around it, and then align all the components of the organization to achieve desired results (Kouzes and Posner, 1987, 1993; Bennis and Nanus, 1985). To accomplish these goals, leaders must possess a set of behaviors and skills that enable them to effectively manage organizational change. Interestingly, despite the proliferation of leadership models, there is increasing convergence of opinion about the key dimensions of effective leadership (Locke, 1992). To develop leadership talent, cutting-edge companies look for these competencies:

- *Vision.* Ability to articulate an image of a future state that is realistic and compelling and better than the present state. Having a broad, long-term, big-picture view of the business and the organization as a whole.
- *Managing complexity.* Ability to process and interpret information and knowledge at multiple levels; capacity to organize information into logical sequences and to see the relationships between sets of data and changing circumstances.
- *Business and industry insight.* Having exceptional knowledge and awareness of the business or industry; ability to understand and anticipate customer and market trends as well as changes occurring in the competitive marketplace.
- *General manager perspective.* Capacity to understand the broad-

based requirements of the business; capable of integrating multiple, sometimes conflicting, processes and functions into a coherent business proposition.

- *Drive for success.* Deep-seated need for achievement and excellence; thriving on challenges and persevering despite obstacles; balancing personal needs for power with need to contribute to the common good (socialized power).
- *Personal integrity.* Evoking trust in others by being appropriately open and by behaving in predictable ways; being consistent in behavior and maintaining consistency between words and actions; being clear and consistent in values and acting accordingly.
- *Flexibility.* Ability and willingness to adapt quickly to changing conditions. Can see both sides of an issue and avoids locking in to a particular position or point of view.
- *Self-awareness.* An accurate understanding of personal strengths and weaknesses; ability to admit mistakes and be open to constructive feedback from others.
- *Active learning.* Seeking out new information and knowledge; gaining insight and knowledge from experience; ability to learn and profit from mistakes.
- *Influencing without authority.* Insight into others' behaviors and motivations; ability to motivate through words and deeds; ability to empower others through shared vision and persuasive communications.
- *Developing talent.* Ability to identify and develop management and work force talent and skills; commitment to the development process; providing a challenging climate to encourage development.
- *Teamwork.* Ability to build and mold teams within and across organizational boundaries; ability to balance individual and team goal setting, learning, and performance.

But leaders must do more than acquire leadership competencies; they must also cultivate an understanding about how people and organizations learn and adapt to change. Without this understanding, they will lack the focus and determination to see change through—a deficiency that undermines many strategic change efforts. What qualities, then, distinguish managers who can lead change from those with less potential to lead the change process? Our experience suggests that leaders with requisite change skills share the following knowledge and common set of assumptions.

The defining characteristic of change-oriented leaders is their determination to close the gap between what is and what could be. Change-oriented leaders focus on the future. They ask what has to be done to make their vision—and everyone else's vision—a reality. In pursuing this goal, they exploit incongruencies and anomalies in the present to gain insight on what is needed in the future. They also assume that a leader's vision must be externally focused to be effective, that is, it must align with business realities such as changing customer needs, competitive pressures, technological trends, and so on.

Finally, change-oriented leaders adhere to a straightforward formula for success: they set high performance standards and hold themselves and others accountable for achieving them. Change-oriented leaders, in sum, seek to achieve their vision by reinventing the present and by continually pursuing the highest performance standards measured against ever-changing business realities.

Another characteristic of change-oriented leaders is that their investment in personal learning is matched or exceeded by their commitment to team and organizational learning. They accept what time-based theorists have been saying: that the speed at which organizations learn is the only sustainable source of competitive advantage (Meyer, 1993; Stalk and Hout, 1990). But knowing that it takes more than intent to make organizational learning real, change-oriented leaders establish forums where individuals and groups can learn from one another. Their goal is to create ongoing learning processes that will drive organizational change and lead to success in the marketplace.

Change-oriented leaders view people as strategic assets needed to achieve competitive advantage. They realize, however, that human assets erode unless nurtured and developed. They also understand that developing individual competencies provides the underpinning for team and organizational learning. If organizational learning is to occur, then individual learning must be accelerated within an environment where personal insights are leveraged throughout the organization. For this reason, change-oriented leaders seek to maintain investment in people despite business downturns. Their logic is simple: it is people—not capital, technology, or work processes—that hold the key to developing new sources of competitive advantage.

Finally, change-oriented leaders believe passionately in the value of distributed leadership. While recognizing their unique responsibility as executives, they understand that discontinuous change requires that everyone exercise initiative and be empowered. They see the need for leadership at every level in the organization, not as a role reserved for the few who manage at the top of the pyramid. The most effective organizations, then, are ones whose cultures support a wide range of people exercising leadership.

"Leadership," by this definition, is as much a situational as an individual phenomenon, evident when anyone initiates change or effectively influences other members of the organization to take constructive action. Thus change-oriented leaders understand that strategies that fail to empower the work force are doomed to failure. Hence the most formidable challenge leaders face is to a foster a climate where people throughout the organization will assume ownership of the change process.

To recap, change-oriented leaders possess discrete leadership competencies along with a set of assumptions and beliefs about how people and organizations learn and adapt to change. Leaders with these qualities are more likely than others to manage the realities of complex organizational change. As noted earlier, however, an array of barriers typically inhibits the identification and development of people with the characteristics and perspective required to lead radical change. The critical challenge, then, is to design a selection process that overcomes these barriers.

Strategic Selection

If organizations are to successfully manage radical change, they must systematically identify and develop leaders with the necessary competencies. Strategic selection is a process for improving the quality and effectiveness of selection decisions (Nadler and Gerstein, 1992b; Gerstein and Reisman, 1983). For an organization undergoing radical change, the purpose of strategic selection is twofold: to ensure that the organization's immediate leadership requirements are met, and to begin the longer-term process of developing a new generation of leaders with the competencies to lead in the future. The process is strategic in the sense that it connects leadership selection and development to the long-term business requirements of the organization. An effective strategic selection process has certain specific requirements:

Recognize the Need for a New Approach. The first and most difficult challenge is for senior managers involved in this process to acknowledge that past approaches to selection are inadequate to meet current and future needs. Such recognition is neither trivial nor easy since managers entrusted with this responsibility are often products of the system that must now be changed. Thus, while many of these managers are survivors of the Darwinian selection process described earlier, they now have to discard outdated assumptions about selection while embracing a systematic approach to the development of leadership talent.

Such recognition must be coupled with the conviction that a fresh approach to selection will catalyze organizational change. However, one obstacle is that prior incremental change efforts in many organizations have generated skepticism among a number of employees who have seen too many pronouncements about "new leadership" ending up with the same people being placed in jobs with new titles. While making selection a key element of the change agenda does not imply the wholesale replacement of the existing leadership, it does mean defining new leadership criteria and being willing to make tough decisions about who should occupy new leadership positions. If senior managers are unable or unwilling to shake up the existing organization, the selection process will lack credibility and in the end will undermine the entire change process.

Be Willing to Take Ownership of the Process. Another requirement for success is that senior managers take close and direct accountability for the selection process, including defining future leadership requirements and making critical selection decisions. While human resources staff or outside consultants need to play a significant support role, senior managers must translate their vision into choices about the leadership characteristics required to guide the organization forward.

The hands-on involvement of senior management in the selection process sends several key messages to the organization. It communicates that people are critical in bringing about successful organizational change. If significant senior management attention is devoted to selection, leadership will be seen as a valued strategic asset in the new organization. Additionally, as the authors of the new leadership requirements, senior managers are creating a powerful vehicle for communicating the behaviors, skills, and competencies that will be valued in the organization of the future.

Behaviors Must Reflect Values That Underlie the Process. A final requirement for success is that senior managers involved in the selection process convey the operating style and values of the new organization through their own behaviors and actions. As each step of selection is planned and implemented, choices will be made in terms of openness, participation, and sharing ownership that either galvanize the organization in a positive direction or create greater skepticism, perhaps even despair. By designing and managing the selection process in a way that openly communicates selection criteria and future expectations, and also invites involvement and collaboration, senior managers can help jump start the organization in the desired direction.

The team taking a new approach to leadership selection must recognize that the process, while offering great leverage for change, also generates considerable anxiety and uncertainty for the organization. People are legitimately concerned with what changes of that order will mean for their career and position, and whether or not they will continue to be valued by a changing organization. Because change disrupts the status quo, it is always perceived as threatening. However, by being sensitive to how people react to change, the team can manage the selection process in ways that tend to maximize the excitement and promise that are the positive aspects of change and that deal constructively with some of the fear and apprehension that are its negative parts.

Steps in the Selection Process

The strategic selection process has five distinct steps.

1. Identifying Expectations and Success Factors

Defining the competencies required in the new organization accomplishes two distinct but related objectives: first, it helps crystallize the views of senior managers about the strategic requirements, culture, and leadership skills needed in the new organization; and second, it serves as a benchmark against which to formulate leadership development strategies.

Defining leadership competencies begins with discussions among senior managers about key organizational challenges and the overall approach to the change process. Through individual or group interviews, senior managers articulate their vision of the future, including, for example, key strategic issues facing the company, anticipated changes in the marketplace, critical success factors, structural changes altering spans of control and reporting relationships, and changing demands of the work force.

Besides defining leadership success criteria, a byproduct of this process is help in building a change agenda. Such discussion, for example, surfaces divergent views among senior managers about critical issues confronted by the organization. These discussions frequently help senior managers resolve differences while creating a climate of cooperation and teamwork. Although unanimous agreement among senior managers is rare, and indeed not always desirable, this process often helps create significant alignment around a vision for the organization.

2. Defining Leadership Competencies

The next step in the process is producing a general list of competencies that can be used to make selection decisions and devise development strategies. Such competencies are often a combination of organization-specific requirements and a set of change-oriented characteristics similar to those discussed earlier in this chapter. The task at this stage is not inventing leadership competencies from scratch—there is a high degree of consensus about the core competencies—but making a thoughtful appraisal of which leadership dimensions are most critical, given the specific challenges the organization faces.

Observations about future requirements are translated into a set of behavioral dimensions that define critical success factors for future leaders. Senior managers, for example, discuss how changes in business strategy translate into changed behavior within the organization. The step is analogous to the difference between a picture of an apple and a real apple. The image must be translated into something textural and three-dimensional that people can actually bite into. The final dimensions are arrived at through an iterative process, until the team concludes that the list of skills and abilities truly reflects their thinking about the leadership needs of the organization. The dimensions should be defined in sufficient behavioral detail to allow anyone using the criteria for assessment to be able to reliably judge whether an individual possesses the skill or quality in question. Generic leadership skills that are not adequately described in behavioral language introduce unreliability into the system as each rater decides for himself or herself what a dimension actually means.

A special advantage of this approach is that it captures the description of competencies in the unique language of the organization. Every group, by virtue of history, culture, and shared experience, has its own ways of describing behavior, both desirable and undesirable. What is for one organization "personal drive" is for another "fire in the belly." Each dimension may be describing identical behavior or personal qualities, but the language used creates a unique template for the organization, thus creating a customized set of leadership dimensions. Senior managers participating in this process have a sense of shared ownership and commitment to the skills and abilities articulated in their own language.

Another subtle outcome of the competency-determination process is the opportunity it provides for senior managers to clarify for themselves what they are trying to accomplish in changing their organization. Articulating leadership competencies thus becomes an extension of strategic vision and direction. In fact, abstractions such as "flatter, less-hierarchical organizations" take on a new cogency when the organization begins selecting leaders with exceptional interpersonal skills, networking ability, and value systems that are consistent with diversity, empowerment, and learning. The choices that senior managers make about who will lead the organization in the future is one of the clearest, most powerful signals about the precise nature of the change agenda.

One caution about the process of defining requirements. While there is value in thinking through the challenges an organization is facing and selecting leaders with skills that align with them, there are limits to the matching process. The environment is changing so rapidly that flexibility and breadth are more critical for success than a narrow skill set that connects with a specific strategic challenge. For this reason it is useful to think about leadership criteria in terms of two basic areas of competence.

The first relates to competencies that are relatively enduring—the change-oriented leadership characteristics described earlier. These qualities have to do with the ability to manage change, to see organizations through perpetual whitewater and constantly changing external demands. Competencies in this area, we believe, are common across organizations and are likely to be relevant into the indefinite future. On the other hand, there is a second set of competencies that are more situational or organization-specific. These skills are unique to each business situation, generally involve technical knowledge or skills, and are required to execute a specific assignment at a given point in time. Both sets of competencies are important, but they are different, and these differences must be recognized during the selection process.

3. Identifying Talent Pools

Once leadership competencies have been defined, the next task is to identify the talent pool from which future leaders will be selected and developed. Most organizations today have compiled formal or informal lists of succession candidates and high-potentials. When important job openings are created, senior managers usually rely on these lists to produce a candidate pool. The problem is that when organizations are undergoing radical, discontinuous change, succession and high-potential lists seldom reflect the range and depth of competencies needed to meet the new leadership requirements. It's important to explore this point further, starting with the issue of high-potentials.

It is usually impractical in the short term to assess an entire succession pool against a new set of criteria. However, as high-potential lists are scanned to generate candidate pools, new criteria can be employed to screen for candidates. For example, as general management perspective is of growing importance for many jobs, lists can be screened for those candidates who have had crossfunctional experience or who have demonstrated their ability to work effectively across organizational boundaries. By using screening criteria that reflect emerging skill requirements, senior managers shape the pool toward the capabilities that will be significant in the future. As high-potential lists are reviewed, there may be incremental changes as certain individuals clearly ill suited to future leadership roles are dropped from the list entirely and others are added whose skills were not as valued in the old organization.

This strategy addresses the use of high-potential lists, but for the near-term leadership shortfall, we need to examine how using succession-planning lists differently can play a role. In most organizations, succession-planning candidates are chosen because of their past record of performance. Typically, candidates are judged against a set of requirements defined at a given point in time and reflecting candidates' track record against the organization's current operating demands. However, as the pace of change increases, leadership requirements inevitably shift to reflect the primacy of new skills and abilities. While succession lists will be redefined over time, during the early phases of the change process senior managers are limited by the existing succession pool.

Given this constraint, what can senior managers do to increase their likelihood of success in selecting managers for important positions in the new organization? There are two general strategies at this early stage: making selections from the existing succession pool but using different criteria and post-selection support, and going outside for talent. In the first case, the leaders are chosen from the current pool whose skills, abilities, and attitudes fit best with the new selection criteria. The challenge is in demonstrating by word and action that the new criteria are crucial for future success and that therefore any abilities that selectees are lacking will be aggressively addressed via short-term developmental efforts. While new leaders are entitled to have the confidence of senior management—else they shouldn't be selected at all—it is equally important that they understand the organization has a new set of expectations and they must collaborate immediately in establishing developmental plans that address the areas in which they are weak.

A second approach to using the existing pool of talent has to do with where in the organization you choose people from. There is evidence that where leaders with long tenure in an organization have been successful in leading radical change, they have tended to come from the periphery of the organization or at least to have spent long periods of time away from the center of the organization. Leaders who have grown up in the midst of a particular organizational culture have a very difficult time changing it. The lesson is this: when selecting from the existing succession pool—all things being equal—consider candidates who have earned their stripes running divisions abroad or in other than the core business. They may have greater capacity to bring about change in the short term.

The second strategy for meeting short-term leadership needs is to bring in talent from outside the organization. That strategy has both benefits and risks. On the positive side, once an organization has recognized the leadership competencies it requires for future success, these competencies can be more quickly imported via outside hires than they can be developed within the organization. In addition, outside hires are a breath of fresh air in that they often see the strengths and weaknesses of organizations they are entering more clearly than those who have been living there. Also, they tend to have greater freedom of action because they are not extensively involved in the existing political system.

There are, however, several risks to outside hires. Internal candidates who have lost jobs to outsiders are often angry and demotivated, at least in the short term. They need to be helped to see selection decisions in perspective and shown what their own continuing opportunity for contribution will be. Also, outside hires, while seeing some things with great clarity, may not understand the subtler aspects of the organization, including how things actually get done. They have to be quick learners and capable of building their own political base in very short order. Organizations that bring in people from the outside often have unrealistic expectations, idealizing outsiders who they think have the "right stuff." It is important that insiders temper their expectations and be prepared to play an active role in helping outsiders to succeed.

4. Rating Candidates

Turning back to the selection process, the next step is rating candidates against the agreed-upon selection criteria. The critical success factors at this stage relate to choosing the right raters. One virtue of a competency-based approach to selection is that once the selection criteria have been defined, candidates can be rated against the criteria by managers who know them best; they do not have to be rated by the same managers who developed the criteria or who will ultimately make the selection decision.

The most effective raters are managers who have had sufficient work experience with a candidate to be able to accurately assess that person's strengths on key leadership dimensions. Prior to rating candidates, raters should meet in a group session to review the selection criteria and resolve any questions or ambiguities about the dimensions. This process helps create a shared understanding of each dimension and the overall intent beyond the selection criteria. Once individual ratings have been collected, raters meet to work through differences of opinion and to reach a consensus rating for each candidate.

5. Making Decisions

Once the candidate ratings have been completed, senior managers responsible for hiring decisions compare the ratings against the leadership requirements. If proper attention has been given to articulating leadership requirements and to candidate rating, they are now in a position to make well-informed decisions about the candidates. As no candidate fully meets all requirements, the decision process involves weighing the tradeoffs that each candidate presents. At this point it is often useful to focus on the dimensions that are most critical for job success and also on the distinction between those skills that are probably trainable versus those that are not. It facilitates the decision process if the group decides ahead of time how decisions will be made—by consensus, majority vote, or some other measure.

Besides enhancing the quality of selection decisions, the strategic selection process has other benefits for the organization. Being data driven, it inherently represents "management by fact." It sends a message to the organization that decisions will be made based on information and not on personal bias or prejudice. In addition, the process provides an opportunity for managers who serve as raters to be exposed to the change agenda and to develop, through their participation, a sense of ownership for it. Lastly, in the midst of discontinuous change, which by its very nature is psychologically unsettling, a thoughtful and deliberate selection process reassures the organization that there are rational processes by which the future can be actively anticipated and mastered.

Developing Leadership Capability

Creating an effective selection process is a prerequisite to developing enduring leadership capability. But it is not enough that the managers with the requisite skills are identified, they must also be given a chance to broaden and develop their skills through systematic job-related developmental experiences. What strategies are needed to accomplish this objective? What role should senior managers play in building an organization's leadership development capability? Equally important, what must senior managers do to deliver the leadership talent needed to meet near- and long-term organizational requirements?

Much has been learned in recent years about developing leaders. In the last decade alone, numerous articles, books, research studies, and reports have described and analyzed different development strategies and methods. At the same time, managers and human resource practitioners have been experimenting with strategies that improve the quality and effectiveness of leadership development. These strategies range from job rotation and assignment management through education and training to comprehensive leadership questionnaire feedback and coaching. Some of the development approaches that many leading-edge companies employ include:

- *Job rotation and assignment management.* Planned movement of selected individuals into "stretch assignments," changes in job scope, and other assignment opportunities designed to broaden their experience and exposure to different parts of the organization. Especially useful in accelerating the development of high-potentials or experienced professionals who are being groomed for senior leadership positions.
- *360-degree feedback process.* Systematic feedback from superiors, subordinates, peers, and customers designed to provide insight into people's strengths, weaknesses, and developmental opportunities. Provides impetus—and a nice baseline—for developing focused plans for individual development.
- *Task forces and teams.* Assignment of high-visibility task forces and teams whose charter addresses critical organizational needs. Typically provides cross-functional exposure and practice in using innovative methods of problem solving and breakthrough thinking.
- *Education and training.* Includes customized internal training as well as external training courses and seminars. The intent is to match an individual's learning requirements to specific curricula delivered at a point when the individual's learning needs are at a peak.
- *Mentoring and coaching.* Assignment of senior managers to support and facilitate the development needs of less experienced executives. When practiced widely, mentoring and coaching create a climate conducive to personal development and change.

The problem, of course, is that formidable barriers exist to applying these strategies in a systematic way. A few companies, most notably PepsiCo and GE, have demonstrated the strategic value of leadership development (Pearson, 1987; Tichy and Sherman, 1993). But the capacity to produce a sufficient supply of leaders on an ongoing basis remains the exception. Most organizations don't acknowledge the importance of development; others apply development strategies on a hit-or-miss basis, failing to meet the organization's required leadership needs. This dilemma, prevalent for years, has been exacerbated by the permanent whitewater conditions found in most organizations today. The net result is a widening leadership gap. What needs to be done to reverse this trend?

A critical first step is for senior managers to recognize that the root cause of the problem often begins with them. The problem isn't a lack of knowledge but a commitment on their part to make leadership development a strategic priority. Unless leadership development is defined as a source of competitive advantage, efforts to develop leaders invariably lose momentum as short-term pressures arise or the novelty of the initiative wears off. To avoid this all-too-frequent scenario, a clear line of sight must be developed between the organization's strategic objectives—including its short- and long-term leadership requirements—and its plan for meeting these requirements.

Senior managers willing to make this commitment must start by initiating a multiphase leadership development process that begins at the top and that eventually extends throughout the company. This process starts with selection and placement and continues through iterative cycles of developmental planning, assessment of performance, reflection and organizational learning, followed by a new cycle of selection and placement. This process is shown in Figure 12.1.

To provide structure to the process, regular development review sessions need to be instituted throughout the organization, starting at the top. In these meetings, managers come together to discuss ongoing organizational and staffing requirements, initiate targeted development strategies, and evalute the organization's progress in developing adequate leadership talent and bench strength. These meetings may be run as part of strategic selection sessions or sequenced to complement such meetings. In either case, the aim is for managers to meet regularly in a safe and constructive environment to examine leadership needs, to implement organizationwide development strategies, and to monitor the progress of high-potentials and key managers throughout the organization.

Development reviews provide the structure for a leadership development process capable of meeting an organization's strategic objectives. To be effective, however, development initiatives must be

Figure 12.1. Selection-Development Cycle.

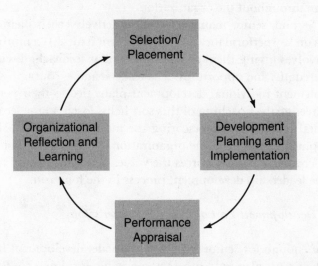

coupled with a set of principles that breathe life and credibility into the development process. Consistently adhered to, the following principles will significantly enhance an organization's capacity to meet its strategic leadership requirements.

Model Development Behaviors

The most important principle is for senior managers to model leadership development behaviors and practices. It is one of the few widely accepted axioms in organizations that people respond to what leaders do, not what they say. If leadership development is to be taken seriously, then senior managers must align their actions and stated intentions, demonstrating their values in ways that others can see. First, they must make every effort to understand their own leadership style, including their strengths and weaknesses, and to use this to advance their personal learning. Increased self-awareness, important for everyone, is especially critical for senior managers, whose actions shape the attitudes and behaviors of countless others throughout the organization. The more insight managers gain about themselves, the better able they are to act consistently with their intentions, an accomplishment that sends a powerful message throughout the organization.

Second, senior managers need to actively coach their direct reports on key performance and development issues. At a minimum, this involves giving them candid and regular feedback, discussing their strengths and opportunities as leaders, and encouraging them to implement individual development plans tied to their personal and career goals. Coaching of this sort helps foster a broader developmental climate by underscoring the message that feedback and development are vital in the organization. When carried out effectively, coaching also reinforces the values and skills needed to sustain the leadership development process in the long run.

Make Development Part of Every Manager's Job

It's not enough for senior managers to model development behaviors; they must also hold others accountable for doing so. Regrettably, many managers pay lip service to development, either because they don't understand what their organization expects of them or, when they do, they are not consistently held accountable for their actions.

In a classic *Harvard Business Review* article, A. E. Pearson, former president of PepsiCo, exhorts senior managers to step up to this challenge by implementing an aggressive "people development" strategy. He describes the five-point plan PepsiCo used to "muscle build" an organization: (1) continuously raise the performance bar; (2) aggressively identify and develop high-potential managers; (3) align every facet of the organization—corporate culture, organizational structure, and policies—to reward development and upgrading efforts; (4) infuse the organization with outside talent; and (5) deploy human resources professionals to assist line managers in the development process (1987, p. 50).

While one can debate Pearson's tactics, it is hard to refute his success at PepsiCo or, for that matter, his underlying thesis: that setting clear development goals and holding managers accountable for achieving them are effective means of achieving competitive advantage. In the end, unless senior managers set aggressive developmental targets and are willing to hold themselves and others accountable, organizations are unlikely to close today's significant shortfall in leadership talent.

Embrace Fast-Cycle People Development

Changes taking place in organizations today require new sets of skills and new ways of thinking. As organizations shift from incremental to discontinuous change, they must simultaneously replace outmoded development strategies with fast-cycle approaches that accelerate the development of leaders. While there are limits to the speed individuals can learn new skills, today's realities require organizations to find radically more efficient development strategies.

An obvious first step is to identify and deploy managers whose talents and skills lend themselves to accelerated development. Whereas a premium in the past was placed on experience and a single-minded drive for success, the demand today is for people with strong interpersonal and influence skills, change-management competencies, and the ability and desire to learn from experience. A second, related strategy for accelerating development is to abandon assumptions about the type of job assignments or sequenced steps needed for optimal learning to take place. As hierarchically based, functional organizations give way to horizontally structured cross-functional organizations, how managers are assigned to developmental opportunities will have to be radically rethought. Instead of a logical stepwise progression, organizations will need to be more opportunistic in developing talent.

Consider the unique learning opportunities available during the early phases of large-scale organizational change. Most organizations initiating radical change establish high-performance, cross-functional teams to redesign core business processes and to help "architect" key components of the new organization. Given the breakthrough nature of these teams, managers participating on them have the chance to develop competencies in a few months that would normally take years to develop.

Link Leadership Development and Organizational Learning

Leadership development has traditionally focused on individual learning. Managers develop personal development plans and attend seminars to acquire specific competencies and skills. They are assigned to special task forces or given "stretch" assignments to broaden their experience and to learn new skills. Such person-centered strategies are effective in developing individual competencies, but don't ensure that leaders will develop the capacity to lead in increasingly complex, horizontal, team-based organizations. Yet this is precisely the environment that leaders will have to master in the future.

More and more the challenge is to develop leaders who possess superior individual talent but can apply it in the context of constantly changing team and organizational structures and processes. Senge (1990) makes this point when he observes that "one of the paradoxes of leadership in learning organizations is that it is both collective and individual" (p. 360).

Let's consider briefly the link between individual and organizational learning. According to Garvin (1993), learning organizations are skilled at five core activities: (1) basic problem solving; (2) experimentation with new ideas and approaches; (3) the ability to learn from past experience; (4) learning from others' experiences and best practices; and (5) transferring knowledge quickly and efficiently throughout an organization (p. 81). The first three of these strategies lie at the heart of individual learning, while the last two pertain to how personal learning is facilitated through discussion, dialogue, and shared experiences.

Opportunities to develop team and organizational learning skills have increased dramatically in recent years. Teams and networks of teams—not individuals—are emerging as the building blocks of the future. At an operational level, high-performance teams carry out the work individuals used to perform, creating new, radically different learning opportunities for prospective leaders. Cross-functional teams are redesigning business processes and managing across permeable boundaries, again affording new, team-based experiences. Similarly, action learning teams are tackling critical business issues while fostering the development of new leadership competencies and skills (Wick and Léon, 1993). Even at the top of organizations, teamwork is replacing traditional approaches (Nadler and Ancona, 1992).

If leaders capable of managing in new, team-based organizations are to be developed, then opportunities have to be created that link traditional development strategies with team and organizational learning opportunities. Sharing best practices at senior management conferences, encouraging benchmarking efforts, sponsoring action learning teams, and actively participating in company-sponsored culture change seminars are but a few of the initiatives that will develop new leadership competencies while simultaneously accelerating the pace of organizational change.

Summary

The turmoil and stress of discontinuous change are exacerbating existing gaps between needed leadership talent and available bench strength. This gap can be traced to the mindset and experiences of many senior managers and is reflected in the lack of attention and resources devoted to the selection and development of new leaders. To address this issue, senior managers must examine their underlying assumptions about leadership and be willing to increase their involvement and support for selection and development processes that will fill the leadership gap. For leaders willing to make this commitment, a process called strategic selection process can significantly enhance the quality of selection decisions.

Identifying talent is only the first step in a multiphase process that includes iterative cycles of selection and placement, development planning and implementation, performance appraisal, and reflection. To institutionalize this process, organizationwide development forums need to be established. These forums provide a context for discussing leadership issues and for monitoring the progress of development efforts throughout the organization. This work, in turn, is reinforced through development strategies including active coaching and mentoring by leaders at all levels; establishing aggressive development goals and holding leaders accountable for achieving them; implementing fast-cycle people-development strategies; and integrating person-centered training with innovative team and organizational learning opportunities. These initiatives, when fully implemented, will increase the supply of new leadership talent while enhancing the capacity of organizations to adapt to and lead discontinuous change.

PART FOUR

Leading Change

13

Beyond the Heroic Leader

David A. Nadler

This chapter will focus on the role of leadership in strategic organizational change, particularly *reorientations*—changes initiated in anticipation of future events. Re-creations, the other type of discontinuous change (see Chapter Two); often fail and leaders are then replaced. Thus, the key challenge for current organizational leadership is to learn how to effectively initiate, lead, and manage reorientations.

It appears that there are certain aspects of reorientation that are dependent upon the leader. The first is *strategic anticipation.* Reorientation requires the organization to accurately anticipate that the conditions for strategic change will arise in the future, and to determine the most effective responses. Unless the leadership somehow becomes involved in this anticipation, no change will be initiated. Second, reorientation requires a *created sense of urgency.* Since by definition the need for change is not apparent to all, some urgency is needed to stimulate behavior. Usually, only the leadership can create such a sense of urgency throughout the organization. Third, reorientation requires effective *creation and management of pain*. Urgency frequently results from pain, either immediate or anticipated. Pain, however, can motivate both functional and dysfunctional behavior. Again, only the leadership has the capacity both to create pain and shape the responses to it. Finally, reorientations succeed when people perceive the required change is *central*, that it is truly critical to the core issues of the organization. Centrality, if not apparent, can be defined only by leadership.

Therefore, it is understandable why no successful reorientations occur unless leaders play a major role, whether that be the existing leadership or new leadership brought in from the outside. The question, then, is what constitutes effective leadership in these situations?

The Heroic Leader

While the subject of leadership has received much attention over the years, the more specific issue of leadership during periods of change has only recently attracted serious attention (Burns, 1978; Bennis and Nanus, 1985; Tichy and Ulrich, 1984; Tichy and Devanna, 1986). What emerges is a picture of the special kind of leadership that appears to be critical during times of discontinuous organizational change. While various words have been used to portray this type of leadership, we prefer the term "heroic leader." It refers to a special quality that enables the leader to mobilize and sustain activity within an organization through specific personal actions combined with perceived personal characteristics. In many cases this is evidenced by the development of a very personal bond between the leader and the people in the organization.

At the core of the concept is the model of the charismatic leader. This is not the popular version of the charismatic leader— the great speechmaker, the television personality. Rather, this model has emerged from recent work aimed at identifying the nature of a particular type of leadership that successfully brings about changes in an individual's values, goals, needs, or aspirations (Berlew, 1974; House, 1977; Bass, 1985). Building from the general concept of charismatic leadership, what specifically characterizes the heroic leader of organizational change? We believe they demonstrate three major types of behavior, as outlined in Figure 13.3.

The first component of heroic leadership is *envisioning*—creating a picture of the future with which people can identify and which can generate excitement. By creating vision, the leader provides a vehicle for people to develop commitment, a common goal around which people can rally, and a way for people to feel successful.

Envisioning is accomplished through a range of different actions. The simplest form is articulation of a compelling vision in clear and dramatic terms. The vision needs to be challenging, meaningful, and worthy of pursuit, but it also needs to be credible. People must believe that it is possible to succeed in the pursuit of the vision. Other ways that leaders communicate the vision include the expectations that they express and their own actions—leaders must consistently demonstrate behaviors that symbolize and further that vision.

The second component is *energizing*. Here the role of the leader is the direct generation of energy—motivation to act—among members of the organization. How is this done? Different leaders engage in energizing in different ways, but some of the most common include demonstrating their own personal excitement and energy, combined with leveraging that excitement through direct

Figure 13.1. The Heroic Leader.

Envisioning
- Articulating a compelling vision
- Setting high expectations
- Modeling consistent behaviors

Energizing	**Enabling**
• Demonstrating personal excitement	• Expressing personal support
• Expressing personal confidence	• Empathizing
• Seeking, finding, and using success	• Expressing confidence in people

personal contact with large numbers of people in the organization. They express confidence in their own ability to succeed. They find, and use, successes to celebrate progress toward the vision.

The third component is *enabling*. The leader psychologically helps people act or perform in the face of challenging goals. Assuming that people are directed through a vision and motivated by the creation of energy, they then may need emotional assistance in accomplishing their tasks. This enabling is achieved in several ways. Heroic leaders demonstrate empathy—the ability to listen, understand, and share the feelings of those in the organization. They express support for individuals. Perhaps most important, heroic leaders express their confidence in people's ability to perform effectively and to meet challenges.

When leaders act in these ways, what functions are they performing that help bring about change? First, they provide a psychological focal point for the energies, hopes, and aspirations of people in the organization. Second, they may serve as the embodiment of some type of organizational "ego ideal." They represent what the organization hopes to become. Through their personal effectiveness and attractiveness they build a very personal and intimate bond between themselves and the organization. Thus, they can become a source of sustained energy, a hero with whom people can identify.

However, even successfully accomplishing all those things might still not be enough. There are a number of inherent limitations to the effectiveness of the heroic leader, many stemming from the risks associated with leadership revolving around a single individual. Some of the key potential problems are:

- *Unrealistic expectations.* In creating a vision and getting people energized, the leader may create expectations that are unrealistic or unattainable. These can backfire if the leader cannot live up to the expectations.

- *Dependency and counterdependency.* A strong, visible, and energetic leader may spur different psychological responses. Some people may become overly dependent on the leader; in some cases whole organizations become dependent. Everyone else stops initiating actions and always waits for the leader to provide direction. They may become passive or reactive. On the other extreme, others may be uncomfortable with strong personal presence and may spend a lot of time and energy demonstrating that the emperor has no clothes.

- *Reluctance to disagree with the leader.* The heroic leader's approval or disapproval becomes an important commodity. People may become hesitant to disagree or come into conflict with the leader, which may lead to stifling conformity.
- *Need for continuing heroism.* The leader may become trapped by the expectation that the heroic actions will continue unabated. This may cause the leader to act in ways that are not functional, or (if the heroism is not produced) cause a crisis of leadership credibility.
- *Potential feelings of betrayal.* When and if things do not work out as the leader had envisioned, then the potential exists for individuals to feel betrayed. They may become frustrated and angry, and some of that anger may be directed at the individual who created the expectations that have now been betrayed.
- *Disenfranchisement of next levels of management.* A consequence of the strong heroic leader is that the next levels of management can easily become disenfranchised. They lose their ability to lead because no direction, vision, exhortation, reward, or punishment is meaningful unless it comes directly from the heroic leader. The heroic leader thus may end up underleveraging the senior management.
- *Limitations of range of the individual leader.* When the leadership process is built around an individual, management's ability to deal with various issues is limited by the time, energy, expertise, and interest of that individual. This is particularly problematic during periods of change when different types of issues demand different types of competencies that a single individual may not possess. Different types of strategic changes make different managerial demands and call for different personal characteristics. Finally, there may be limits to the number of strategic changes that one individual can lead over the life of an organization.

In light of these risks, it appears that the heroic leader, while necessary for effective reorientation, is not sufficient. Effective leaders of change need to be more than just heroic.

Instrumental Leadership

Successful reorientations also seem to be characterized by the presence of another type of leader, who focuses not on exciting people and changing their goals, but on making sure that individuals throughout the organization do indeed behave in the ways needed for the change to occur. The role of leadership is to clarify required behaviors, build in measurement, and administer rewards and punishments so that people perceive that behavior consistent with the change is instrumental for them in achieving their own goals. We call this type of leadership *instrumental leadership,* since it focuses on managing structure to create individual instrumentalities. The basis of this approach is in expectancy theories of motivation, which propose that people will perform those behaviors that they perceive as instrumental for acquiring valued outcomes (Vroom, 1964; Campbell, Dunnette, Lawler, and Weick, 1970). Leadership, in this context, involves managing environments to create conditions that will motivate the required behavior (House, 1971; Oldham, 1976).

In practice, instrumental leadership of change involves three elements of behavior. The first is *structuring.* The leader invests time in creating structures that make it clear what types of behavior are required. This may involve setting goals, establishing standards, defining roles, and similar activities. In reorientations it involves detailed planning about what people will be needed to do and how they will be required to act during different phases of the change.

The second element of instrumental leadership is *monitoring.* This involves creating systems and processes to measure, monitor, and assess both behavior and results and to administer corrective action (see Lawler and Rhode, 1976). The third element is *rewarding*—which involves both rewarding behavior that is consistent with the requirements of the change and punishing that which is not.

The Role of Mundane Behaviors

Typical descriptions of both heroic and instrumental leaders tend to focus on significant events, critical incidents, and "grand gestures." The vision of the change manager is frequently exemplified by the key speech or public event that is a potential watershed event. While these are important arenas for leadership, change leadership (both heroic and instrumental) frequently occurs through an accumulation of less dramatic, day-to-day patterns of activity, which have been called mundane behaviors (Peters, 1978). Through relatively unobtrusive acts, the leader can help to shape the patterns of events that people see. Examples of mundane behavior that can have a great impact include:

Allocation of time and calendar management
Shaping of physical settings
Control over agendas of events or meetings
Use of events such as lunches, meetings, and so on
Summarization—post hoc interpretation of what occurred
Use of humor, stories, and myths
Small symbolic acts, including rewards and punishments

In these and many other ways, the leader can use daily activities to emphasize important issues, identify desirable behavior, and help create patterns and meaning out of the various transactions that make up organizational life.

The Complementarity of Leadership Approaches

It appears that effective organizational reorientation requires both heroic and instrumental leadership. The heroic leader excites individuals, shapes their aspirations, and directs their energy. In practice, however, this may not be enough to sustain patterns of desired behavior. Employees may be committed to the vision, but over time other forces (information, rewards, feedback) may influence their behavior, particularly when they are not in direct personal contact with the leader. This is particularly relevant during periods of change when the formal organization and the informal social system may lag behind the leader, communicating outdated messages or rewarding traditional behavior. Instrumental leadership is needed to create the systems that will support the continuation of new behaviors, to ensure that people really do act in a manner consistent with their new goals. Either one alone seems insufficient to achieve change.

The complementarity of leadership approaches (House, in press) and the necessity for both creates a dilemma. Success in implementing these approaches seems to be associated with the personal style, characteristics, needs, and skills of the individual who is the leader. Thus, a person who is adept at one approach may have difficulty executing the other. For example, heroic leaders may have problems with the tasks involved in achieving control. Many heroic leaders have narcissistic tendencies—in fact a certain degree of narcissism may be necessary to be an effective heroic leader. The problem is that these individuals are frequently motivated by a strong desire to be loved or to receive affection from those around them. They therefore have problems delivering unpleasant messages, dealing with performance problems, or creating situations that could attract negative feelings. Only the truly exceptional individual can handle the range of both approaches. While such individuals exist, an alternative may be to involve others in leadership roles, thus complementing the strengths and weaknesses of one individual leader.

The limitations of the individual leader (of either type) pose a significant challenge. Heroic leadership has a "broad reach." It can influence many people, but is limited by the frequency and intensity of contact with the individual leader. Instrumental leadership is also limited by the degree to which the individual leader can structure, observe, measure, and reward behavior. These limitations present significant problems for achieving reorientation. One implication is that structural extensions of leadership should be created in the process of managing reorientations. A second implication is that human extensions of leadership need to be created to broaden the scope and impact of leader actions. This leads to a third aspect of leadership and change—extending leadership beyond the individual leader, or creating institutionalized leadership.

Institutionalizing the Leadership of Change

Given the limitations of the individual heroic leader, the challenge is to broaden the range of individuals who can perform the critical leadership functions during periods of significant organizational change. There are three potential leverage points for extending leadership—the senior team, the broader senior management, and the development of leadership throughout the organization (see Figure 13.2).

Leveraging the Senior Team

The group of individuals who report directly to the individual leader—the executive or senior team—is the first logical place to look for opportunities to extend and institutionalize leadership. Development of an effective, visible, and dynamic senior team can be a major step in getting around the problems and limitations of the individual leader. Several actions appear to be important in enhancing the effectiveness of the senior team.

Visible Empowerment of the Team. A first step is the visible empowerment of the team, or "anointing" the team as an extension of the individual leader. There are two different aspects to this empow-

Figure 13.2. Institutionalized Leadership.

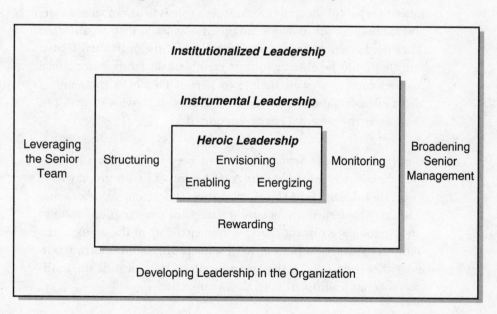

erment: objective and symbolic. Objective empowerment involves providing team members with the autonomy and resources to serve effectively. Symbolic empowerment involves communication messages (through information, symbols, and mundane behaviors) that show the organization that these individuals are indeed extensions of the leader, and ultimately key components of the leadership. Symbolic empowerment can be done through the use of titles, the designation of organizational structures, and the visible presence of individuals in ceremonial roles.

Individual Development of Team Members. Empowerment will fail if the people on the team are not capable of capitalizing on their anointed status. A major problem is that the members of the senior team frequently are the product of the very systems, structures, and values that the reorientation seeks to change. Participating in the change—and, more important—leading it—may require a significant switching of cognitive gears. It demands that the senior team members think very differently about the business and about managing. This need for personal change at the most senior level has implications for the selection of senior team members. It also may mean that part of the individual leader's role is to help coach, guide, and support people in developing their own leadership capabilities. They need not (and should not) be a clone of the individual leader, but all should be able to initiate credible leadership actions in a manner consistent with their own personal styles. Ultimately, it also puts a demand on the leader to deal with those who won't or can't make the personal changes required.

Composition of the Senior Team. The need for the senior team to lead change may mean that the composition of that team may have to be altered. Different skills, capacities, styles, and value orientations may be needed. In fact, most successful reorientations seem to involve some significant changes in the makeup of the senior team. This may require outplacement of some people and importing others, either from outside the organization or from outside the coalition that has traditionally led the organization.

The Inducement of Strategic Anticipation. A critical issue in reorientations is *strategic anticipation*. By definition, a reorientation is a strategic organizational change that is initiated in anticipation of significant external events. Reorientation occurs because the organization's leadership perceives competitive advantage from initiating the changes earlier rather than later. The question is, who is responsible for thinking about and anticipating external events, and ultimately deciding that reorientation is necessary? In some cases, the individual leader does this, but the task is enormous. This is where the senior team can be helpful, because as a group it can scan a larger number of events and potentially be more creative in analyzing the environment and the process of anticipation.

Companies that are successful anticipators create conditions in which anticipation is more likely to occur. They invest in activities that foster anticipation, such as environmental scanning, experiments or probes inside the organization (frequently on the periphery), and frequent contacts with the outside. The senior team has a major role in initiating, sponsoring, and leveraging these activities.

The Senior Team as a Learning System. For a senior team to benefit from its involvement in leading change, it must become an effective system for learning about the business, the nature of change, and the task of managing the change. The challenge is to bond the team together while avoiding insularity. One of the down sides of such team structures is that they become isolated from the rest of the organization, they develop patterns of dysfunctional conformity, avoid conflict, and over time develop patterns of learned incompetence. All of this diminishes the team's capacity for effective strategic anticipation, and it decreases the team's ability to provide effective leadership of the reorientation process.

There are several ways to avoid negative consequences. One approach is to work hard and keep the team an open system, receptive to outside ideas and information. This can be accomplished by creating a constant stream of events that expose people to new ideas—speakers or visitors brought in to meet with the team, visits by the team to other organizations, frequent contact with customers, and planned "deep contact" in the organization (informal and nondisruptive regular data collection through personal contact, such as breakfasts and focus groups).

A second approach is to shape and manage the internal group process of the team itself. This involves working on effective group leadership, building effective team-member skills, creating meeting-management discipline, acquiring group problem-solving and information-processing skills, and ultimately creating norms that promote effective learning, innovation, and problem solving.

As a final note, it is important to remember that frequently there are significant obstacles to developing effective senior teams to lead changes. The issues of skills and selection have been mentioned, but more important is the question of power and succession. A team is most successful when there is a perception of common fate. Team members have to believe that the success of the team will, in the long run, be more salient to them than their individual short-run success. In many situations, this can be accomplished through appropriate structures, objectives, and incentives. But this fails when there are pending (or anticipated) decisions to be made about senior management succession. In these situations, the quality of collaboration tends to deteriorate significantly and effective team leadership of change becomes problematic. The individual leader must manage the timing and process of succession in relation to the requirements for team leadership so that conflicting (and mutually exclusive) incentives are not created.

Broadening Senior Management

A second step in moving beyond individual leadership of change is the further extension of the leadership beyond the executive or senior team to include a broader set of people who make up the senior management of the organization—people one or two levels down from the executive team. This set of individuals, generally ranging in size from 30 to 120 people, is in fact the senior operating management of most sizable organizations, and is looked upon as senior management by most employees. In many cases (and particularly during times of change) they do not *feel* like senior management, and thus they are not positioned to lead the change. They feel like participants (at best) and victims (at worst).

This group can be particularly problematic since they may be more embedded in the current system of organizing and managing than some of the senior team. They may be less prepared to change, they frequently have molded themselves to fit the current organizational style, and they may feel disenfranchised by the very act of developing a strong executive team, particularly if that team has been assembled by bringing in people from outside the organization.

The task is to make this group feel like senior management, to get them signed up for the change, and to motivate and enable them to work as an extension of the senior team. Many of the implications are similar to those mentioned above in relation to the top team; however, there are special problems of size and lack of proximity to the individual heroic leader. Part of the answer is to get the senior team to take responsibility for developing their own team as leaders of change. Other specific actions may include:

- *Rites of passage.* Creating symbolic events that help these individuals to feel more a part of senior management.
- *Senior groups.* Creating structures (councils, boards, committees, conferences) to maintain contact with this group and reinforce their sense of participation as members of senior management.
- *Participation in planning change.* Involving these people in the early diagnosing of the need to change and planning the change strategies associated with the reorientation. This is particularly useful in getting them to feel more like owners of the change, rather than its victims.
- *Intensive communication.* Maintaining a constant stream of open communication to and from this group. It is the lack of information and perspective that psychologically disenfranchises them.

Developing Leadership in the Organization

A third arena for enhancing the leadership of reorientation is through the organizational structures, systems, and process for the development of leadership. These frequently lag behind the reorientation, when they should be in tune with the focus on strategic anticipation. The management development system of many organizations frequently works effectively to create managers who will fit well with the organizational environment that the leadership seeks to abandon.

Chapter Twelve describes many techniques for developing the new breed of leaders needed for change. Here we will only recap the main points.

- *Definition of managerial competence.* Factors that have contributed to managerial success in the past may be the seeds of failure in the future.
- *Sourcing managerial talent.* Significantly different sources for acquiring leaders or potential leaders are usually needed. Because of the lead time involved, managerial sourcing has to be approached as a long-term task, five to ten years.
- *Socialization.* As people move into positions of leadership, deliberate actions must be taken to teach them how the social system works. During periods of reorientation, the socialization process ought to lead rather than lag behind the change.
- *Management education.* Reorientation may require managers and leaders to use new skills, competencies, or knowledge. This creates a demand for effective management education.
- *Career management.* The most potent factor in the development of effective leaders is the nature of their job experiences; the challenge is how to ensure they get the appropriate experiences. Preparing people to lead reorientations may mean a major rethinking of the types of experiences they need and building in processes to ensure that they get those experiences. It calls for a deliberate strategy of balancing current contribution with investment for the future when placing people in job assignments.
- *Seeding talent.* Developing leadership for change may also require deliberate leveraging of the available talent. This implies very thoughtful placement of individual leaders in different situations and parts of the organization, the use of transfers, and the whole notion of strategic placement.

Summary

At the broadest level, leadership of organizational change has three basic components:

1. *Excitement* of the organization and individuals to change through the concept of the heroic leader
2. *Instrumental direction* of behavior through structuring, monitoring, and rewarding
3. *Enterprise* of leadership: moving beyond the individual leader and focusing on the senior team, the broader senior management, and leadership development through the organization

Leadership is an area that has stimulated years of exploration and still eludes full understanding. The relationship between leadership and organizational change poses even greater challenges. The task is critical, however, if our knowledge of how to build more effective organizations is to continue to grow.

14

The Emerging Role
of the CEO

Jeffrey D. Heilpern

In recent years American competitive performance and corporate asset values have been under siege. CEOs face intense scrutiny from all angles—above and below, external and internal. Leading large, complex organizations in an era of discontinuous change is a staggering challenge. The rules of engagement are changing—and so they should: Our survival and prosperity as a postmodern society are at stake.

Seven Key Trends in Corporate America

Important trends are now visible that are fundamentally changing the nature of the leadership responsibility and accountability facing CEOs. These trends raise a number of difficult challenges for CEOs in today's charged context. In particular, seven key trends in corporate America are fundamentally reshaping the arena of corporate governance and the multiple relationships that a CEO must manage with great skill to be a successful leader.

1. *Many venerable benchmark companies have gotten into enormous difficulty.* Few would have ever predicted that so many U.S. corporations with sustained growth and success records would tumble so far and so fast. Prominent examples include IBM, GM, American Express, Westinghouse, Kodak, Sears, and Digital Equipment Corporation. Hundreds of billions of dollars of corporate value have disappeared, to the chagrin of shareholders, managers, employees, board members, the financial community, customers, and suppliers. What was assumed to be safe and predictable has proven to be uncertain and unreliable. The national corporate psyche has been damaged. Ultimately, this is probably a healthy development, because it forces change, learning, and improvement on all levels.

2. *Job security for CEOs has greatly diminished.* We are witnessing an unprecedented and uncharted period of massive CEO removals. Outright firings and forced early retirements are increasing dramatically. This changing reality of power at the top has been discussed with painful detail in the business press. For example, a recent "News/Trends" column in *Fortune*® magazine, poetically called "A Week of Woe for the CEO," lists no less than thirteen major CEO departures in the last year alone. "In one tumultuous week at the end of January 1993, John Akers and Paul Lego joined the parade of embattled CEOs forced into retirement in the past 12 months. And James Robinson III of American Express finally departed, after first facing down his fractious board" (Saporito, 1993, p. 10). The notion of the CEO with close to the divine right of kings has itself been dethroned.

3. *Involvement and accountability of boards of directors for corporate and CEO performance are increasing.* As a direct result of the dramatic performance problems and financial losses of so many esteemed companies, not only have many highly regarded CEOs been forced out, but boards are feeling an increased level of heat and pressure to be more accountable. The pain and embarrassment some board members (who often are chairmen and CEOs in

other top corporations) are experiencing during this seismic shift
was dramatically reported as follows (Saporito, p. 68):

> The voice was Tennessee drawl, but the sentences were
> clipped and pointed. "There is going to be change.
> This is a tough board. This is not American Express."
> The speaker was IBM director, Thomas Frist, chair-
> man of Hospital Corp. of America in Nashville. He
> was talking on the evening of January 26, only hours
> after the end of a long IBM board meeting, after Chair-
> man John Akers had announced he would step down
> and after the directors had officially launched a search
> for a new chief executive. One day before, the Amer-
> ican Express board, supposedly on the way to tossing
> out Chairman James Robinson III, had made itself a
> laughingstock by letting him stay—changing his job,
> yes, but leaving the business world with the impres-
> sion that the deck chairs had been rearranged, nothing
> more.

That decision was extremely short-lived. But it was only after
additional howls of protest from the largest and most powerful
institutional investors that Robinson finally agreed to step down
completely and leave the company.

4. *More tangible, proactive, and meaningful board roles
are being called for by a growing chorus.* John Smale, the retired
chairman and CEO of Procter & Gamble, now the nonexecutive
chairman of General Motors after leading the assault on Bob Stempel, the previous, struggling chairman and CEO, has recently proposed the following eight rules to "build a better board" (Martin,
1993, p. 10):

1. There clearly should be a majority of outside
    directors.
2. The independent members of the board should
    elect a lead director.
3. The independent directors should meet alone in
    executive session on a regularly scheduled basis.

4. The independent directors should take responsibility for all board procedures.
5. The board should have the basic responsibility for selection of its own members.
6. The board should conduct regularly scheduled performance reviews of the CEO and key executives.
7. The board must understand and fully endorse the company's long-term strategies.
8. The board must give an adequate amount of attention to its most important responsibility: the selection of the CEO.

These rules will in many cases change the very nature of corporate governance and remove a serious degree of power from CEOs, especially those whose performance is less than stellar. For those CEOs, notes *Fortune*® magazine, "It would put them where they should be, beholden, employees of the stockholders" (Martin, 1993, p. 10).

5. *Shareholders' views and desires are having unprecedented impact on corporate decisions, including the question of who is allowed to stay at the helm as CEO.* Such increased involvement is a mixed blessing for CEOs and boards of directors. It clearly ups the ante for performance and provides some additional tonnage to the board's weapons in managing the CEO. Former Westinghouse CEO Paul Lego commented at the time he was forced to resign, "The entire market and structure in the United States relative to the relationship between shareholders and companies is changing—it's in a dynamic mode" (Saporito, 1993, p. 10).

In addition to large institutional investors becoming much more activist, signs of unrest appear from new and surprising quarters. Consider the following (*New York Times,* June 11, 1993, p. D3):

Shareholder Sues Utility

Merle Thorpe, Jr., a longtime shareholder of Citizens Utilities, broke with the company yesterday and sued its directors for approving an unusually generous pay package for Leonard Tow, the company's chairman and chief executive.

The suit, which accuses the directors of breaching their fiduciary duty for not standing up to Mr. Tow, was filed in Delaware Chancery Court, joining four others that were filed last month by plaintiffs' attorneys.

Mr. Thorpe, a 76-year-old Washington lawyer who has practiced securities law for five decades, said his suit is different in that he has been a shareholder of Citizens for nearly 30 years and owns at least $4 million of its stock. Thus, unlike many plaintiff's lawyers who can be partial to quick settlement, Mr. Thorpe contends he wants a full airing of the issues that have been raised concerning the company's pay practices and direction. The 11 directors on Citizens' board are the focus of Mr. Thorpe's anger.

The stakes and negative consequences of lackluster performance and self-serving practices are getting louder and clearer.

6. *Increasing use and value of a "lead director" role.* Many experienced executives and board members are calling for an additional power player at the top beside the combined chairman and CEO. Some favor a nonexecutive chairman, which has recently proved helpful at General Motors. Others, including Harvard Business School professor Jay Lorsch and General Motors chairman John Smale himself, are calling for the independent members of the board to select a lead director in all companies. The balance of power will shift as the responsibility, involvement, and authority of the board members increase.

7. *Teamwork at the top.* The role of chief operating officer in large corporations is increasingly held not by one person but by a senior management team led by the CEO. This development adds yet another dimension and challenge for the CEO, who now must be an effective team builder and team leader, not just a strategist, decision maker, and motivator of key individuals. (See *Teamwork at the Top,* Nadler and Ancona, 1992, for an in-depth examination

of the problems, pitfalls, and promising solutions facing such senior teams.)

These seven trends have brought into sharper focus the multiple relationships with key constituencies that the CEO must ad-
roitly manage. It is to these key audiences, or constituencies, that
we turn next to better understand the leverage points that successful
leaders must master and juggle.

A 360-Degree Map of CEO Constituencies

To understand better the CEO's world in our era of discontinuous
change, it is useful to map out the various stakeholder groups that
form key constituencies for the CEO's leadership. (See Figure 14.1.)
Each of these constituencies has a unique set of demands and benefits that can both challenge and assist the CEO. While these groups
overlap and interact to a significant degree, it is important to examine each constituency to identify their particular hot buttons and
unique requirements. Ultimately, the CEO, as the most highly leveraged change agent in the entire enterprise, must create and *market*
a vision and plan for a different future to each of these segments,
who look to the CEO as the ultimate supplier of personal
leadership.

1.   *The board of directors.* The best CEOs recognize that the
board serves as the fulcrum in the triad of corporate governance,
balancing the roles and needs of the shareowners and management.
A highly regarded statesman in the arena of corporate governance,
Ira M. Millstein, has recently put forward the provocative notion of
the "certifying board," one that works cooperatively but with meaningful checks and balances as the "focal point of the governance
process, serving as the fulcrum of accountability in the triad of
shareholders, boards, and managers" (from a presentation to the
Conference Board on May 18, 1993). The benefits of such an arrangement are manifold to CEOs who are both effective and secure.
Those CEOs who are underperforming or prefer not to collaborate
with the board will be displeased and even threatened. But greater
involvement by the board will be an increasing fact of life, so all

Figure 14.1. CEO Constituencies.

chief executives should actually welcome and encourage such involvement. The best CEOs proactively and often seek meaningful input, guidance, and "air cover" from the leaders on their boards.

2. *The shareholders and the financial community.* These two constituencies have several similar requirements for the CEO. They want candor, realistic assessments of current and future situations and scenarios, accurate information, and accessibility when appropriate. The multitude of questions asked of CEOs at analyst meetings shows the thirst that the financial community has for straight talk and being kept "in the loop." Openness and candor, coupled with the authority of knowledge that a good CEO has, is a core competency and leadership behavior that pays great dividends over time for the CEO and the company. Those who shun contact, try to manipulate, or dismiss with imperial arrogance the financial community and key institutional shareowners make a se-

rious mistake. They only end up hurting themselves and their companies.

3. *Governmental and regulatory bodies and decision makers.* As the interdependence and complexity of the global village dramatically increase, a judicious mix of cooperation and confrontation will be required. While alignment and collaboration are always the preferred mode, situations exist where a CEO must take on regulators or elected officials. The political and regulatory realities call for effective coalition building, stakeholder management, and some high-stakes gambles led personally by the CEO. These dramas occur at the local, state, regional, federal, and international level. The diplomatic and negotiating skills needed by CEOs will only increase over time.

4. *The senior management team and the organization's top leaders.* As the chief change agents and marketers of the vision, values, and strategies of their corporations, effective CEOs recognize and actively work with their senior team and the company's top one hundred or so leaders as true customers of their personal leadership. Alignment across and down through an organization serves as a fundamental building block for successful performance over time and the capacity to successfully change. Highly empowered leaders at all levels of a company are motivated, helped, and enhanced by clear, consistent, and challenging priorities, decisions, and messages from the top.

5. *Customers and suppliers.* The total quality movement worldwide has profoundly and permanently increased the importance and centrality of treating both customers and suppliers as partners in the never-ending journey to meet or exceed customer requirements at reduced cost. Good CEOs today spend a meaningful amount of time with customers and suppliers, serving as a lead problem solver and ambassador of total customer satisfaction.

6. *Employees throughout the company.* Just as quality improvement is the job of every single employee, so too the entire employee body is a key constituency of the CEO for the transmission of the vision and change agenda. Enriched jobs, self-managing teams, and broader spans of control all reinforce the importance of all members of an organization. In fact, often those farthest away from the CEO have the most contact and influence on customers

and their "moments of truth." (See Jan Carlzon's book, *Moments of Truth,* for a fuller exploration of the high-impact moments of encounter and interaction with customers.) Managing by walking (and traveling) around, town hall meetings, live telecasts with remote input of questions, open voice mail and electronic mail systems, and educating senior management through exposure to improvement efforts at all levels—all these serve to increase understanding and communication between a CEO and the massive segment of employees. Truly effective leaders know that only by capturing the *discretionary effort* of every human being in the enterprise—and recognizing that all are members of the same team—will an organization continue to improve.

Anticipating and responding effectively to the needs and concerns of each of these six constituencies above are fundamental requirements for CEO success in today's world of tumultuous change. Let us now look at some of the specific personal and psychological challenges that arise for a role model CEO.

Personal and Psychological Challenges Facing the CEO

The CEO has a unique amount of power and responsibility in all that he or she does, especially as the chief corporate change agent. That position includes the pressure and challenge of being all of the following, often simultaneously:

• *Heroic leader.* Whether wanted or not, the CEO must accept that others project onto him or her their desires for a powerful, knowing, confident, capable leader. Such projections create a useful increase in perceived power but can also carry with it certain burdens: the pressure to continue to work magic, the inevitable failures and disappointments as some wrong choices are made, and the loneliness of being the leader to whom all others look for answers and solutions (see Chapter Thirteen).

• *Architect.* The CEO must directly take on the tasks of thinking through possible design options and the important trade-offs and preferences involved in creating an effective and adaptive organizational architecture. Because form follows function, no

CEO should allow an enterprise design to emerge that he or she does not personally believe will enhance sustained competitive advantage and bring the shared vision to fruition.

- *Captain and navigator.* Not only is the CEO the principal architect but also the real-time captain and navigator in the rocky shoals of the 1990s. Adjustments must be made frequently as the winds and weather conditions change abruptly, and the responsibility of being on duty twenty-four hours a day, 365 days a year, is enormous. The ability to hold steady under severe stress and pressure and still convey a sense of confidence and inner security that any and all difficulties can be handled is a differentiating characteristic of gifted leaders.

- *Guardian of the themes.* Over a period of years, the CEO must continually sound the trumpets for the key themes and values that serve as both a rallying cry and guideposts—even to the point of boredom. CEOs must not become scattered by too often following their intellectual and personal hunger for new ideas, emerging concepts, and additional initiatives, no matter how inviting and seductive they might appear.

- *Contrarian.* The contrarian rallies the troops and boosts morale and confidence when times are difficult, but raises the bar and ensures that no one gets too smug or complacent when times are good.

Playing all those roles simultaneously raises a number of personal and psychological challenges:

1. *Living in a fishbowl,* where everything is amplified and scrutinized. It may be painful, but ignoring this reality can be perilous. Ironically, most CEOs want to have more influence than they feel they now have on other people, yet they are often surprised or even annoyed by how closely their every word and move are noted and interpreted.

2. *Avoiding false modesty,* which can truly be harmful. Even though humility is a sincere virtue, leaders need to *want* something, and they need to inspire confidence. No leader ever got very far saying "I'll be glad if I can lead this company half as well as my predecessor."

3. *Tapping one's full self.* To draw on the deepest values,

energy, aspirations, and power, the CEO must be willing to become friendly with his or her "shadow" side, the inner world where the soul abides. Exploring the inner world is not something most people are trained to do or rewarded for divulging, even though its benefits can be profound. Such travels often require long and lonely hours of introspection as well as adequate time with those select people with whom one can let one's hair down.

4.   *Recognizing the fine line between a healthy expansive personality and too much narcissism and selfishness.* Seeing oneself objectively is impossible. Therefore the CEO must have some trusted sources of feedback and counsel to help identify and travel along that fine line. Subordinates typically fear upsetting their boss. The more self-centered or narcissistic the CEO, the less likely feedback will be volunteered or accepted. Denial is a very strong defense mechanism—until it cracks. Special efforts must be made not to fall victim to one's lofty self-image and too fully believing one's good press, either as an individual or a company.

5.   *Seeking feedback and acknowledging weaknesses.* All human beings have certain blind spots or areas in which they are in effect tone deaf. But for the CEO, such limits and human frailties are magnified. As an antidote, feedback needs to be solicited and worked with to ensure that damage is not unintentionally inflicted on the team and the organization. As Carl Rogers (1972) so profoundly stated in his masterpiece *On Becoming a Person,* "The facts are friendly," even if painful, because only when one accepts what is can one change. Soliciting and responding to meaningful feedback on a periodic basis are critical CEO success factors.

6.   *Really letting go of some things.* No one ever likes to plan a future they won't be part of, and few leaders in history have voluntarily given up power. But in this age of growing empowerment at all levels of organizations and society, the best leaders are those who know when and how to step back and let others play a greater role, even when they could do it better themselves.

Helpful Resources and Promising Solutions

Fortunately, a number of mechanisms and sources of support have emerged and been rigorously field tested. Some of the most helpful include the following:

- *A real senior team.* It takes sustained effort and commitment, and the willingness to take some risks, but a high-performing senior team can be created. Done well, profound leverage and power result. But all too often what passes as teamwork is a veneer of politeness, covering masks, competition, and gamesmanship. A CEO can only develop a truly high performing senior team if he or she insists upon it.

- *The kitchen cabinet.* Beyond the formal senior management team or official cabinet, successful leaders, both business and political, need a small number of loyal and trusted associates who can candidly talk through what needs to be done and help the CEO think through options, tradeoffs, and possible unintended consequences of key decisions and choices. Some overlap usually exists between the kitchen cabinet and the formal management team. A well-documented and successful example in the political world is John Kennedy's sessions during the Cuban missile crisis that included a mix of cabinet officials and personal aides.

- *One-on-one discussions with a trusted personal adviser.* Most leaders have one or two special sources of personal counsel, occasionally someone inside the organization but usually not; all those who work full time in the enterprise are actors in the corporate drama with their own agenda and personal needs. More often, an outsider, either an experienced personal friend, colleague, or consultant, has the objectivity, independence, perspective, and requisite expertise to be helpful. Providing honest feedback and challenging the CEO's assumptions and personal behavior are not easy to do. At times this can be risky and unpleasant for both sides. But such interventions are essential for a CEO to continue to learn, grow, and improve. As one particularly forward-looking CEO, Phil Quigley of Pacific Telesis, likes to put it, "It's important for you to be in my face on this stuff."

- *Open boundaries with customers and suppliers.* These are a source of tremendous learning and enhanced performance. Almost all organizations and their senior executives are still too insular. With feedback and information from outside, long-held assumptions can be tested and revised, personal trust and lines of communication can be established, and more real-time data and facts are made available. All these provide the CEO with powerful tools to enhance credibility and capability as a leader grappling with discontinuous change.

• *CEO benchmark discussions.* Noncompetitive discussions between CEOs in different industries or through industry associations provide a rare source of perspective, reality testing, encouragement, and solace. Such benchmark visits and discussions are a useful product of the total quality benchmarking practice. For CEOs, the most valuable discussions are held one on one, to ensure privacy, confidentiality, and directness. Having corresponding staff members from both organizations present frequently lowers the level of disclosure to a less personal, safer common denominator. Sometimes, however, a third-party facilitator who knows both participants and their companies can be helpful in guiding the discussion and debriefing both CEOs after the session to maximize learning.

• *Organization learning.* CEOs are in the best position within an organization to create both the mechanisms and the climate for productive organizational learning to occur. A key factor that helps or hinders learning is the degree to which blaming and judging are part of the learning process. Effective CEOs serve as role models, acknowledging their own fallibility along with their desire to face problems as a stimulus to learn and to improve. To be a wise leader one must be a wise person. And as Scott Peck notes, "Wise people learn not to dread but actually to welcome problems . . . because it is in meeting and solving problems that life has its meaning. Problems are the cutting edge that distinguishes between success and failure. Problems call forth our courage and our wisdom" (1978, p. 16).

• *Productive and friendly bickering.* Too often in corporate environments genuine differences are not allowed to surface and be worked through in a productive way. A powerful approach is to explicitly give all involved permission to engage in friendly and productive bickering. Two prerequisites seem to be necessary. First, those involved must have a shared vision of the enterprise they are committed to build together. Second, they must have a genuine respect and personal regard for one another. With those two elements in place, people can allow a great deal of both heat and light to be generated that is productive. Ironically, in organizational life, we need more genuine respect and caring as well as more productive bickering.

Conclusion

Each of the resources and solutions described above has helped willing CEOs enhance their own capability as the chief agents of change in their organizations. In this era of discontinuous change, the CEO's ability to fulfill this role has become all the more important and difficult. Without a dramatic increase in the effectiveness of chief executives as change agents, our preeminence in the hypercompetitive global village of the twenty-first century is at significant risk.

A "Virtual" Interview
with Five Change Leaders

A. Elise Walton
Robert B. Shaw

As part of our objective of testing our models, and continually learning about change, we interviewed several corporate leaders on their view of change. We selected executives who had managed or were managing major organizational transitions:

> Bob Allen, CEO of AT&T
> Jamie Houghton, CEO of Corning, Inc.
> Jon Madonna, CEO of KPMG
> Jeff Stiefler, president of American Express
> Craig Weatherup, president and CEO of PepsiCo

We examined several areas, such as how to initiate change, types of resistance, the role of the CEO and leadership teams, and words of advice on change management. Our interviews were conducted separately, and we organized their responses by common themes.

Note: We would like to thank Kathleen Morris and Charles Raben for conducting several of the interviews in this chapter.

When did you first realize that radical change was needed in your corporation? What factors impressed upon you the need for major change?

- *Allen:* I felt the need for significant change in my bones. It came from my daily experiences with customers and with my own people. My interactions with AT&T's customers left me with a high level of concern. The pressing issue was how to be more effective in serving their needs with satisfaction. We were high priced and we were losing market share. It wasn't rotten, but it wasn't good.

  It was also obvious that our employees were worried about the future. There weren't a lot of offers of good ideas about how to solve our problems, but a lot of criticism and a lack of enthusiasm for the (then) current condition. I knew we needed to change, though I wasn't sure exactly what, nor how to make the necessary changes. I began by trying to answer a few fundamental questions—Where are we going as a company? What are the values that bind us? What do we stand for? What's our competitive edge—real or potential?

  I came at it with the belief that you have to change or you stagnate—and if you stagnate, you die. We were driven by a fear that you don't want to be like other companies who did well for a while and then stopped doing well. My personal set of values and beliefs makes me uncomfortable with stability and the status quo. I am fundamentally incapable of being satisfied for very long with these types of things.

- *Houghton:* I realized early in my tenure as CEO of Corning that something had to change and change in a major way. The morale was terrible and we just had to do things differently. We were in the middle of a major recession, and Corning was in really tough shape, barely breaking even in operating profits.

  I'd been vice chairman for several years before assuming the top job. Therefore I was not "the-new-guy-with-lots-of-never-been-thought-of-ideas." Nevertheless, I knew we had to create a very different operating environment. We absolutely had to improve our financial performance. I was beginning to feel comfortable with the concept of quality as a way to break out of our bureaucratic ways. The problems in our organization reinforced my willingness to trust my instincts about what was needed.

• *Madonna:* On an operating basis, I knew we had to make changes in the basic way we ran the business. The nature of our business was changing and traditional sources of revenue were shrinking. The impetus for change was primarily that the bottom line was not what we wanted and declining profitability was a sure and early sign that we needed to change. There were also some other important external factors that set the stage for the changes we initiated. We were the first big firm to undergo a major international merger and a couple of others had quickly followed, for example. In addition, accounting firms were increasingly dealing with issues of "risk" and it was around this time that Leventhal [a major competitor] collapsed. Still, I didn't know until after I assumed my new role just how much radical change was needed.

• *Stiefler:* On becoming president of IDS, I inherited an organization that was extraordinarily successful. I was also following a remarkable leader in Harvey Golub. By any of the dimensions that we use to look at the business, we felt pretty good about our performance.

• *Weatherup:* The years prior to our change effort were very good years for PepsiCola. Earnings were strong. There were no market share issues and no consumer issues. We had the most admired advertising in the industry. In short, there were few obvious reasons to say "Hey, we're in trouble and need to change the way we operate." But a number of factors came into focus and it became clear to some of us that we needed to systematically transform our business. Changing individual pieces of the organization would not work given our need to operate in a fundamentally different way. The biggest single factor driving the change was the recognition that our new environment was much more complex than in the past. Over a several year period, we went from 600 customers to 600,000 customers. This was a result of strategically moving into the operations end of our business, primarily through acquisitions of bottlers. We had to make customer focus the core of our business philosophy. That required a fundamental change in our culture. We recognized this early on and, as a result, avoided false steps.

What were your initial steps in starting down the path to large-scale change?

- *Stiefler:* We talked about building the company that would put our current organization out of business, and we talked about the fact that we were approaching our hundredth year. We talked a lot about building something for the next century, what kind of company we wanted that to be, and what the strong foundations were for building it.

  We began to talk about a mechanism for challenging ourselves. We certainly didn't have any grand plan at this point. We decided to use, at least as a starting point, our planner field force retention. We felt pretty good about our field force retention, which was almost world class by competitor standards, but was a disaster in absolute terms. At that point, only half the planners we'd been hiring in a given year would survive the first year, and 75 percent would leave in the fourth year. And we were in a business in which we promised people, at least indirectly, a long-term relationship with a trusted financial adviser.

  That information produced a platform that served as the front end of the organizational change process. When we looked across the board at the root causes of planner turnover, we realized they were systemic. They touched most areas of the company, so in order to fix that planner turnover—our number-one quality defect—we were going to have to change much of what happened in the company. We began, in a very systematic way, to focus on the gaps between where we were as an organization and where we really needed to be, instead of focusing on how we were performing relative to ourselves or relative to our competitors. Against all of those prior standards, we were doing very well. We needed some other set of standards, some more absolute kind of standards.

We also determined what would *not* change. One of the things that we talked about a lot was the fact that our mission, our strategy, and our values, would not change. The planner force, as our primary distribution system, won't change. So, there were some anchors for people.

• *Weatherup:* Some people saw me making a big deal of the need for change. We were strong as a company and they didn't understand why I was talking about the danger we faced if we didn't operate differently.

After we had made the case for change, we generated a host of potential answers—essentially how to turn these challenges into opportunities. We then came up with five agreed-on options and assigned these to five foxhole teams. These two-person teams were my staff of ten and they were allowed to select the option they wanted to work on. The teams spent 50 percent of their time over the next thirty days working on this. We moved quickly once the need for change was clear to me and my team. We decided to start with our "right-side-up initiatives."

We set a date when we would announce the organizational change. It was the time for action. We wanted no further delay. We needed to crash ahead because that's the way we work best as a company. You can't get going without a lot of thought about the need for change and your basic change strategy, but your up-front analysis shouldn't prevent you from action. You need to start the effort, create some momentum, and then assess what is working and what is not. I kept saying that we were about to get hit by a freight train. We talked about financial pain, customer pain, and employee pain. At first, we just went over the issues, without any attempt to answer these challenges.

• *Allen:* Going back to the idea that we have to be successful in the marketplace, we didn't have data, the systems, or the structure to do what we needed to do. That led me to write a white paper about a redirection—one that focused on the business unit as the core building block of our company. We decided to focus initially on clarifying roles and accountability, and to work on collaboration later. If we couldn't win in our several markets, collaboration didn't matter.

It was more than structure, I knew we didn't have the right level of passion . . . probably because of the lack of clarity and the shellshocks of radical change. I hoped redirection would result in an attitudinal change. I had confidence in the people. If they *knew* the marketplace, were given the direction, they would take appropriate action—albeit with imperfect skills.

It was a radical change for a lot of people. It was not a perfect answer, but I knew if we could get focus we could understand the customer. And if we understood the customer, we could win.

- *Houghton:* In October of 1983, we had our first large-scale top management meeting (150 managers worldwide) since I'd taken over as chairman six months before. We'd had off-site meetings like that many times over the years, and they'd generally been very harmonious and gentle affairs. My instinct told me this one had to be different.

So my opening speech was not polite. I pointed out that our financial results were appalling, the organizational morale worse, and that as organizational leaders we were disgraceful. I said that our first task was to admit we were at the bottom and had nowhere to go but up.

I likened our condition to that of an alcoholic. Professional evidence suggests that the curing process begins only when the patient admits the condition and begins on his or her own to crawl out of the hole. I told our group, "You know, we are at the bottom right now. Let's admit it. Then let's agree that, starting tonight, we're going to begin the process of turning ourselves once again into a healthy, living organization. We'll start right after dinner." I then strode off the stage—to dead silence.

Early in that meeting, I announced we were going to make a major investment in total quality management. I said we were going to spend several million dollars in setting up a quality institute, in training all our people around the world (six languages, over a two year period), in establishing a corporate director of quality (a senior officer who was on our board of directors and who agreed to delay his retirement to do this), and on and on.

I must tell you I was a very lonely fellow. The organization was demoralized and very cynical. How could we spend that much money when we were just breaking even? Was this "quality" idea just the new chairman's way of trying something out? I believe they looked upon the suggested quality initiative as being just another "new flavor of the month." This translates as "every-new-chairman-must-have-a-new-concept-but-don't-worry-because-he'll-tire-of-it-in-six-months-so-just-stay-down-in-the-foxhole-and-it-will-all-go-away."

So, in a sense, my first major initiative—quality—began by my holding my nose and jumping in the water, by taking a chance. I had a gut feeling that pursuit of quality in its broadest sense would be a key to our success. But I must admit I was bloody lucky. Looking back it's easy to see what a powerful impact it had on the company. In 1983, I had not a clue of this—but thank God we made the move.

- *Madonna:* Initially, I thought we could downsize the old way since everyone agreed we had too many partners. We put a "partner rights" committee together and agreed about the need to reduce the number of partners. But, when we tried to take action, we failed. The will to do it just wasn't there without some kind of forcing action.

   I personally came from an environment that led me to never want to be part of a drastic downsizing. I went through this early in my career and vowed it would never happen on my watch. But when I saw what we were dealing with when we took over, it was clear that we needed to take action. The significance of the downsizing is that it allowed us to get rid of some senior guys that just weren't doing their jobs. We never had an actual number in mind; it was a bottoms-up number. Instead, we emphasized the need to be able to compete in today's more competitive environment, coining the phrase "Partner for the 1990s" as a descriptor of this requirement or capability. It would become the measure for making the cut.

After downsizing, the second thing we did was institute a pay-for-performance system. We decided to tie everyone's compensation to individual performance, and we indexed performance for each practice. In the past everyone was treated the same, but not with the new performance system. This caused a redistribution of compensation among the partners. We took partners that weren't performing and cut them.

After managing the downsizing, we got into "Future Directions" to evaluate where we should be in the year 2000. We needed a Future Directions initiative because while we were good historically at managing costs we were not so good at growing revenue, and this would be the challenge for firms like ours with revenue from our traditional business declining. The whole notion of a Future Directions initiative was an intuitive move at first and ultimately an approach that broke the old model. It gave people a chance to look at the firm from a different perspective.

What type of resistance did you meet? How did you enroll the organization, especially your senior team?

- *Houghton:* I was the new chairman. I think people (especially the five people reporting to me) were testing. I think they were cynical themselves. Their attitude was "Who's this new guy? Let's see what he does." This was a pretty tough group just sitting there waiting to see what happened. I didn't have their immense devotion, I'll tell you that.

  Quality was the major platform on which I built change around here. Compared to 1983, there are probably only a few cynics around today. That's due to two factors. First, remember that nobody at the beginning thought I'd stick with this initiative for more than a few months. That view changed over time as I continued to talk about virtually nothing else. Second, the organization has slowly realized the pursuit of total quality is not just "Jamie's idea"; it's a matter of survival in today's world. I had three presidents running groups reporting to me. I wanted to get my arms around the business and I didn't want to have anybody in between. I got them on board because I was very clear about my expectations. I started to say, "Okay, guys. We are the quality improvement team for the corporation. We are going to set the example. We are going to meet together 20 percent of our time." That's a lot and they were not happy about that either. I said, "Occasionally I have to make the final decision, but ninety times out of a hundred, I want it to be group decision. I want to have meetings that are talking about issues and then we will come to a consensus." We just spent a lot of time together, in Corning and at off-site meetings. We had some of our most creative discussions late in the evening over red wine, just yelling like hell. It was great, great stuff—and molded us together as a team.

- *Weatherup:* Looking back, the top seventy were the hardest to enroll in the need for change. It got significantly easier as we went closer to the front line. Those working with customers didn't care about our positive reputation in the *Fortune* ratings. They were asking the important questions, like "Where's my two-liter Pepsi?" Getting our senior executives aligned around the need for change was difficult. This was a surprise to me, in that I assumed that the senior people would understand the need to change the way we operated. The resistance was a genuine question of "Why do it?" They had successfully mastered the current system and had turned in a number of strong years, performancewise. Convincing them of the threat was difficult in that they were both the architects and beneficiaries of the current organization.

    We moved very quickly in the change effort. At each level of the organization, we sought buy-in through a systematic enrollment process. We presented the case for change and asked people to do specific tasks to advance the effort. You could not enroll the next level in the organization if you were not enrolled. The approach we used—taking a customer assignment, learning about customer needs, etc.—was helpful. The ninety-day assignments were very good too. The concept was that in ninety days you'll be signed up or you won't be here. If I had recognized the difficulty some would have, I would have done more spade work with the senior group. Perhaps we should have given the top seventy enough time to internalize the need for change and recognize our commitment to it. Still, moving quickly was critical in making the change happen.

- *Madonna:* The biggest single issue in change is making the case for why change has to occur. This was relatively easy in downsizing. Downsizing served several purposes for us. It was a wake-up call to the organization, it allowed us to balance our size, and it resulted in helping us get the right people into the right jobs. In the pay-for-performance area, people got angry but they knew changes had to be made. The same is true for risk management.

  But in Future Directions—our vision for the future state—the "why" issue is critical. This was where we encountered the most resistance. We had to determine who, what, and why! If we had interjected "how" at that early point, it would have been death. We first had to invest time and energy in getting people to see the need for change; then we could deal with how we implement the change. We took our story to the partners, and that made everything else easier.

  In the elected environment Jim Brocksmith (deputy chairman) and I are in, you can't function totally on your own. You need to have key allies. By ourselves, we couldn't have brought about this level of change. I can't sit here in this room and get it done. We had to sell change to the board, and our management team. Both groups had doubts about the need for fundamental change because we had been operating with the same formula forever. And doing quite well at that. So you have to really understand the organization and how to get things done within it. You cannot have a whole new set of players; you must convince your current team that what you are proposing makes sense and get them to help you get it done.

  The structure of firms like ours has always been an important component of identity within the organization, and we all had shared fundamentally similar structures throughout nearly one hundred years of history. There was, for example, always an audit, tax, and consulting structure. This was a given, and givens in a professional services firms are, I believe, much stronger than in other businesses. This led us to conclude that ultimately we were going to need to deal with the structure issues as a way of truly redefining ourselves.

- *Allen:* I expected my senior team to aid and abet the change. I ask much of them. They're each responsible for a huge business, and also for assisting me with strategic issues for the corporation. I have had a high level of loyalty to, and belief in, those people—it's very much on a personal level. It helped us break through tough situations. My team was with me; very supportive and motivated. The next level I think, signed on as well. That doesn't mean we always agreed on all issues.

  There was at that time, however, an inert level of mid-level managers that slowed the progress of change. Different cultures play out differently, too. There was a point when I thought one of our large businesses would never sign up. Bell Labs had to make a fairly dramatic change.

What changes in the organization's structure or hardware did you make?

- *Weatherup:* We invested a lot of time in the principles to redesign the organization. We had over two hundred people on that design team, and we took ninety days to do the operational design. We had a principle: if the design didn't fit the principles of action you had to redo the principle (0 percent of the changes were this) or redo the design (100 percent of the time, people redid the design). Moreover, we forced them into tremendous detail and made sure the new roles were very clear.

  The reorganization was painful, but pivotal. This made the change effort real. Even if they didn't like the new titles (people complained about alphabet soup), almost everyone had a new boss. At a minimum, this touched everyone and it was a structural consolidation of our cultural changes. For everyone who had been a holdout, this was the last gate.

- *Allen:* As I said earlier, my first step was to focus on clarifying the structure, roles, and accountability. It took two or two and a half years to really implement a business unit approach. We began in '89 and it was 1991 before we really got it right. Even now, we're still learning.

- *Houghton:* After we got the values clear, we focused on the strategy. And as the team developed, we really began to work well together. We put a lot of money on two *major* horses, which are our two big profit producers today. In 1983, those were tiny little pesky businesses that weren't making any money. Today, they represent over 50 percent of our profit at the operating level.

    We sold electronics, clearly a business that wasn't going anywhere. We've probably sold a billion dollars worth of assets. We've bought about a billion dollars of assets. We've reorganized three-quarters of a billion dollars of assets. It's been a real period of change. But, in the end, our values helped us get through this period of turmoil.

What changes in the organization's culture or "software"?

- *Allen:* We made the business units strong, but that approach has created some problems in getting the groups to work together. Prior to the business unit implementation we had an array of businesses, some large, some small, but most were indistinct. Bell Labs had only a small alignment with Network Systems and virtually none with other groups.

    After we put the business units in place, and those units really began to focus and work, we began to think about "what binds us together." That led to Our Common Bond—the statement of our values. During 1991, I felt a sense of a "mission" on values. It was coming from the people. The changes in accountability were having side-effect changes. We had made some mistakes along the way, and our people realized that. There was growing recognition that lack of coordination, and business unit "independence" was about being seen by the customer. This led people to ask questions about our beliefs; about what binds us. That precipitated Our Common Bond. I wrote the first draft towards the end of the year in 1991. We did testing, used focus groups, and worked one on one. It was nearly one and a half years later before we actually launched the "product."

- *Houghton:* One of the first tasks we (the top management) set ourselves was to agree on and articulate our corporate values. After several months of pulling and tugging, we agreed on what we call our "seven big V's." These were and remain: quality, integrity, performance, leadership, technology, independence, the individual. The interesting thing about these values was not that most of them had been around forever (i.e., integrity and technology), but they'd never been articulated and communicated before. So we said in a statement to our employees, "These are our seven big V's. On these we stand." Strategies will change. These will not change.

    That helped. It wasn't an absolutely necessary thing to do—we could have gone along without doing that. But values to me are like buoys in the channel of commerce. In other words, one is changing directions and testing and making strategic decisions all the time, but if one doesn't have values to guide one, there is a disorientation. So, deciding early on, even before you start fooling around with your strategy, what you believe in and what's this company all about, is important.

- *Weatherup:* As I said earlier, we started with a focus on software. A lot of people act as though "when in doubt, change the organization." But often it's just the case that the grass is always greener. You change one set of problems for another. It's an easy fix, but most reorganizations that I've lived through haven't really done much. I believe nine out of ten reorganizations are a total waste of time. It's much more difficult to change the way people think. We took the attitude "we'll get to reorganization later." We wanted a total change in mindset, in orientation and thinking. For example, instead of people spending a great deal of time thinking "How am I going to present my ideas to Craig?" we wanted them thinking "How do I make sure we have enough supply on the truck and satisfy our customers." That type of change requires a dramatic shift in perspective.

What changes in the people side of your business?

- *Stiefler::* The impact is that the organizations who succeed may need people who have higher tolerances for ambiguity, more flexibility, more willingness to make their own day-to-day decisions on what they think is important, and the leader may simply not be able to provide the level of clarity of focus that people would like.

  People really want and are capable of doing what's right. And their standards, if given the appropriate environment, will tend to be as high as they need to be. I think you have to place a standard there. But I don't feel that you have to drive people to that standard as much as I used to. In fact I think of the driving as being counterproductive at times.

  I think I'm much more relaxed about that now. I'm much more interested in people than I used to be, because I've given myself the opportunity to do that. I really find myself caring about people as people. Not just as humans in production. The only difference—in organizations that have duplicate or similar functions, like retail banks, retail stores in many cases—the only fundamental difference in performance is the quality of leadership. And where that difference plays out is in the ability, the differential ability of leaders to get people to perform to their potential rather than to the minimum standard they need to perform to do their job. That's the difference. We have recognized the power of developing a team of people who can share and own the change process with you. It is very hard to do it alone.

- *Houghton:* I believe the *only* competitive advantage in the future is going to be people. Money goes around the world at a rate of billions of dollars a second. Technology, because of information flows, moves around the world. Raw materials are much less important. So you can make the case that the only competitive advantage in the world is going to be people. To say that, you better sincerely value the individual. Talented people, especially knowledge workers, can pick up and leave. They don't have to stay. They don't have to stay anywhere.

- *Allen:* Bringing people in from the outside has been a strategy since '83, '84. I knew that the people that were here couldn't do it all, not because they weren't good people. We just needed some new thinking—most of "us" had the same-shaped heads. My obligation to the shareholders subsumed my concern for insiders' promotion opportunities. We had to bring in outsiders. If we had been in a competitive environment for many years, I probably would have had a different opinion. The final test is how well those [outside] people contribute, and whether they are respected. I think they have demonstrated their worth and value. In most cases, there's been a learning process taking place between so-called insiders and outsiders. It has made both sides stronger, and now we are one. And the more normal business practice of bringing in new talent is almost routine.

- *Weatherup:* We staffed 280 jobs and one of the selection criteria was to have a right-side-up attitude—that is, having the values, the customer focus, living empowerment, and so on. And everyone knew this. They knew that they had to fit with the company and had to fit closely. One of the most frequent problems that would arise was someone saying, "It's not happening with my boss; my boss hasn't changed." What I said was, "Eventually, the day will come when the people who have gone underground (and are not internalizing the values) will no longer be here. They'll find that their talents are better used elsewhere." "Taking their talents elsewhere" was a code sentence we had set up during the enrollment sessions; it essentially meant that those that couldn't fit would be gone after a period of time. When someone left a year later, I would say, "He found his talents were better used elsewhere."

- *Madonna:* Moving to a new structure, I became aware that we needed new systems, and we needed new skills, too. Either they have to be acquired, taught, or learned on the job. Professional services firms have led very protected lives, that is, not particularly subject to adapting to market changes. A major example of this would be in the area of competitiveness; we simply haven't trained our people for all these changes brought on by a more competitive environment. That's all changing today— and fast. Today we are training our people to manage and lead in a different world. There's a quiet revolution going on in professional services firms.

What is the most important role for you to play in the change effort?

- *Madonna:* Leaders [of change] have to have strong personal convictions—they need inner strength. They need a strong sense of doing what's right. They need the ability to size things up and to call a spade a spade. They need the ability to communicate; this is critical. You've got to communicate at a down-to-earth level so people can relate and understand. You've got to provide continuous communication. We've done this well, targeting constant and candid communications with our partners, including a lot of face-to-face meetings, and introducing tools to aid our employees' understanding, such as a video series, etc.

    When we started [this change process] I knew it was going to be a very different game. While I wasn't sure what we would be able to accomplish, I felt that what we were doing was right. We had to follow our own instincts. Whatever was right, that's what we had to do. But when you step into a new leadership position, you have to give people a wake-up call.

    I was probably the catalyst for the changes, the champion of the change, but I received tremendous support from Jim. I'm reminded of the saying, "Leaders should never ask people to go where they won't go." In the past, the leader was a king; in many respects titular heads. In contrast, we had to be active participants involving people to make things happen. We felt we were doing what was right and we had to follow our own instincts.

- *Allen:* When you try to make a change in an organization this big, you should be relatively sure of what you are doing. I don't know how it all comes together. There was no elaborate system for creating our change effort. You need to let potential actions "soak" for a while as you consider your options—and a lot comes from the gut. Some of the best synthesis comes in the middle of the night. Change leadership is a very personal thing, particularly on such things as our redirection and values. It's very much a reflection of what I believe is important for us to do to be competitive in the future. In the final analysis, the best information comes from the people in the business. Processing it is the challenge.

- *Stiefler:* There are a lot of definitions of a leader's role. The leader must define reality. And the reality may be in part, in this case, that the world is complicated and ambiguous. And it defies one's effort and one's desire to make it simple or easy. I motivate people to question that status quo while recognizing that the struggle to define a new reality will be difficult and require all of us to deal with the complexity of the new business environment.

  I think the leader has to create an environment in which people can do their best. And I believe absolutely that the leverage in an organization is the quality of leadership at all levels. The longer I do what I do, the more strongly I believe that I think I've grown more trusting, less intense, less needing to control everything around me.

  A leader must never, ever, ever, ever let themselves be satisfied. Always run scared and wonder actively where the next problem or opportunity is going to come from. I think leaders need to be haunted, in a sense. We have to avoid arrogance or complacency, which is tough if you have had a series of good years and are respected in your industry.

  The leader's fundamental honesty and integrity is critical. People need to believe in you as an individual, and they need to believe that you're doing what you say. They need to believe you'll deliver on your commitments. Fundamentally, if trust doesn't exist, then it's pretty difficult to do anything else.

  But I'm beginning to migrate toward the view that our world is extremely complex; there is no way to make it simple. There is no way to make it comfortable, or as uncomplicated as people would like to have it made. Thus, you need to build trust in a complex world that creates tension and anxiety.

- *Houghton:* Your customers are your bread and butter and they're going to pay for your product or services. But the leader has to spend an inordinate amount of time inside, just being visible, just walking around. You've just got to be out there and be visible all the time. Since I became chairman, I've made a vow to go around the company, to visit every location in the company on a regular basis. I visit about forty or fifty places around the world a year. I've made approximately four hundred of these visits over the past several years.

  My leadership model is to keep it simple, put a few major messages out there, and sustain those messages. I think that's been very helpful because I just constantly reinforce my three messages—that's all I do. I talk about and ask questions about how each organization is doing in quality, performance, and diversity (the individual). People are not stupid. They have 20/20 hearing. They understand now that these are important to me and to the company.

- *Weatherup:* One of the key roles of leaders is to push people to do things they would not do on their own—and in most cases, people will not embrace large-scale change. You have to know, at a deep level, that the more painful thing is *not* to change. In other words, the pain of going forward has to be less than the pain of staying where you are. You have to make sure that quitting is feared, and will be more difficult than going on.

  Radical change requires that the senior person believes in his or her bones that the change must occur. Then, the leader must move and move fast to make the change happen. People at each point of the change effort told me to slow down. But we couldn't afford to slow down or do less as an organization. I had to keep the pressure on and force us to do more and in less time. You have to have conviction to move forward when people you trust are telling you to slow down. You have to start the change process and sustain it when others lose faith. Most of the change management efforts that fail do so because leadership quits. You must push ahead and act on your convictions.

As a leader, you need to be caring and willful. I had to create the impression that "if he says we'll do it, we'll do it." It was important to have a gut-level feeling for the business. You have to be relentless. I was always pounding away. There were no delays accepted, no postponements. You have to say "so what?" to a lot of things that could slow down the change. People would find all types of reasons for slowing down what we needed to do.

As a leader in our change effort, I had to be more clear, more direct, more blunt than usual. I had to be very singular about what we were doing. The CEOs have to do some of the change management work themselves. You can't subcontract it out. We had a motto: Customer Time Is Prime Time. I did a lot of customer calls during the first twelve months of the change. This was important learning for me and important behavior as well.

I believe that each leader must determine what is the best approach for his or her organization and craft a change strategy that will impact a particular culture.

What was the single biggest challenge you faced personally in leading the change?

- *Stiefler:* I had this concern that I would screw up this very good company that Harvey had built during his years at the helm— that I'd let myself and the rest of the organization down. But I also had a sense of history that companies tend not to do well forever and you can't rely on past accomplishments. I began to think about what that all meant, how that all came together in a fundamental way that would help me shape a vision of where the company needed to go.

  And when you come off the kind of record that we had, it was hard to find what that mechanism, what that forcing mechanism was. You can't create a crisis. That's dishonest. But you have to avoid arrogance and smugness that ends up stifling an organization.

And that's what I spend a lot of time thinking about. What's the device, or the set of devices? What's the mechanism? What creates the motivation in an organization for change? And I started to think about how do you institutionalize discontent in an organization? How do you literally make an organization as uncomfortable as I am personally with things the way they are, however good that is? And how do you do it without screwing up things?

At one point, I got anxious, scared, and very concerned about whether or not the people to whom we gave the responsibility would be able to do the job. Whether we'd wind up with a flood of recommendations, or an organization with the wrong expectations, whether the work would ever get done, whether it would meet my standards. And, you know, as has always been the case, when you put good people on a job, and you give them support, they want to succeed as much as you do. I would swoop in and I would get involved and concerned in ways that sometimes were productive and sometimes not. I really had to learn to trust the process and the people.

- *Weatherup:* There's a perpetual dilemma in managing change. You can communicate that you don't know all the answers, but then people say, "Hey, this guy looks pretty stupid." Or you can wait to communicate, and you'll look good, but it's a delay. It's important to be sure enough about what you're doing to be unsure—to be able to say, "That's a good question, and I don't know the answer. We will figure it out together."

I have people looking to me for the answers to very complicated questions. I think I know our business inside and out and, in many cases, can provide direction based on my experience and business judgment. But the world is complex and, in some cases, you need to tell people that we simply don't know enough to make a final decision. People don't like to hear that.

In the end, I think my answer—my approach and my organizational solution—was the exact right answer for my organization. My approach to change reflects my personal values and style. Another executive I know used a very different approach, and his approach is right for his organization. But we could not have switched. I could never have done what he did, and I doubt he could do what I did.

- *Allen:* I have always understated the importance of my own persona. I don't have large ego needs, and I am relatively laid back, as they say. I always had to be encouraged by my team and by outsiders to be more front and center. I need coaching to be out in front, and I've always recognized that. But it's very important in this job. People want to know where I stand on issues, when my inclination is to listen and learn. I'm still learning to deal with this challenge.

In retrospect, would you alter anything in how you approached the change effort?

- *Allen:* If I were to do it over, I'd do everything we did (and probably more) but faster. One should always test hypotheses, but then we have to act fast. I'd also say that by and large, our instincts are right, and we probably ought to act on them sooner. I would have moved quicker in hindsight. You can't move fast enough. You have to try to find a way. In retrospect, I despair to think of AT&T without many of those changes and actions. We made them, in many cases, without balance sheets and profit statements, just on instinct, belief, and common sense.

    I would do more of getting people engaged—through communications plans, through involvement in the entire process. And I recognize that the human asset requires a lot more care than we sometimes gave it. We were trying to be caring, but we also wanted to move quickly. We did not always take full advantage of the value of our people in implementing the change. Neither did we understand the full implications of such radical change so quickly.

- *Madonna:* I don't like to look back. Paul Allaire of Xerox told me, "You'll look back and wish you could have done more, but that you can't. In a perfect world we might have done more but the system wouldn't let us." You are always told that you moved too fast, or the change was too dramatic, but you look back in a couple of years and realize that you moved too slowly and you should have changed more. That captures how I feel.

We weren't forced to do any of this. At the time, the need to change wasn't obvious. Now, two years later, I can see it would have been a serious problem if we didn't begin this change. The next phase of change work is of serious concern to me at this moment. We've left the dock but we're far from the other side. And different people are in different places in terms of getting on board. Our progress is all over the lot, but we are clearly making progress.

- *Houghton:* I think, in retrospect, I would have moved a lot quicker on quality, and I would have moved the quality effort towards the outside customer faster. I'm a firm believer that you've got to start internally because you've got to get people talking the same language, walking the same way, etc. But then what you want to do, as quickly as possible, is shift it to the outside. And did we do that fast enough? Probably not.

- *Stiefler:* Managing change is such a seductive process. One can get sucked in and lose one's perspective. The people who were doing this work were very committed, very bright, very able people, but they had never done this either. And not everything they did worked out or was right. Not all of the approaches made sense. As a leader, there's a very fine balance between supporting the team and questioning them. And both roles weighed very heavily on me, and I remember having that feeling.

But I really had to learn to trust the process and the people. I was not able to give it constant attention. As the process unfolded, I would swoop in and I would get involved and concerned in ways that were sometimes productive and sometimes not. At some point, a light did go on, and I began to realize that I needed to play a different role than I had been playing. And what I did is, I called people out. And I said, "Look, this may make some of you uncomfortable, but I want to be clear about the role that I'm going to play here. If you gauge my support of you by the degree the completeness and the speed with which I agree with you, then you're going to have the opportunity to prove that I don't support you."

- *Weatherup:* In every instance, we underestimated the ability of the organization to change. Tighter time frames would have been better in retrospect. I think you need to move through change quickly and believe that people can manage more than you expect. For example, we finished our initial enrollment meetings in May and June. Then we reorganized. If there had been a vote, everyone would have voted to delay it. But this reorganization simply consolidated what we had been saying all along. And once you accept compromise, it's hard to turn it around.

  You have to integrate. The whole change plan has to make sense to you and the organization. This evolves over time, but it is important for the leader to see the linkages. For example, we had 450 teams working and we received hundreds of proposals. It became a morass. Everyone was confused about how it all fit together. That led to the development of an integrating framework that helped all of us pull the various initiatives together.

In sum, what two or three points of advice would you give to other executives about to take their companies through large-scale change?

- *Stiefler:* Be very clear about the reasons for change, the value of change, the benefit of change, and the penalty of not changing. Distill those reasons into the set of messages that an organization can understand and internalize and simply not get tired of saying them.

- *Weatherup:* Recognize that you need a compelling reason to change that is as powerful and sizable as the change you expect. And I don't mean compelling to your board, but compelling to the people who have to make the change. You can't expect people to make a significant change if they don't perceive an equally significant threat or missed opportunity if they don't change. The size of the change is directly correlated to the need for change. Many of our senior people were struggling with the question: "Do we really have a big reason to dramatically change this organization?" Many believed the risk of changing was greater than the potential benefit. You can't expect people to embrace a large change if they only see a need for incremental change. We had to create a very persuasive case, but it was difficult. Only about 20 percent of our problems were current; 80 percent were projected for the future. That made the change more difficult and made my role as the leader all the more important.

I think leaders of change efforts need to look for opportunities to illustrate the importance of change symbolically. For example, I missed some important PepsiCola strategic review sessions in order to spend time with my team focusing on the change effort. That sent a strong message to my team and the organization regarding the importance of what we were doing.

- *Madonna:* An important key to success is getting an outside perspective. We could never have brought about these changes without outside help. Without outside help you'd have little chance of success, especially with the soft stuff.

    Another key is you have to do a real good job of convincing people why things have to change. Once you understand why, you can act. The hardest part of solving any problem is identifying it.

    A third key is to understand at a deep level your own environment. If you look just internally for awareness, you'll never see what's going on. You have to look outside for an objective point of view. We spent a lot of time looking at our firm from the outside in to understand what was needed.

- *Houghton:* My advice to others is keep it simple. The world is complex but you must keep to a few key themes. Our values are simple; our strategic statement is simple. I get battered around here all the time by people wanting me to talk about various things as being my hot buttons. The point is that I have talked about three things and three things only: performance, quality, and the individual (or diversity). I get some people saying, "Well geez, you ought to talk about technology or you ought to talk about this." Well, I do of course but in a different context. I don't confuse the main message.

I happen to believe that the people that try to run their businesses like the 1950s are going to be in deep trouble, because I don't think people will stand for it. People in today's environment need to be more involved than was true even ten years ago. They need to be empowered, to contribute to the limit of her or his ability. But I am very cautious about recommending anything to anybody else because I just think everybody is different and every situation is different. I guess my only recommendation is, if you've done a lot of analysis and your gut says do something, do it. Act boldly rather than get caught in analysis. It may be wrong. You may have to change your approach. But I think that the worst thing to do is to do nothing. So my recommendation is, once you've got it in your head and your gut and you think it's a good thing to do just go ahead and do it. When you make a decision, you may make a mistake. But you must keep going and pushing the organization forward.

Common Lessons

The challenges and experiences of these CEOs reflect different business challenges and leadership challenges. However, there are some commonalities among their experiences that allow us to draw out some theories and dilemmas in managing change.

1. *There are many roads to successfully managing discontinuous change.* Each CEO had a different approach. Some started with clear environmental indicators of problems. Others sensed a problem but worked to define an agenda without clear environmental indicators. AT&T changed its structure first, and then moved on to emphasize values. PepsiCola built a set of values, and followed it up with a change in structure. The key lesson is that there is no one right way—many ways work. The challenge seems to be work-

ing out the right process for the right business. In the business of managing change, customization is key.

2.   *Discontinuous change often demands action without complete information.* A common theme was expressed around need to act fast without in-depth analysis. These CEOs would have liked to move faster, but faced some constraints on speed. As a trend, this has implications for managing discontinuous change and the ability of organizations and their members to act rapidly.

3.   *It's easy to underestimate the task.* In retrospect, most felt they had underestimated the depth and scope of change. As Weatherup pointed out, at the time he initiated the changes, people felt he was overestimating the need for change. Looking back, he felt he had probably underestimated it. Madonna pointed out that although he didn't know it at the time, the firm would have been in trouble without the change.

4.   *A key role of the leader is to sell the need for change.* Most felt that they played a key role in terms of being out in front, and in Stiefler's words, to "define reality." Houghton was constantly among employees preaching his three themes. Clearly, their role as energizers and directors of change was paramount. It is hardest to create a case for change when that case is based on the future. For Madonna, the future-oriented change—the Future Directions program—was harder to sell than the downsizing or pay-for-performance initiative. For Weatherup and Stiefler, making a case despite great business performance was a challenge.

5.   *Change leadership is a highly personal activity.* Each recognized that change posed personal dilemmas, but worked with them to build a change style. Though shy, Allen worked hard to spend a lot of informal time with employees. Stiefler learned to trust the change process and the change teams. Weatherup stressed the fit between his change strategy and his style. In the best sense, these leaders show the value of individual difference and working with one's own unique persona to build the change agenda.

Conclusion:
The Lessons
of Discontinuous Change

Robert B. Shaw
A. Elise Walton .

Consider the challenge facing the leaders of an organization that must move from a traditional command-and-control functional hierarchy to one of temporary teams operating in a far-reaching network of suppliers and customers. Incremental approaches will not produce this type of transformation. Also consider the challenge facing those who must move their organizations into global markets. Today's leading-edge organizations are no longer constrained by space and time; people work in all regions of the world at all hours of the day. Building global operations that span geographical, cultural, and temporal boundaries is changing the very nature of the organization. These types of shifts are not addressed by incremental steps; they require a more fundamental shift in an organization's essence.

Charles Handy has noted that change is not what it used to be. He suggests that new change rules are needed: "To embrace discontinuous change means . . . completely rethinking the way in which we learn things. In a world of incremental change it is sensible to ape your elder in order to take off where they left off, in both knowledge and responsibility. But under conditions of discontinuity it is no longer obvious that their ways should continue to be your ways; we may all need new rules for new ball games and need to discover them for ourselves" (1989, pp. 9–10).

In this chapter, we summarize what we have learned about leading discontinuous change.

- *The core competency for business leaders in the twenty-first century will be change management.* Those seeking to sustain competitiveness must be capable of developing and implementing integrated change agendas for their organizations. The multiple dimensions of change suggest that different situations require different types of change approaches and leadership will be required to craft an appropriate strategy for each situation. In some cases, the necessary change will be incremental, in others more dramatic shifts will be required.

- *We are moving from an era dominated by incremental change to one of discontinuous change.* Increasingly, we are seeing companies faced with the need to change the essence of their identity. AT&T in the 1980s and IBM in the 1990s are examples of firms altering the fundamentals of how they operate. In the 1970s and early 1980s, the focus was more on incremental change, often under the banner of quality improvement. While necessary, incremental change will be insufficient in situations requiring more extreme measures. In the 1990s and beyond, the focus will be on altering the fundamentals of an organization, rather than merely improving them. This type of change is far riskier, given the potential for strategic miscalculation and poor execution.

- *Discontinuous change transforms three core aspects of organizations: leadership capability, corporate identity, and organizational architecture.* We have found three broad concepts helpful in working with executives responsible for discontinuous change. The first involves change leadership, beginning with the CEO, the executive team, and the key stakeholders. Managing change is a process requiring skill and motivation—both are needed in key positions throughout the organization. Corporate identity is a broader concept than vision or mission. It reflects the fundamental essence of what the organization is about and how it will operate in the future. Organizational architecture is the broad blueprint of the organization's form and includes both formal and informal structures and processes.

• *Discontinuous change is more about improvisation than management.* In change management, there are no strict guidelines, no linear sequence of appropriate actions. Those leading change need to be capable of adjusting to shifting conditions and opportunities that surface as the change unfolds. Discontinuous change, in many respects, is planned spontaneity and deliberate opportunism. The bad news is that change of this type is, in some cases, beyond the control of those seeking to control it. Change occurs sometimes in response to our efforts and sometimes in response to other forces. Our task is to recognize the shift and seize the opportunity.

• *Effective change leaders allow change to emerge and develop within a common set of values.* Discontinuous change requires leadership that develops an overall map of the future organization and then supports the realization of that future through the actions of people at all levels. This approach is very different than traditional micro-managed efforts that use traditional command-and-control approaches. However, this approach is far from passive. It is forceful leadership at all levels of the organization. Norms, values, and common operating principles rather than rules and direct supervision will furnish the cohesion necessary to provide direction and coordination. Leaders will spend an increasing amount of time and energy shaping the vision and values of the organization, as this will become their primary point of leverage. In addition, they will spend a significant amount of personal time focusing on the development of people, particularly selecting team leaders and managers at all levels. In the more diffused organization, the principal means of control will be a strongly held culture and a network of individuals who use their own leadership skills to build the organization along the lines consistent with an overall vision.

- *Discontinuous change is not simply top-down direction or a series of bottom-up initiatives.* Wide-scale change requires an appropriate combination of central, lateral, and local initiatives. Some initiatives must originate with the senior team, such as the overall strategy and form of the corporate enterprise. Others, such as reengineering, are typically sponsored by the senior team but supported by a group of individuals who work horizontally to change an organization. Other initiatives are most appropriately owned locally by individual units. For example, the redesign of a plant requires both broad-based and local ownership. The artistry in leading change is determining the appropriate ownership for each initiative and how they link together into an integrated whole.

- *The soft part of discontinuous change is the hard part.* Most executives look to organizational structure for the answer to the problems or opportunities they face. Changing structure without changing the informal organization will not produce long-lasting results—but it is far easier. Change leadership will thus requires skill at understanding and altering informal aspects of organization life in conjunction with more formal changes. The hard/soft axes of organizational change need to be integrated to produce the greatest impact over time. Changing the soft part of organizational life requires a different set of change management techniques and greater sophistication on the part of change agents.

- *Change is design; design is change.* A key aspect of leading change will be designing the various aspects of an organization's architecture and creating an environment that allow for ongoing design at all levels. Design and change are nearly synonymous, and individuals at all levels will be required to design new ways of operating. This approach contrasts with a top-down perspective where only the most senior executives engage in design work. The "federal" model will require coordination of design efforts at the center and the periphery but most of the power will reside in the local organizations and teams. A "local" approach to design will result in better decisions and more effective implementation. Individuals at all levels will become architects of organizations. Designing, creating, implementing, and refining the architecture of the organization will become a key part of the job and will become more so in the future.

• *Organizational renewal will become more important as change becomes more dramatic.* Discontinuous change will result in organizational turmoil and individual stress. Leaders will need to do more than damage control to build resilient organizations that can recover and sustain discontinuous change. Most change methodologies neglect the need for renewal and assume that it will occur naturally. Experience suggests otherwise. A critical element of leadership's role is to pay attention to the need to the human element of living through significant change.

The emerging era of discontinuous change requires that we develop new organizational and managerial capabilities in the years ahead. Those skilled at quickly evolving new capabilities—and abandoning those that become outdated—will clearly have a competitive advantage. Our goal in writing this book was to share what we have learned from working closely with those responsible for transforming their organizations and capitalizing on discontinuous change. While the challenges of leading organizations through periods of turmoil are becoming increasingly arduous, the benefits of doing so successfully are all the more rewarding.

References

Ackley, D. "The Secret of Communicating Bad News to Employees." *Communication World,* Aug. 1992, pp. 27–29.

Bass, R. M. *Leadership and Performance Beyond Expectations.* New York: Free Press, 1985.

Bazerman, M. H., and Neal, M. A. *Negotiating Rationality.* New York: Free Press, 1992.

Beckhard, R., and Harris, R. *Organizational Transitions.* Reading, Mass.: Addison-Wesley, 1977.

Beer, M., Eisenstat, R. A., and Spector, B. *The Critical Path to Corporate Renewal.* Boston: Harvard Business School Press, 1990.

Bennis, W. *On Becoming a Leader.* Reading, Mass.: Addison-Wesley, 1989.

Bennis, W. G., and Nanus, B. *Leaders: The Strategies for Taking Charge.* New York: HarperCollins, 1985.

277

Berlew, D. F. "Leadership and Organizational Excitement." In D. A. Kolb, I. M. Rubin, and J. M. McIntyre (eds.), *Organizational Psychology*. Englewood Cliffs, N.J.: Prentice-Hall, 1974.

Biggadike, E. R. "Strategic Profiling." New York: Conference Board Report No. 1080, 1994.

Bliss, D. "Strategic Choice: Engaging the Executive Team in Collaborative Strategy Planning." In D. A. Nadler, M. S. Gerstein, and R. B. Shaw (eds.), *Organizational Architecture: Designs for Changing Organizations*. San Francisco: Jossey-Bass, 1992.

Brockner, J. "Managing the Effects of Layoffs on Survivors." *California Management Review*, 1992, *34*(2), 9–28.

Brown, J. S. "Research That Reinvents the Corporation." *Harvard Business Review*, 1991, *69*(1), 102–111.

Brown, J. S., and Walton, E. "Reenacting the Corporation." *Planning Review*, 1993, *21*(5), 5–8.

Burns, J. M. *Leadership*. New York: HarperCollins, 1978.

Cameron, K. S., and Quinn, R. E. *PRISM 4: Changing Organizational Cultures/An Assessment Instrument*. San Francisco: Jossey-Bass, forthcoming.

Cameron, K. S., and Quinn, R. E. *PRISMS: Changing Organizational Cultures/A Change Workbook*. San Francisco: Jossey-Bass, forthcoming.

Campbell, J. P., Dunnette, M. D., Lawler, E. E., and Weick, K. *Managerial Behavior, Performances, and Effectiveness*. New York: McGraw-Hill, 1970.

Carlzon, J. *Moments of Truth*. New York: HarperCollins, 1987.

Coch, L., and French, J.R.P., Jr. "Overcoming Resistance to Change." *Human Relations*, 1948, *1*, 512–532.

Cooper, M. R., Morgan, B. S., Foley, P. M., and Kaplan, L. B. "Changing Employee Values: Deepening Discontent?" *Harvard Business Review*, Jan.-Feb. 1979, pp. 124–125.

Corporate Memory. Promotional brochure. Austin, Tex.: Corporate Memory, 1993.

DeGeus, A. "Planning as Learning." *Harvard Business Review*, Mar.-Apr. 1988, pp. 71–81.

Drucker, P. F. *Managing for Results*. New York: HarperCollins, 1964.

Drucker, P. F. *Managing for the Future: The 1990's and Beyond.* New York: Penguin, 1992.

Evans, P. A. "Management Development as Glue Technology." *Human Resource Planning,* 1992, *15*(1), 85–106.

Falbe, C. M., and Yukl, G. "Consequences for Managers of Using Single Influence Tactics and Combination of Tactics." *Academy of Management Journal,* 1992, *35*(3), 638–652.

Gabarro, J. *The Dynamics of Taking Charge.* Boston: Harvard Business School Press, 1987.

Garvin, D. A. "Building a Learning Organization." *Harvard Business Review,* July-Aug. 1993, pp. 78–91.

Gerstein, M. S. "From Machine Bureaucracies to Networked Organizations: An Architectural Journey." In D. A. Nadler, M. S. Gerstein, and R. B. Shaw (eds.), *Organizational Architecture: Designs for Changing Organizations.* San Francisco: Jossey-Bass, 1992.

Gerstein, M. S., and Reisman, H. "Strategic Selection: Matching Executives to Business Conditions." *Sloan Management Review,* Winter 1983, pp. 33–49.

Glance, N. S., and Huberman, B. A. "The Dynamics of Social Dilemmas." *Scientific American,* Mar. 1994, pp. 76–81.

Greiner, L. E. "Evolution and Revolution as Organizations Grow." *Harvard Business Review,* 1972, *50,* 37–54.

Hammer, M., and Champy, J. *Reengineering the Corporation.* New York: HarperCollins, 1993.

Handy, C. *Age of Unreason.* New York: McGraw-Hill, 1992.

Heider, F. *The Psychology of Interpersonal Relations.* New York: Wiley, 1958.

Hickson, D., Pugh, D., and Pheysey, D. "Operations Technology and Organization Structure: An Empirical Reappraisal" *Administrative Science Quarterly,* 1969, *14,* 378–397.

Hitt, M. A., and Tyler, B. B. "Strategic Decision Models: Integrating Different Perspectives." *Strategic Management Journal,* 1991, *12,* 327–351.

House, J. S. *Work Stress and Social Support.* Reading, Mass.: Addison-Wesley, 1981.

House, R. J. "Path-Goal Theory of Leadership Effectiveness." *Administrative Science Quarterly,* 1971, *16,* 321–338.

House, R. J. "A 1976 Theory of Charismatic Leadership." In J. G. Hunt and L. L. Larson (eds.), *Leadership: The Cutting Edge*. Cardondale: Southern Illinois University Press, 1977.

House, R. J. "Exchange and Charismatic Theories of Leadership." In G. Reber (ed.), *Encyclopedia of Leadership*. In press.

Howard, R. "The CEO as Organizational Architect." *Harvard Business Review*, 1992, *70*(5), 107–119.

Huberman, B. A., and Glance, N. S. *Diversity and Collective Action*. Palo Alto, Calif.: Xerox Palo Alto Research Center, 1992.

Katzenbach, J. R., and Smith, D. K. *The Wisdom of Teams: Creating the High Performance Organization*. Boston: Harvard Business School Press, 1993.

Keller, M. *Rude Awakening: The Rise, Fall, and Struggle for Recovery of General Motors*. New York: Morrow, 1989.

Kerr, S. "On the Folly of Rewarding *A* While Hoping for *B*." *Academy of Management Journal*, Dec. 1975, pp. 769–783.

Kilmann, R. H., Saxton, M. J., Serpa, R., and Associates. *Gaining Control of the Corporate Culture*. San Francisco: Jossey-Bass, 1985.

Kotter, J. P. *A Force for Change: How Leadership Differs from Management*. New York: Free Press, 1990.

Kotter, J. P., and Schlesinger, L. A. "Choosing Strategies for Change." *Harvard Business Review*, Mar.-Apr. 1979, pp. 106–114.

Kouzes, J. M., and Posner, B. Z. *The Leadership Challenge: How to Get Extraordinary Things Done in Organizations*. San Francisco: Jossey-Bass, 1987.

Kouzes, J. M., and Posner, B. Z. *Credibility: How Leaders Gain and Lose It, Why People Demand It*. San Francisco: Jossey-Bass, 1993.

Lavin, D. "Robert Eaton Thinks Vision Is Overrated and He's Not Alone." *Wall Street Journal*, Oct. 4, 1993, pp. A1, A8.

Lawler, E. E. "Strategic Choices for Changing Organizations." In A. M. Mohrman and Associates (eds.), *Large-Scale Organizational Change*. San Francisco: Jossey-Bass, 1989.

Lawler, E. E. *The Ultimate Advantage: Creating the High Involvement Organization*. San Francisco: Jossey-Bass, 1992.

Lawler, E. E., and Rhode, J. G. *Information and Control in Organizations.* Glenview, Ill.: Scott, Foresman, 1976.

Levin, D. P. "G. M. Plans to Shift Power to Outside Director." *The New York Times,* Mar. 29, 1994, p. D6.

Likert, R. *New Patterns of Management.* New York: McGraw-Hill, 1961.

Locke, E. A. *The Essence of Leadership: The Four Keys to Leading Successfully.* New York: Free Press, 1992.

Loomis, C. "Dinosaurs?" *Fortune,* May 3, 1993, pp. 36–42.

McCall, M. W., Jr. "Developing Leadership." In J. R. Galbraith, E. E. Lawler, and Associates (eds.), *Organizing for the Future.* San Francisco: Jossey-Bass, 1993.

McCall, M. W., Jr., Lombardo, M. M., and Morrison, A. M. *The Lessons of Experience.* Lexington, Mass.: Lexington Books, 1988.

Marks, M. L. *From Turmoil to Triumph: New Life After Mergers, Acquisitions, and Downsizing.* New York: Lexington Books, 1994.

Martin, J. "Directors' Feet to the Fire." *Fortune,* Nov. 29, 1993, p. 10.

Mason, D. H. "Scenario-Based Planning: Decision Model for the Learning Organization." *Planning Review,* 1994, *22*(2), 6–11.

Meyer, C. *Fast Cycle Time: How to Align Purpose, Strategy, and Structure for Speed.* New York: Free Press, 1993.

Mintzberg, H. *Structuring of Organizations.* Englewood Cliffs, N.J.: Prentice-Hall, 1978.

Nadler, D. A., and Ancona, D. G. "Teamwork at the Top: Creating Executive Teams That Work." In D. A. Nadler, M. S. Gerstein, and R. B. Shaw (eds.), *Organizational Architecture: Designs for Changing Organizations.* San Francisco: Jossey-Bass, 1992.

Nadler, D. A., and Gerstein, M. S. "Designing High Performance Work Systems: Organizing People, Work, Technology, and Information." In D. A. Nadler, M. S. Gerstein, and R. B. Shaw (eds.), *Organizational Architecture: Designs for Changing Organizations.* San Francisco: Jossey-Bass, 1992a.

Nadler, D. A., and Gerstein, M. S. "Strategic Selection: Staffing the Executive Team." In D. A. Nadler, M. S. Gerstein, and R. B.

Shaw (eds.), *Organizational Architecture: Designs for Changing Organizations*. San Francisco: Jossey-Bass, 1992b.

Nadler, D. A., and Gerstein, M. S. "What Is Organizational Architecture?" *Harvard Business Review*, 1992c, *70*(5), 120–121.

Nadler, D. A., Gerstein, M. S., and Shaw, R. B. *Organizational Architecture: Designs for Changing Organizations*. San Francisco: Jossey-Bass, 1992.

Nadler, D. A., and Tushman, M. L. *Strategic Organization Design: Concepts, Tools, and Processes*. New York: HarperCollins, 1988.

Oldham, G. R. "The Motivational Strategies Used by Supervisors: Relationships to Effectiveness Indicators." *Organizational Behavior and Human Performance*, 1976, *15*, 66–86.

Ouchi, W. G. *Theory Z*. Reading, Mass.: Addison-Wesley, 1981.

Pearson, A. E. "Muscle-Build the Organization." *Harvard Business Review*, 1987, *65*(4), 49–55.

Peck, M. S. *The Road Less Traveled*. New York: Simon & Schuster, 1978.

Peters, T. J. "Symbols, Patterns, and Settings: An Optimistic Case for Getting Things Done." *Organizational Dynamics*, 1978, *7*(2), 2–23.

Porter, L. W., Lawler, E. E., and Hackman, J. R. *Behavior in Organizations*. New York: McGraw-Hill, 1975.

Porter, M. E. "From Competitive Advantage to Corporate Strategy." *Harvard Business Review*, 1987, *3*, 43–59.

Prahalad, C. K., and Hamel, G. "Core Competence of the Corporation." *Harvard Business Review*, 1990, *68*(3), 79–91.

Rogers, C. *On Becoming a Person*. Boston: Houghton Mifflin, 1972.

Rumelt, R. P. "How Much Does Industry Matter?" *Strategic Management Journal*, 1991, *12*, 167–185.

Saporito, B. "A Week of Woe for the CEO." *Fortune*, Feb. 22, 1993, pp. 10, 68.

Schein, E. H. *Organizational Culture and Leadership*. San Francisco: Jossey-Bass, 1985.

Schwalbach, J. "Profitability and Market Share: A Reflection on the Functional Relationship." *Strategic Management Journal*, 1991, *12*, 299–306.

Senge, P. *The Fifth Discipline: The Art and Practice of the Learning Organization.* New York: Doubleday, 1990.

Shaw, R. B., and Perkins, D.N.T. "Teaching Organizations to Learn: The Power of Productive Failures." In D. A. Nadler, M. S. Gerstein, and R. B. Shaw (eds.), *Organizational Architecture: Designs for Changing Organizations.* San Francisco: Jossey-Bass, 1992.

Smith, D. K., and Alexander, R. C. *Fumbling the Future: How Xerox Invented, Then Ignored, the First Personal Computer.* New York: William Morrow, 1988.

Stalk, G., and Hout, T. M. *Competing Against Time: How Time-Based Competition Is Reshaping Global Markets.* New York: Free Press, 1990.

Stewart, J. M. "Future-State Visioning Technique at National Rubber Company." *Planning Review*, 1994, *22*(2), 20–24.

"A Survey of Employee Communication Practices." New York: William M. Mercer, Inc., 1993.

Tichy, N. M., and Devanna, M. A. *The Transformational Leader.* New York: Wiley, 1986.

Tichy, N. M., and Sherman, S. *Control Your Destiny or Someone Else Will.* New York: Currency Doubleday, 1993.

Tichy, N. M., and Ulrich, D. "The Leadership Challenge: A Call for the Transformational Leader." *Sloan Management Review*, 1984, *26*(1), 59–68.

Tushman, M. L., Newman, W., and Romanelli, E. "Convergence and Upheaval: Managing the Unsteady Pace of Organization Evolution." California Management Review, 1986, *29*(1), 29–44.

Tushman, M., and Romanelli, E. "Organization Evolution: A Metamorphosis Model of Convergence and Reorientation." In B. Staw and L. Cummings (eds.), *Research in Organization Behavior*, vol. 7. Greenwich, Conn.: JAI Press, 1985.

Ulrich, D., and Lake, D. "Organizational Capability: Creating the Competitive Advantage." *The Academy of Management Executive*, 1991, *5*(1), 77–92.

Vroom, V. H. *Work and Motivation.* New York: Wiley, 1964.

Whyte, G. "Decision Failures: Why They Occur and How to Prevent Them." *The Academy of Management Executive*, 1991, *5*(3), 23–31.

Wick, C. W., and Léon, S. L. *The Learning Edge: How Smart Managers and Smart Companies Stay Ahead.* New York: McGraw-Hill, 1993.

Yates, J. *Control Through Communication: The Rise of System in American Management.* Baltimore, Md.: Johns Hopkins University, 1993.

Zahra, S. A., and Chaples, S. S. "Blind Spots in Competitive Analysis." *The Academy of Management Executive,* 1993, 7(2), 7–28.

Index